# Lesbian and Gay Couples

# LESBIAN AND GAY COUPLES

## Lives, Issues, and Practice

Ski Hunter

LYCEUM
BOOKS, INC.
Chicago, IL

© 2012 by Lyceum Books, Inc.

Published by

LYCEUM BOOKS, INC.
5758 S. Blackstone Avenue
Chicago, Illinois 60637
773-643-1903 fax
773-643-1902 phone
lyceum@lyceumbooks.com
www.lyceumbooks.com

6 5 4 3 2 1   12 13 14 15 16

ISBN 978-1-933478-74-6

Printed in the United States of America.

**Library of Congress Cataloging-in-Publication Data**
Hunter, Ski.
   Lesbian and gay couples : information and practice / Ski Hunter.
     p. cm.
   Includes bibliographical references and index.
   ISBN 978-1-933478-74-6 (pbk. : alk. paper)
  1. Gay couples.  2. Lesbian couples.  I. Title.
   HQ76.34.H86   2011
   306.84'8—dc22
                                  2011001120

# Dedication

*To all lesbian, gay, bisexual, and transgender persons, and especially those who have helped lessen oppression*

*To the Safe Zone Group at the University of Texas at Arlington, whose goal is to lessen oppression for lesbian, gay, bisexual, and transgender students, staff, and faculty*

*To the School of Social Work at the University of Texas at Arlington. I have had a wonderful career there and have supportive friends who I treasure.*

# Contents

# Introduction

This book is on lesbian and gay adult couples. The purpose is to describe for readers the basic issues these couples deal with, their differences from and similarities to heterosexual couples, and how they deal with heterosexism and the marriage issue. In addition, there are several chapters on practice with these couples for practitioners. What are the issues these couples bring to a practitioner, and what interventions might help them? This introduction presents demographics of lesbian and gay couples, research history, the constant backdrop of heterosexism in the lives of gay and lesbian couples, and postmodern and queer theory.

In this book, I use *lesbian and gay communities* in the plural form because there are a variety of lesbian and gay communities across the country and around the world. No monolithic lesbian or gay community exists. In addition, *gay* refers to men and *lesbian* to women, even though some women refer to themselves as gay instead of lesbian, and some gay men and lesbians use no labels at all.

## Demographics of Lesbian and Gay Couples

Approximately 601,000 same-sex couples live together according to the 2000 U.S. census (Gates & Ost, 2004). Other estimates are that of 5.5 million unmarried couples living together, about one in nine are same-sex couples. Of those couples, 301,026 are male couples and 293,365 are female couples (Simmons & O'Connell, 2003).

These population data are estimates. Some couples may be reluctant to reveal their sexual identity or the nature of their romantic attachments to the government on census forms. Also, many same-sex couples do not live together (Cahill, South, & Spade, 2000). In addition, hardly any legal marriage or divorce records exist on lesbian and gay couples. Marriage is so infrequent that the data on same-sex marriage are not significant. Nor are there data on how many lesbians and gay men have experienced the loss of a serious relationship through death of a partner (Kurdek, 2005).

Lesbian and gay couples live all over the United States, in 99.3 percent of all counties (Smith & Gates, 2001), though they are most likely to live in urban areas (Gates & Ost, 2004). An analysis of data from several large studies, including the General Social Survey and the National Health and Social Life Survey, showed that 60 percent of partnered lesbians and gay men live in only twenty cities. Partnered gay men are more concentrated in those twenty cities than are partnered lesbians (Black, Gates, Sanders, & Taylor, 2000).

Lesbian and gay couples represent every ethnic, racial, income, and adolescent and adult age group. This book addresses adults because of the many unique issues adolescents deal with (for reviews of lesbian and gay adolescents, see Hunter, 1998; Hunter & Hickerson, 2003). Same-sex couples are two times more likely than heterosexual married couples to be of mixed race or ethnicity (Simmons & O'Connell, 2003). For example, approximately 16 percent of same-sex couples include a Hispanic partner, and 14 percent include an African American partner (Black et al., 2000). The number of interracial lesbian and gay couples may partly reflect the fact that fewer opportunities exist for racial and ethnic minority lesbians and gay men to find same-race or same-ethnicity partners in their communities of origin. Also, by migrating to more cosmopolitan, urban settings, lesbians and gay men intermingle with diverse cultural groups, thus increasing their possibilities for dating outside of their race or ethnicity (Peplau, Cochran, & Mays, 1997).

## Research to Date on Lesbian and Gay Couples

Although a long history of research exists on lesbians and gay men, the literature on couples is modest. Research on same-sex couples began slowly in the 1970s and grew in the 1980s. It diminished as the AIDS epidemic in the gay community in the 1980s began to receive more attention. In recent years, however, research on same-sex couples has drawn more interest. That research, however, has been problematic. Many research projects have relied on questionnaires, and different researchers have used incomparable questions. This, along with use of different samples (mostly unrepresentative), has resulted in some of the contradictory findings mentioned in this text. Most of the studies have been small scale; only a few major research studies have been done. Most respondents have volunteered to participate, and usually they are young, well educated, white, and middle class. In addition, many research projects obtained reports from only one partner in a couple (Peplau & Fingerhut, 2007).

The literature that provides direct comparisons of same- and different-sex couples is small. Nonetheless, since the 1980s, a few researchers, including Blumstein and Schwartz (1983) and Kurdek (e.g., 1988a, 1988b, 1995a, 1998a, 1998b, 2004, 2008), have conducted comparative studies focused on lesbian, gay, and heterosexual romantic relationships.

## Heterosexism and Its Effects on Lesbian and Gay Couples

All lesbian and gay individuals and couples contend with the oppression of stigma and discrimination that results from heterosexism. Defined by Herek (1995), heterosexism is "the ideological system that denies, denigrates, and stigmatizes any non-heterosexual form of behavior, identity, relationship, or community" (p. 321). It operates at both cultural and individual levels. An example of how heterosexism manifests itself at the cultural level is the way that the media portrays, or does not portray, lesbians and gay men. For example, the media does not often highlight happy, satisfied, and successful same-sex couples (Ossana, 2000). Another example of cultural heterosexism is the widespread belief that the only acceptable affectional and sexual expression is that which occurs between women and men. This reflects belief in the inherent superiority of one form of loving over all others (Sanders & Kroll, 2000). We take this belief for granted, and it is reinforced through social customs and institutions (Herek, 1995). This belief and other heterosexist beliefs are acquired and reinforced by society over the life span (Bigner, 2000). We barely acknowledge beliefs such as the inherent superiority of heterosexual love until something brings the issue to the surface. For example, when lesbians and gay men want to legally marry, then there are calls for laws to prevent this—many state laws state that legal marriage exists only between a woman and a man (see chapter 9).

Cultural heterosexism is also seen in the lack of legal recognition and protection for lesbian and gay couples, including child custody rights (Ossana, 2000; Shernoff, 1995; Slater, 1995), medical decision-making power for the nonlegal parent (Ossana, 2000), employment (Slater, 1995), shelter (Slater, 1995), and social services (Granvold & Martin, 1999). More than 50 percent of lesbian, gay, and bisexual (LGB) participants in a study by Mays and Cochran (2001) reported lifetime experiences of discrimination such as being fired from a job or being prevented from renting or buying a home. These couples' civil rights are regularly challenged through court cases, ballot initiatives, and legislative proposals.

Individual heterosexism includes people's own negative feelings about lesbians and gay men, such as disgust and indignation. Examples of individual behaviors are jokes and derogatory terms that make fun of lesbians and gay men or put them down (Berrill, 1990; Herek, 1993, 1995). A study by Swim, Pearson, and Johnson (2007) used daily experience accounts to assess lesbians' and gay men's encounters with everyday hassles. Over one week, participants reported experiencing an average of two hassles focused on their sexual identity. Two-thirds of the hassles were verbal, including jokes, comments based on stereotypes, hostile or threatening comments, and comments expressing general dislike of lesbians and gay men.

In most circumstances in the United States and around the world, lesbian and gay couples still risk being gawked at if they hold hands in public. Stress can result from other hassles, such as when same-sex couples request a shared bed in a hotel room. In an experimental study, Jones (1996) found that same-sex couples requesting that hotel arrangement were denied a room significantly more often than were heterosexual couples making the same request. In addition, stress can result from rejection of the couple or their children by family, neighbors, or peers at work or school (Todosijevic, Rothblum, & Solomon, 2005). In a national survey (Kaiser Family Foundation, 2001), 34 percent of lesbians and gay men reported that their family or a family member had refused to accept them because of their sexual identity. Families of origin might also ignore their family member's sexual identity (Lewis, Derlega, Berndt, Morris, & Rose, 2001).

Hate crimes, also called bias crimes, are influenced by both cultural and individual heterosexism and mostly target men because of their sexual identity. Extreme forms of physical attacks can result in serious injuries or death (McDougall, 1993; Neisen, 1990). Most lesbian and gay research respondents (95 percent) report having experienced some degree of violence (Dean, Wu, & Martin, 1992; Von Schulthess, 1992). Berrill (1992) reported from twenty-four local, regional, and national samples of gay and bisexual men the proportion of different types of harassment and violence that they experienced: assault with weapons (9 percent), physical assault (17 percent), vandalization of property (19 percent), threats of violence (44 percent), and having objects thrown at them (25 percent). In addition, they were spit at (13 percent) and experienced verbal harassment (80 percent).

Balsam, Rothblum, and Beauchaine (2005) reported findings from one of the largest studies of victimization among LGB women and men, covering the life span. The study compared the violence experienced by 557 LGB and 525 heterosexual adults. The LGB respondents experienced more of every type of violence than heterosexual respondents in childhood and adulthood, including psychological, physical, and sexual violence. Within the same family, an LGB sibling or siblings were at greater risk for victimization by their parents. In another large-scale study, approximately 20 percent of sexual minority women reported being the victim of a sexual identity–based crime or attempted crime (e.g., physical assault, sexual assault, robbery, vandalism; Herek, Gillis, & Cogan, 1999).

Roberts, Austin, Corliss, Vandermorris, and Koenen (2010) found that lesbians, gay men, bisexuals, and heterosexuals who were ever in a same-sex relationship are between two and two and a half times more likely than the general population to experience violence especially in childhood. They have double the risk of experiencing posttraumatic stress disorder (PTSD) as a result of the violence. The authors suggested five ways that sexual minorities are at risk for victimization and PTSD: hate crimes, gender nonconforming behavior in childhood, social isolation and discrimination, elevated risk-taking behavior due to social isolation and stigma, and limited access to mental health care.

In 2002, a lesbian couple and their infant son barely escaped with their lives after arsonists set their home on fire. This happened a few days after the women had filed suit against the University of Montana for not providing domestic partner benefits. In 1999, two brothers claiming to be carrying out "God's will" brutally murdered gay partners, forty and fifty years old, while they were asleep in their bed (Kaiser Family Foundation, 2001). These are only a few examples of life-threatening or murderous episodes against lesbians and gay men. Lesbian and gay couples can also experience stress from the fear aroused when violence happens to others. Vulnerability to these dangers requires lesbian and gay individuals and couples to be vigilant, especially in unfamiliar surroundings.

Using minority stress theory (Meyer, 2003) as an interpretive framework, Rostosky, Riggle, Gray, and Hatton (2007) conducted a qualitative analysis of forty lesbian and gay couples (twenty female and twenty male). The analysis was based on the couples' conversations about their committed partnerships. Of the participants, 85 percent were white, 6 percent identified as African American, and 8 percent identified as other nonwhite and non–African American racial or ethnic identities. The mean age of the couple members was 34.5 years. The mean

length of relationship was 5.33 years; 35 percent had been in a relationship between six months and two years, 31 percent had been together between two
and five years, and 34 percent had been together more than five years (up to
twenty-three years). The majority of the couples lived together (89.5 percent).
The study defined minority stress as the chronic social stress that results from belonging to a stigmatized social category and is over and above the general stressors of daily life. Minority stress was composed of five factors: (1) experiences of
discrimination, (2) anticipated rejection, (3) hiding and concealing of identities,
(4) dealing with internalized homonegativity, and (5) development of coping
strategies (Meyer, 2003).

Most of the couple members (94 percent) were out to their families of origin, but only 34 percent believed that their family was supportive or accepting
of their sexual identity. Only 36 percent reported that their family accepted their
partner into their lives. They experienced their families as expressing discomfort
with the couple relationship, refusing to acknowledge their partner or their relationship (e.g., by not sending invitations or holiday cards to the partner), and
attempting to cause dissolution of the relationship. Confrontations or verbal attacks came from family members, as well as from friends, coworkers, and
strangers (Rostosky, Riggle, Gray, et al., 2007).

Most of the participants reported being verbally harassed at some point in
their life because of their sexual identity. Almost half (46 percent) reported that
they had been verbally harassed five or more times. Fewer (19 percent) reported
having been physically assaulted at least once (Rostosky, Riggle, Gray, et al., 2007).

Of the forty couples, thirty-three discussed their stigmatized status in the
larger culture or society. More than half of the couples discussed discrimination
by institutions, most commonly religious and legal institutions. Couples discussed
their lack of legal rights, such as civil marriage, and the lack of legal protections
for their partners. More than half of the sample mentioned society's negative
stereotypes and attitudes, such as the common stereotype that same-sex relationships are fleeting and impermanent. Another stereotype assumes that lesbians and gay men are promiscuous, predatory, immoral, and therefore incapable of stable couple relationships. Another stereotype is that same-sex couples
play out gender roles (one partner is the "man," and the other is the "woman").
The couples often expressed their perception that society disapproved of and devalued their committed relationships. They also lamented the lack of visible, positive role models for same-sex couples (Rostosky, Riggle, Gray, et al., 2007).

It is reasonable to assume that discrimination based on sexual identity places strains on lesbian and gay couples (Mays, Cochran, & Rhue, 1993). Researchers have consistently shown that lesbians and gay men who experience discrimination are at greater risk of poor psychological adjustment and stress-related psychological disorders (e.g., Mays & Cochran 2001; Meyer, 1995, 2003). Ultimately, the various stressors that lesbian and gay couples experience can affect mental well-being (Otis & Skinner, 1996) and perceptions of relationship quality for couple members, as well as diminish the self-esteem or mental health of the partners or their ability to function effectively in a relationship. In a study of same-sex couples in civil unions, Todosijevic et al. (2005) found a significant association between reports of gay-specific stressors and lower relationship satisfaction for lesbian couples, though not for gay couples.

Another study (Balsam & Szymanski, 2005) has examined the role of minority stress in lesbian and bisexual women's same-sex relationships. Participants were 272 women age 18–66, with a mean age of 34.75 years (standard deviation = 10.27). The sample comprised 85 percent European American, 6 percent African American/black, 2 percent Hispanic/Latina, 1 percent Asian American/Pacific Islander, 1 percent Native American, and 4 percent biracial women. Consistent with DiPlacido's (1998) theoretical model, the study operationalized minority stress to include both internalized heterosexism and external experiences of heterosexist discrimination. Consistent with clinical and theoretical reports, internalized heterosexism was negatively associated with relationship quality. Contrary to expectations, however, recent and lifetime heterosexist discrimination was not related to relationship quality. It may be that same-sex couples can cope better with experiences that happen outside of their relationship than with internal beliefs that may be more hidden. It is important to consider that when studies measure only the occurrence of discriminatory events, they miss the perceived impact of those events. It is possible that the extent of discriminatory events that gay and lesbian couple members experience as stressful may play a more important role in relationship functioning.

Despite the stigma and stressors experienced by lesbians and gay men, most of them function well. Like members of other stigmatized groups, they develop strategies to cope with their status. In the Rostosky, Riggle, Gray, et al. (2007) study, in response to stressors, couples used coping strategies that included reframing negative experiences, concealing their relationship, creating social support, and affirming themselves and their partnership. Balsam and Szymanski

(2005) suggested that it is also possible that the couple relationship can serve as a safe haven that buffers couple members from the effects of discrimination. Nevertheless, assault and other victimization can create considerable distress. Attacks directed toward lesbians and gay men because of their sexual identity have a more powerful negative impact than other crimes against them. Even a minor incident of harassment can be frightening, because one never knows what it will lead to. Sexual identity–based crimes also have consequences for lesbian and gay communities, as they give a message that lesbians and gay men are not safe (Herek, Cogan, & Gillis, 2002).

## The Postmodern and Queer Theory Challenge

This book is traditional in that it uses binary categories of "lesbian" and "gay." But there are other ways to view lesbians and gay men, as well as gender and sex. Starting with gender and sex, in standard usage, *sex* distinguishes males and females mostly on the basis of biological characteristics (Rutter & Schwartz, 2000). A person is assigned to categories of "male" or "female" because of characteristics of genitalia, chromosomes, reproductive organs, gametes, and hormones. *Gender* is what society expects persons to be on the basis of their sex (Maurer, 1999). This includes roles and stereotypes (Stein, 1999). Gender, however, can be projected onto experiences that may have no relation to the sex of a person (Bohan & Russell, 1999; McKenna & Kessler, 2000).

Many of the biological factors used to classify persons as male or female do not easily divide persons into two distinct groups (Coombs, 1998), such as for persons who are born with different combinations of genitals, chromosomes, and secondary-sex characteristics such as body hair or breasts not classifiable as male or female (Stein, 1999). Transgender persons also defy "male" and "female" categories. Some cultures recognize more than two sexes (Blackwood, 1984). Our current views about what biological features distinguish males from females may be inaccurate.

McPhail (2004) also questioned gender and sexuality binaries. Such categories for classifying people as "gender" and "sexual orientation" can be limiting and harmful, as well as inaccurate. McPhail's view of postmodern and queer theory brings new ways of conceptualizing people and social movements. We usually classify people by membership in groups. Group status is often divided into binary categorizations: male-female, white-nonwhite, heterosexual-nonheterosexual, wealthy-poor, and able-disabled. The first group has power; the second group does not. These groups are also divided into categories of "valued or privileged" or "devalued or marginalized." But people in the same groups often have considerable differences rather than commonalities. And some people do not fit into binary categories, such as those who are bisexual, intersex, and transgender. Queer spirituality also adds to this discussion. It opposes dominant religious worldviews that favor a heterosexual perspective. It also rejects heterosexual privilege, patriarchy, and male hegemony (Bosivert, 2007; Jordan, 2007).

The most common criticisms of gender and sexuality conclude that there is no objective truth. Instead, truth and realities are multiple, subjective, and socially constructed, and often they serve those in power. Queer theory separates gender from sexuality and from the continuities between anatomical sex, social gender, gender identity, sexual identity, sexual object choice, and sexual practice. For example, the labeling of a person who is not heterosexual in a category distinct from "heterosexual" helps the medical and scientific communities label the person "abnormal." Once those communities create the "abnormal" category, then the people in it are regulated and policed. But research shows that gender and sexual orientation may be socially constructed, dynamic, and multivariate over time (Klein, Sepekoff, & Wolf, 1985). Many lesbians and gay men believe that they were born as lesbian or gay. Some believe that they chose their same-sex identity. Women have a more fluid sexuality than do men, and there is considerable variation in their same-sex and other-sex attractions (Diamond & Savin-Williams, 2000). Women's identity can be altered by cultural, social, and situational factors. Women are also more likely to adapt multiple identities (Rust, 2000).

McPhail (2004) pointed out that two of social work's core values are self-determination and the dignity and worth of each person (National Association of Social Workers, 1996). Much of the postmodern critique is to allow people to define themselves rather than to be defined and categorized by others. McPhail recommended that social workers use continua of gender and sexualities instead of discrete categories; they should hesitate to speak of categorizations of people. "Sexual identity" may be more preferable than "sexual orientation" or "sexual preference." Nothing is as simple as being born gay or heterosexual or choosing what one will be.

McPhail's (2004) suggestions for social workers include the following: Ask questions such as, Who do these categories serve? Who do they include or exclude? Who has power to define these categories? How do categories change over time and across cultures? She recommends that social workers question gender and sexuality binaries, and that social work curricula include postmodern and queer theories as another view along a continuum of views.

When working with persons around issues of gender and sexuality, we should not make assumptions about anything on the basis of a category. As practitioners, we should ask a lesbian or gay couple to tell us their own narrative about themselves and their being in a couple. I suggest that readers keep these ideas in mind in the chapters to come. I challenge us to go beyond categories.

## Chapters and Audience

This book has three parts: "Life Span of Couples," "Micro-Level Practice with Lesbian and Gay Couples," and "Other Issues That Affect Lesbian and Gay Couples." The chapters in these parts address the major themes of how lesbian and gay couples meet (chapter 1); couples who have or want children (chapter 2); relationship satisfaction, benefits, and maintenance (chapter 3); relationship dissatisfaction and breakup (chapter 4); micro-level practice with lesbian and gay couples (chapters 5–7), heterosexism and coping strategies (chapter 8), and the marriage issue (chapter 9).

In summary, the purpose of this book is to address adult lesbians and gay men in couples with empirical evidence. The book does not present practice models. Instead, practitioners can adapt their preferred models to the issues and suggested practice ideas presented here.

This book is intended to be a supplemental textbook (rather than the main text) for a course on lesbians and gay men, lesbian and gay couples, or for a course on couples generally. It is also a guide to practice for practitioners. The primary audiences include undergraduate and graduate students in courses on diversity, adult development, and marriage and family. It can be used in the fields of social work, counseling, mental health, nursing, psychology, sociology, and education. Lesbians and gay men themselves can also benefit from reading this book: they will learn about the experiences of others in couples and how to handle difficulties and maintain relationships.

# Part One

## Life Span of Couples

# Meeting **1** Others

What obstacles do lesbians experience in meeting each other?

What obstacles do gay men experience in meeting each other?

How do they overcome obstacles and meet?

What role does the Internet play in meeting?

When lesbians date or gay men date, do they do things differently than heterosexuals who date, or is the process a similar one? If similar, what are their behaviors when dating?

What is the difference in dating between lesbians and gay men?

What dating scripts do lesbians use? Which is the most popular script? Which scripts are used, but less often? Why do you suppose this is the case?

In terms of dating, how are midlife women different from younger women?

What are the rules about dating?

What is available to couples in terms of civil unions, marriage, and other unions?

What are some stereotypes about lesbian and gay couples?

What do lesbian and gay couples want in their relationships?

What are some of the difficulties lesbian and gay couples have to contend with?

What are the similarities and differences in lesbian, gay, and heterosexual couples?

What characterizes a best-friends model for lesbian and gay couples?

The literature on the life span of couples covered in this chapter dates from 1990 to 2010. This is a period that produced only a few findings on couples' life span. What is presented here is based on those data. The data do not cover culture, social class, or nationality, but they do cover some similarities for race/ethnicity. Also, there is much data on comparisons of lesbian, gay, and heterosexual couples.

## Obstacles to Meeting

Several obstacles exist for lesbians and gay men to meet others. For many people, one of those is invisibility. For example, some people are isolated, such as those in rural areas or those who have not disclosed their sexual identity. The small pool of potential partners is another obstacle, and the pool is even smaller for racial and ethnic lesbians and gay men (Greene, 1995). For lesbians, even when a woman recognizes that another woman is also a lesbian, this does not ensure a connection. Moreover, women are not socialized to be forward in initiating relationships (Rutter & Schwartz, 1996). Another obstacle in many meeting places is financial cost, and particularly lesbians with limited incomes may not be able to afford to participate in those places (Greene, 1995), but there are free or less costly places available to meet others. Fear of HIV/AIDS also decreases the dating pool (Linde, 1994). In a study of personal ads by gay men in San Francisco, the mention of HIV-positive status drastically reduced the pool of respondents to the ads (Hatala, Baack, & Parmenter, 1998).

## Meeting

Given the obstacles mentioned here, how do lesbians and gay men meet potential dates and partners? Some of them have informal dating services of friends and family members who match them up with potential partners. If they hide their sexual identity, however, those friends and family members may set them up with heterosexual dates (D. E. Murphy, 2004). Lesbians and gay men also meet others in support networks, which have been developing since the 1970s. Meeting through friends is one of the most common ways to meet others. Lesbians and gay men have also increasingly gone digital as a way to meet others (Peplau & Fingerhut, 2007). Virtual networks for gay men and lesbians to meet others exist on the Internet (Hendrickson, 2007). The Internet provides unmediated communication among people all over the world (Hendrickson, 2007), and it is always available, twenty-four hours a day. In a *USA Today* survey with 474 lesbian and gay participants, 61 percent of couples said they had met online (Jayson,

2010). Gay men appear to meet people online more than lesbians do (Hendrickson, 2007).

Internet social networks are particularly important for those who have little access to other support networks because of their geographical location or fear of disclosure. Some have entire relationships online or use the Internet to find only sexual encounters: about 40 percent of gay men have used the Internet to find sexual partners (Liau, Millett, & Marks, 2006). Online sites, such as Dating.com and Match.com, provide ways to meet others. Other general sites have dating areas or chat rooms. Instant messaging, message boards, personal Web sites, Facebook, MySpace, and blogs are also available for meeting others (Caster, 2008). There are also many lesbian and gay discussion boards where people can meet others. Dating-coach Web sites, such as GayLoveCoach.com, come and go, but with a Google search one can always find other Web sites focused on providing spaces for lesbians and gay men to meet others.

Publications such as *The Gay Yellow Pages* and *International Gay Yellow Pages* list meeting places in urban areas. Bars and nightclubs or dance clubs are gathering places for some lesbians and gay men (Alonzo, 2005). There may be no publications or meeting places other than a bar for those who live in rural areas, and even that may not exist (D. E. Murphy, 2004). But the Internet is everywhere, and those in rural areas can meet others via their computers.

Virtual communication has various levels of anonymity. In decreasing order, they include anonymous exploration, casual posting, online conversations, and offline meetings (Harper, Bruce, Serrano, & Jamil, 2009).

## Desired Matchups

Gay men tend to prefer men who are physically masculine and have traditionally masculine traits (Bailey, Kim, Hills, & Linsenmeir, 1997; Davidson, 1991). Men who are HIV negative are more likely to want to be with other HIV-negative men (Hatala et al., 1998). Lesbians tend to prefer women who are feminine, though this bias is not as strong as the masculine bias is for gay men (Bailey, Kim, et al., 1997). Gay men are also more likely than lesbians to prefer physically attractive partners (Bailey, Kim, et al., 1997; Feingold, 1990).

## Dating

Lesbians and gay men who enter courtships today face an immensely improved social climate than did those who came out decades ago (Rose, Zand, & Cini, 1993). Still, little is known about the dating process among them. Klinkenberg and Rose (1994), however, studied the topic. Their sample included fifty-one gay men (age 21–51) and forty-four lesbians (age 19–55). The researchers reported that, during all stages of a first date, cultural and interpersonal scripts for same-sex dating were the same as the scripts of heterosexual women and men. In Rose et al.'s (1993) study, those dating followed a conventional script with a typical sequence of events, including discussing plans, dressing up, getting to know one's date, going to a movie, going out to eat or out for a drink, and initiating physical contact. Some differences, however, occurred between women and men. Gay men played out traditional male roles in arranging a date and other activities, whereas lesbians more often negotiated first-date activities. In addition, nearly half (48 percent) of the men reported having sex on their most recent first date, compared with only 12 percent of the women. Lesbians were more likely to focus on the emotions they experienced with their date (Klinkenberg & Rose, 1994). African American lesbians (18 percent) were also significantly less likely to participate in sex on the first date than were African American gay men (30 percent; Peplau, Cochran, & Mays, 1997)

Rose et al. (1993) studied three courtship scripts that have been used to describe lesbian dating and couple formation: romance, friendship, and sexually explicit. In the romance script, emotional intimacy and sexual attraction are closely intertwined in women's attraction to each other. The dating phase may be short, and women usually proceed quickly toward commitment. Cini and Malafi (1991) found that lesbians were both sexually and emotionally involved by the fifth date and viewed themselves as a couple.

In the other two major patterns of lesbian courtship, the friendship script and the sexually explicit script, emotional intimacy and sexual attraction are not as intertwined, or perhaps not linked at all. Neither script requires dating for its initiation. The friendship script, believed to be the most common courtship script that lesbians use, emphasizes emotional intimacy over sexuality. Two women become friends, fall in love, and establish a committed relationship with each other that may or may not be sexual. In contrast, the sexually explicit script primarily focuses on sexuality and attraction. In this script, women who are physically attracted to each other initiate sexual contact with possibly no goal of future commitment. Emotional intimacy is less important or may not be present.

Rose et al. (1993) studied responses from thirty-eight lesbian respondents as a function of three age groups, including young adults (age 20–29), adults (age 30–39), and midlife adults (age 40–65). About 29 percent of participants had used all three scripts, 47 percent had used two, and 29 percent had used only one. Again, the friendship script was the most widely used. About 74 percent of respondents reported having been friends with a woman, on at least one occasion, before becoming romantically involved with her. This script generally proceeded in the following way: Two women established a friendship, and both highly valued the emotional intimacy of their connection. The intimacy and companionship of the friendship gradually led the women to a deep emotional commitment that they expressed physically, as well. In contrast to the friendship script, 55 percent of respondents had used the romance script, and 63 percent had engaged in the sexually explicit script. Script preference followed a slightly different pattern, however; across all age groups, half of the women preferred the friendship script and half preferred the romance script. No group indicated a preference for the sexually explicit script, despite the prevalence of its use.

The women whom Rose et al. (1993) interviewed defined dating as a way to get to know another woman and to have a good time or explore the romantic or sexual potential of the relationship without any specific commitment in mind. The characteristics "freedom from gender roles" and "heightened intimacy" indicated that lesbian dating is more egalitarian than heterosexual dating. Women usually shared behaviors, such as who initiates and pays. A majority of respondents (55 percent) rejected traditional gender roles by either mutually negotiating their interactions or switching roles depending on the specific interaction. Others opted more consistently for a particular role as either the initiator (16 percent) or the noninitiator (29 percent). The interaction also appeared to be less geared toward trying to impress the other person by spending money, performing courtship behaviors such as opening doors, or worrying about appearance. The respondents were more interested in getting to know the other person. Participants also pointed out that societal prejudice against lesbians placed limits on how openly they could date (Rose et al., 1993).

Rose et al. (1993) found that a majority of lesbians use direct verbal declarations to convey romantic interest (e.g., "tell her how I feel," "proposition her sexually," and "declare my affection"). When on a date, respondents were not shy in terms of signaling attraction. The second most frequently cited category of sexual signaling involves nonverbal behaviors. Respondents relied heavily on touching. The initiation of sexual contact depended on dating experience. Experienced lesbian daters were found to have initiated physical intimacy on their dates significantly more often than those with less lesbian dating experience. As lesbians grow older and gain more dating experience, they appear to become more comfortable with initiating sexual intimacy. Those with extensive previous heterosexual dating experience, however, rejected physical intimacy more often than did those with little experience.

Most midlife lesbians in the Rose et al. (1993) study also undertook courtship with greater freedom from gender roles and with more maturity. They were found to differ significantly from young adults in terms of perceiving lesbian dating as having the serious goal of commitment. Most were more purposive in their attitudes and behaviors than the young adult or adult group. Midlife lesbians often spoke about having approached relationships more casually in their youth or having been motivated by physical attraction, sexual gratification, or other needs unrelated to what they considered more important at the time of the interview. As they aged, most became more concerned about the "attachment worthiness" of a partner; that is, they determined whether the necessary warmth, respect, and reciprocal liking necessary to sustain a relationship were present before they pursued a sexual relationship. Once they judged those attributes to be present, most acted quickly. Thus, their current behaviors seemed to be motivated by a more accurate assessment of their needs and by greater experience concerning what can sustain a relationship. Midlife lesbians also spoke about other changes over the course of their lifetime that affected courtship. Many mentioned enjoying the fact that they no longer had to conform to the butch-femme roles that dominated the bar scene in their youth. They also appreciated the relatively greater freedom they felt to be openly lesbian and to be able to find partners outside of bars, a result of the growth of lesbian communities. Most preferred using the term *courtship* to signify their goal of a long-term relationship (Rose et al., 1993). A downside for midlife lesbians is that they often have fewer potential partners to pursue and thus may escalate the course of a relationship without being fully sure of the favorability of a partner (Hall & Gregory, 1991). Although midlife lesbians prefer a long-term committed relationship with one other person, on the whole, they are in various states of relationships. These states range from seeing no one to seeing one woman, several women, or many women at once (Coss, 1991; Mitchell, 2000). For at least some midlife lesbians, their experiences have tempered the idea that they will live "forever after" with one partner.

Lesbians often either reject or modify contemporary heterosexual practices. The findings by Rose et al. (1993) imply that, even when lesbians conform to some aspects of heterosexual roles, they do not necessarily reproduce heterosexual power relations in terms of sexual behavior. Furthermore, their courtships may be more sexually satisfying; satisfaction with sex has been shown to be linked to equality in initiating and refusing sex.

Most lesbians value emotional intimacy more than or equal to sexual desire or attractions. They prefer courtship scripts based on friendship and romance (Rose & Zand, 2000). For some women, however, it is ambiguous as to when a relationship shifts from friendship to romance. How does one tell if a friend has sexual interest?

Gordon (2006) reported from a study of dating norms among twenty-three lesbians age 21–63. Most respondents were white and middle class. Nearly all of the women felt that they were not knowledgeable about sex and dating rules in their lesbian community. They could not distinguish when they were on a date from when they were going out as friends. If on a date, they did not know the expectations for behavior. Most felt that they stumbled through dates because they had few guidelines. In contrast, the lesbian community was explicit about some rules, such as the following: a woman has sex with only one woman at a time; monogamy starts when a couple begins dating, even if neither woman verbalizes this; sex is to occur only within the context of a relationship; and casual sex is to be avoided. Having sex for pure physical pleasure or having a relationship primarily for sex were viewed as stereotypically male. Instead, expectations are for women to prioritize the romantic or emotional connection over sexual activity. Sex is not the goal of the relationship but a by-product. In addition, sexual equality is valued; a partner should not be more sexually dominant than the other partner or receive more sexual attention than the other partner.

## Becoming a Couple

When lesbians and gay men become a couple with another same-sex person, that person is usually the central focus of the person's chosen "family" and is an emotional and, typically, a sexual partner (James & Murphy, 1998). Because most lesbian and gay couples are not legally married, they might create a ceremony to validate and celebrate their commitment (D. E. Murphy, 2004). Ceremonies range from a private exchange of rings to a public celebration with family and friends. Various ceremonies that lesbian and gay couples use have been described in the literature (Butler, 1990). Most couples, however, have no ceremony. Of the gay couples in Berger's (1990a) study, who ranged from age 24 to age 74, only 12.6

percent had a commitment ceremony. Bryant and Demian (1994) reported that 16 percent of their sample—with an average age of 36.5 for men and 34.7 for women—had a commitment ceremony. Oswald, Gebbie, and Culton (2001) reported from a sample of 527 nonmetropolitan lesbian, gay, bisexual, and transgender (LGBT) men (93 percent of whom were white) that 55 percent had taken steps to legalize their relationship and 19 percent had celebrated a commitment ceremony.

Same-sex couples can now attain civil unions and domestic partnerships in some U.S. states. At this time, they can marry in only a few states. Many, however, express the desire to marry (Kaiser Family Foundation, 2001). Some state and local governmental entities have offered limited benefits, such as group health insurance, for the same-sex partners of their employees, but most same-sex couples do not have such options (Herek, 2006).

Berger (1990a) found that the time between first meeting and moving in together ranged from less than one week to six years, with a median time of approximately four months. According to Berger (1990a), living together may be a couple's attempt to solidify the relationship because of the lack of external validation for their couple status.

Some partners commit to each other but do not live with each other. Some partners have more than one significant partner or coexist in heterosexual marriages (Cabaj & Klinger, 1996; Hostetler & Cohler, 1997; James & Murphy, 1998; Peplau & Cochran, 1990). Shernoff (1995) pointed out that gay men display diverse patterns in couples, including sexual exclusivity, primarily sexual exclusivity, sexual nonexclusivity and an unacknowledged open relationship, sexual nonexclusivity and an acknowledged open relationship, and primarily exclusive relationships with nonsexual lovers.

Because some men participate in several coupled relationships at the same time, it may be useful to distinguish primary from nonprimary (casual) relationships or from being single (Cohler & Galatzer-Levy, 2000). Yet some men who have only casual relationships with others and no primary link may not self-identify as single. Asking lesbians and gay men to define their relationship situation is the best way to understand what it is to them (Cabaj & Klinger, 1996; Hostetler & Cohler, 1997).

Another source of diversity is the ways lesbian and gay couples refer to themselves. In a national survey of mostly white lesbian (560) and gay (706) couples who had been together for an average of six years, respondents used several terms most often and about equally: *lover, partner,* and *life partner.* More men (40 percent) than women (30 percent) preferred the term *lover;* more women (37 percent) than men (27 percent) preferred the terms *partner* and *life partner* (Bryant & Demian, 1994). Some may not use any of these terms. They might reject the term *partner* because it can imply a business association or because it is often used in other social situations (e.g., tennis partners). The term *lover* can imply primarily a sexual relationship (Berger, 1990a; D. E. Murphy, 2004). Other terms such as *girlfriend* or *boyfriend* can be confusing because lesbians use *girlfriend* to also describe their women friends. Other terms include *significant other, spousal equivalent,* and *domestic partner* (D. E. Murphy, 2004). Again, it is best to ask the members in each individual couple what they prefer to call themselves (Berger, 1990a).

## Couple Patterns

A lesbian or gay pair who declares couplehood may not know exactly how to be a couple. There is no prescribed way to be a same-sex couple. Each couple must develop its own parameters and rules (Rostosky, Riggle, Dudley, & Wright, 2006).

A prevalent belief is that partners in same-sex couples copy traditional heterosexual couples, such as adopting the role of husband or wife. One plays a masculine dominant role and the other a feminine submissive role. This butch-femme pattern, particularly among lesbians (Laird, 2000), was dominant in the United States from the 1920s to the early 1960s (Faderman, 1992; Nestle, 1992), and especially during the 1950s (Nestle, 1992), and it applied to white and ethnic/racial lesbians.

In their study of working-class lesbians between the mid-1930s and the early 1960s in Buffalo, New York, Kennedy and Davis (1993) found that women enacted butch-femme roles through appearance and sexual roles. "Butches" portrayed a masculine appearance in clothes and haircuts, whereas "femmes" had a feminine or even glamorous appearance. Butch-femme roles also determined the sexual relationship: the butch was the doer and the giver, and the femme was the receiver. At that time, lesbians had to adopt a butch or femme role to participate in the community and attain the benefits of collective resistance to oppression.

Butch-femme roles have not lasted (Weston, 1996). Most lesbians today cannot imagine taking on a butch or femme role. The feminist and lesbian feminist movements also have rejected the roles as patriarchic (Kennedy & Davis, 1993).

Some lesbian couples, however, may feel comfortable with such roles and play out some version of them.

A traditional pattern among some gay couples is the mentor-apprentice role (Harry, 1984). Partners using this pattern often differ in age by five to ten years. The older partner is the mentor and dominates decision making. Lesbians are less likely to follow this pattern (Reilly & Lynch, 1990). Most contemporary lesbian and gay couples reject roles of wife and husband, butch and femme, dominant and submissive, active and passive, or powerful and powerless (e.g., D. E. Murphy, 1994; Peplau, 1991, 1993).

The most frequent couple pattern is that of best friends, which reflects flexible and egalitarian roles (Faderman, 1991). In addition, it promotes sharing, reciprocity, companionship, and role flexibility. One partner does not do everything (Peplau, 1993). Gay couples usually have more discretionary income than lesbian couples and might hire outside help for household work (Peplau & Cochran, 1990), which helps contribute to an egalitarian relationship in other tasks.

The downside of having to figure out how to "do" relationships can cause stress and conflict (D. G. Patterson & Schwartz, 1994). For example, when gay partners do housework, they may experience conflict over who does traditionally male versus traditionally female tasks (Crisp, Priest, & Torgerson, 1998; Patterson & Schwartz, 1994).

## Love, Other Positive Aspects, and Commitment

The relationships of lesbians and gay men are the same as heterosexual relationships in terms of deep emotional attachments and commitments (Kurdek, 2001, 2005; Mackey, Diemer, & O'Brien, 2000). Lesbians and gay men also commit for a long time. In a study by Bryant and Demian (1994), most lesbians (92 percent) and gay men (96 percent) reported that they wanted to be together for life or for "a long time." In a study by Rust (1996), close to half of lesbians (48 percent) and even more gay men (80 percent) indicated that they wanted a lifetime monogamous relationship with one partner. Peplau et al. (1997) investigated the relationships of 398 African American lesbians and 325 African American gay men (both groups ranged between age 18 and age 70). On average, they had been in their relationships for more than two years. Most of them (74 percent of women and 61 percent of men) indicated that they were in love with their partners. Only about 10 percent indicated that they were not in love, and the rest were unsure. In general, respondents reported high levels of closeness in their relationships, with mean scores near 6 on a 7-point scale.

Rostosky et al. (2006) found in their sample of lesbian and gay couples (mean age 31.9, age range 19–54) that couples had been together an average of 6.4 years, with a range of 7 months to 22 years, and that they perceived their commitment as involving investments, rewards, costs, and a match with personal values and ideals. Ideals for their relationships were sexual and emotional intimacy, communication, and overall high relationship quality. Respondents perceived obtaining these ideals as central to the commitment of the couple. Commitment was also perceived as involving recognition and negotiation of individual differences. Decisions about monogamy were central to couples' perceptions of commitment. Relationship costs for the couples included limits on personal freedom and conflict and stress from disclosure of their couple status. Constraints such as not having access to legal marriage were also limitations. The results showed no differences between lesbian and gay couples on the variables in the study.

Lesbian and gay couples are also similar to heterosexual couples in many other ways. For example, no discrepancies have been found in the quality of intimate relationships (Gottman et al., 2003; Kurdek, 1994b, 1995a, 2001, 2004, 2005; Mackey, Diemer, & O'Brien, 2000; Peplau & Beals, 2004; Peplau & Fingerhut, 2007; Roisman, Clausell, Holland, Fortuna, & Elieff, 2008), cohesion (Green, Bettinger, & Zacks, 1996), or adjustments (Kurdek, 1995b).

## Summary

Although lesbians and gay men face obstacles in meeting others, they use contemporary means, including the Internet and dating services. When dating, they follow the traditional pattern that heterosexuals follow, but when on dates, there are some differences between lesbians and gay men. Gay men more frequently have sex on the first date, whereas lesbians focus more on the emotions they felt on the date. Lesbians use three courtship scripts: romance, friendship, and sexually explicit. They tend to prefer courtship scripts based on friendship and romance. They usually become friends first; romance and sex come later, although it can be ambiguous when a relationship shifts from friendship to romance. However, they use both direct and indirect ways to express romantic interest. Once lesbians and gay men are in couples, they have a range of statuses, which include living together and not living together. A best-friends model based on equality typically structures their relationship. Older models based on inequality and butch-femme roles for lesbians are rarely used today. Like heterosexual couples, lesbian and gay couples have deep committed relationships. But there are also differences, such as fewer power differences and more equity in lesbian and gay couples.

## Vignette

Twenty-three-year-old Jane met twenty-four-year-old Alicia at a dance for lesbians. They were attracted to each other and decided to see each other again. They went out for dinner, to the movies, on bike rides, and visited friends. Jane wanted to have sex early on, but Alicia did not, because she wanted to get to know Jane better. Jane agreed but was not particularly happy about it. After several months of friendship, Alicia agreed that she was ready to have sex with Jane. This dramatically increased the seriousness of their relationship. They eventually decided to have a commitment service with friends and "officially" became a couple. They bought rings for each other and were quite happy with their new arrangement. When they moved in with each other, they encountered some difficulties over who would do what in the household. They finally wrote down what each person wanted to do and negotiated tasks. Even though Jane and Alicia didn't always feel like they knew how to be a couple, they worked things out and were happy with their relationship, with living together, and with being a couple.

## Resources

### Online

**MeetGayCouples.com**
This site is a social network for gay and lesbian couples to meet other couples. The site aims to help couples find like-minded couples for friendship and support, and it provides an array of articles, advice, and free resources.

### For Further Reading

Campbell, J. E. (2004). *Getting it on online: Cyberspace, gay male sexuality, and embodied identity*. New York: Harrington Park Press.
Marcus, E. (1999). *The male couple's guide: Finding a man, making a home, building a life* (3rd ed.). New York: Harper Perennial.

Nichols, C. (2002). *Dating women: Love, sex, flirting and the happy everafter.* London: Women's Press.

Partners Task Force for Lesbian and Gay Couples. (1995). *Partners national survey of lesbian and gay couples.* Seattle: Author. Retrieved from http://www.buddybuddy.com/survey.html.

Patterson, C. L., & D'Augelli, A. R. (Eds.). (1998). *Lesbian, gay, and bisexual identities in families: Psychological perspectives.* New York: Oxford University Press.

Roberts, S. (1998). *Roberts' rules of lesbian dating.* Duluth, MN: Spinster Ink.

Rose, S. (2002). *Lesbian love and relationships.* New York: Harrington Park Press.

Vernon, S. (2010). Retirement planning for gay and lesbian couples. *Money for Life.* Retrieved from http://moneywatch.bnet.com/retirement-planning/blog/money-life/retirement-planning-for-gay-and-lesbian-couples/1744.

# Couples Who Have or Want to Have Children

Do lesbians and gay men want to be parents?

Are there diverse ways of being a parent?

What is the most common way of bringing children into a lesbian or gay relationship?

What other paths can lesbian and gay couples take to have children?

What are some of the problems of insemination or surrogacy?

What obstacles do some lesbian and gay parents face that are specific to them?

What obstacles does a co-parent face?

How do children affect couple satisfaction?

Do parents share child care equally?

If parents disclose their sexual identity to their children, how are the children likely to react?

How do children deal with disclosure of their parents' sexual identity?

What are your conclusions on how the children of lesbian and gay parents adjust?

Many lesbians and gay men are parents or want to be parents. In a national poll, almost half (49 percent) of lesbians and gay men who were not parents said that they would like to have children or adopt children (Kaiser Family Foundation, 2001).

The 2000 U.S. census estimated that same-sex couples are raising approximately 250,000 children younger than age 18 (Gates & Ost, 2004). Of those couples age 22–55, 34 percent of lesbian couples who lived together and 22 percent of gay couples who lived together have children. By comparison, approximately 46 percent of heterosexual married couples have children (Bennett & Gates, 2004). Same-sex couples with minor children tend to live in communities with greater numbers of children. More same-sex partner households with minor children live in California than in any other state (Gates & Ost, 2004).

The 2000 Black Pride Survey reported that nearly 40 percent of African American lesbian and bisexual women, 15 percent of African American gay and bisexual men, and 15 percent of African American transgender persons have children (National Gay and Lesbian Task Force, 2000). Of those surveyed at black gay-pride celebrations, 25 percent of the women and 4 percent of the men reported that children lived with them (Battle, Cohen, Warren, Fergerson, & Audam, 2002). Mays, Chatters, Cochran, and Mackness (1998) studied a large sample of African American lesbians and gay men (506 women and 673 men). Most of the sample members were low income. One in three women reported having one or more children, and 26 percent reported that a child was living in their household; in contrast, nearly 12 percent of the men reported having one or more children, but only 2 percent reported that a child was living in their household.

The 2000 U.S. census, with a much larger sample than the previously cited studies, reported that eighty-five thousand African American same-sex couples live in the United States. Of all same-sex couples, 14 percent were African American (Gates & Ost, 2004). About one in five same-sex couples with at least one African American partner (21 percent) were interracial. African American female same-sex households were raising children younger than age 18 at nearly twice the rate of white female same-sex couples (52 percent versus 32 percent). African American male same-sex households were raising children at almost twice the rate of white male same-sex households (36 percent versus 18 percent). The 2000 census identified 105,025 Hispanic same-sex couples. Of Hispanic female same-sex couples, 54 percent were raising at least one child younger than age 18, compared with 70 percent of Hispanic married opposite-sex couples and 59 percent of Hispanic cohabiting opposite-sex couples. Female same-sex couples in which both partners were Hispanic were raising children at more than twice the rate of white, non-Hispanic female same-sex couples (66 percent versus 32 percent). Male same-sex couples in which both partners were Hispanic were raising children at about three times the rate of white, non-Hispanic same-sex couples (58 percent versus 19 percent; Cahill, 2008).

Moreover, many lesbians and gay men are parents of children who do not live with them. Their children may be away at college or living on their own as adults. Among those in this situation, between 25 percent and 37 percent of older lesbian and gay persons have had children (Bradford & Ryan, 1991).

A lesbian and gay couple may also agree to have children together and rear them together. The parents may or may not live in the same household. This situation also applies to interracial or interethnic couples (Rosenfeld, 2007).

## Ways to Have Children

Many lesbian and gay persons with children, perhaps still the majority, have children from a previous heterosexual relationship (Bigner, 2006). Growing numbers of lesbians and gay men are choosing to have children in a same-sex relationship. Several paths to parenthood are available to them, each of which involves a different degree of biological relatedness of the child to the parents. Some couples adopt, in which case neither parent is biologically related to the child. Some gay couples use traditional surrogacy, so that the partner who provides the sperm is biologically related to the child. Donor insemination is widespread among lesbians and has been increasingly used since the 1980s. The partner who carries the child is usually biologically related to the child. Other lesbian couples use in vitro fertilization, such that one woman contributes the egg and the other woman is the birth mother. Some states permit two same-sex partners to be the legal parents of a child. In states that do not allow for second-parent adoption by a same-sex partner, only one partner in the couple is the legal parent (Peplau & Fingerhut, 2007).

Both insemination and surrogacy agreements can be problematic. Lesbian couples who use donor sperm insemination have to resolve issues such as anonymity of the sperm donor or possible future legal or social connections with the child and the donor (Hartman, 1999; Patterson & Chan, 1996). Although some states have laws specifying that a sperm donor is not a legal father, not all states have addressed the issue. Lesbians, therefore, sometimes confront issues related to the paternity of the child born as the result of a donor insemination agreement. If they undergo insemination with the sperm of a known donor, the man may demand a parental role in their family. This can happen even if a pre-existing arrangement mandates otherwise. The couple can avoid challenges to their parental relationship by acquiring sperm from an anonymous donor through a sperm bank. Traditional surrogacy can also create problems for gay couples, such as having to contend with a number of legal and moral issues (Hartman, 1999; Patterson & Chan, 1996). The main issue is the possibility of the surrogate suing for custody after the child is born. Because of this, many states discourage or limit the practice of surrogacy.

As noted already, if a couple chooses adoption, then neither parent is biologically related to the child. Nevertheless, many lesbian and gay persons adopt children each year. Some adopt children they are raising with a partner (often a biological child of the partner). Some adopt children because family members or close friends died or became incapacitated and could not take care of their own children. Some persons work through intermediaries who know of women who want to have their babies adopted. Adoptions are handled through private and public agencies, domestic and foreign (Lassiter, Dew, Newton, Hays, & Yarbrough, 2006; National Gay and Lesbian Task Force, 2000; Patterson, 1994). Some states prohibit lesbian and gay persons from adopting children or from being foster parents. Judicial rulings in a few states, however, have allowed for adoption by openly lesbian and gay couples (Human Rights Campaign Foundation, 2002). When adoption is available to couples, partners can adopt a child together or use co-parent or joint adoption. The co-parent (or joint parent), who has no biological relation to the child, has no legal rights regarding the child.

There are also other ways to legally adopt minor children (Patterson, 1995a), as noted earlier. So-called stranger adoptions occur when biological parents are unable or unwilling to take care of a child. In such cases, a court dissolves legal bonds between the child and his or her biological parents and creates new legal ties between the child and the adoptive parents. Another type of adoption can occur when lesbian and gay couples rear children together. In some states, the legal system might recognize only one member of a same-sex couple as a legal parent. In states where second-parent adoptions are available, such families might seek second-parent adoptions to establish legal status for the second parent without terminating the rights or responsibilities of the legal parent. In recent years, both stranger adoptions and second-parent adoptions have occurred across the United States (Richman, 2009). But the laws governing adoption vary considerably across the states (Joslin & Minter, 2008; Patterson, 1995a). Some states allow for second-parent adoptions. In the courts, the issue often reaches appellate courts: some state appellate courts have affirmed second-parent adoptions, but others have rejected them. In some states, the law bars unmarried couples from adopting (and forbids legal recognition of same-sex marriages). This prevents lesbian and gay couples from making any type of adoption. Sometimes, same-sex couples who have been married in one state are not legally able to attain joint adoptions in another state (Patterson, 2009).

Even though state laws vary, adoptions by openly lesbian and gay adults still occur (National Gay and Lesbian Task Force, 2005a, 2005b). Openly lesbian or gay adults have also completed stranger adoptions without the parents' sexual identity becoming a topic of public discussion.

Across the United States today, legal and policy contexts for lesbian and gay parents and their children vary remarkably. At one end of the scale are those states in which the law recognizes same-sex marriages, stranger adoptions, and second-parent adoptions and in which parents' sexual identity is deemed irrelevant for purposes of foster care, child custody, and visitation. At the other end of the scale are those states in which the law does not recognize same-sex marriages and disadvantages lesbian and gay parents in custody and visitation proceedings. Thus, the legal situation for lesbian and gay parents and their children varies dramatically from one jurisdiction to another. This is a situation, however, that is in flux (Patterson, 2009).

Research findings do not support the idea that lesbian and gay adults are less likely than others to provide good adoptive or foster homes. Findings on the development of children with lesbian and gay parents do not warrant legal discrimination against the children or their parents (Herek, 2006; Patterson, 2007, 2009).

## Obstacles for Lesbian and Gay Parents

### Heterosexism

Lesbians and gay men who want to be parents face many obstacles. The overriding obstacle is heterosexism (see the introduction and chapters 5, 6, and 8). Many people in general and in the legal system give lesbians and gay men no validation because they disapprove of their sexual identities and same-sex coupling. Many people believe that lesbians and gay men are unfit to raise children and should have no association with children. Others believe that children of lesbian and gay parents will be psychologically and socially maladjusted, suffer social stigmatization (Matthews & Lease, 2000), experience negative development in gender identity, or become lesbian or gay themselves (Shapiro, 1996). Many children experience stigma because of these false beliefs.

## Fears of Losing Custody

Lesbians and gay men who have custody of their children from a previous heterosexual marriage may fear losing custody of their children or contact with their children because of their sexual identity. This is a realistic fear, as many lesbian and gay parents are denied custody of or visitation rights to see their biological children (Patterson & Chan, 1996). In many jurisdictions, courts have awarded custody to the heterosexual parent or to another person in the extended family, such as a grandparent (Benkov, 1994; Patterson, 1995b). But court decisions on custody have changed since the first same-sex custody cases more than thirty years ago (Arnup, 1999). Some judges have ruled that same-sex sexual identity alone does not render a parent unfit to raise children (Rosenblum, 1991). The National Association of Social Workers, the American Psychological Association, and other professional and human services organizations and associations support the position that a person's sexual identity should have no effect on child custody decisions or in determining whether a person qualifies as a foster or adoptive parent (Benkov, 1994; Cahill, Ellen, & Tobias, 2002). But there is considerable variability on custody and visitation issues across jurisdictions (Brantner, 1992; Joslin & Minter, 2008; Richman, 2009). In some states, parents' sexual identity has no relevance to custody and visitation disputes. In others, parents' sexual identity is considered relevant if (and only if) it can be shown to have a negative effect on the child. Because a connection of this type can be difficult to establish, judgments in such situations often favor lesbian and gay parents (Patterson, 2009). Some state courts, however, presume that the sexual identity of lesbian and gay parents makes them undesirable parents.

In other states, legal standards for custody fall between the two extremes. For example, the law might not explicitly deny rights on the basis of parental sexual identity, but it nevertheless does not look well upon lesbian and gay parents. It is often difficult to anticipate the outcomes in such cases (Richman, 2009).

A consensus has emerged among professional organizations, including the American Psychological Association, the American Bar Association, the American Medical Association, the American Academy of Pediatrics, and the National Association of Social Workers, on the body of research on lesbian and gay parents and their children. These organizations have adopted policies that oppose discrimination based on sexual identity, and they support legalization of second-parent and stranger adoptions by lesbians and gay men.

## Co-parents

A co-parent is the nonbiological parent of a child born into a lesbian or gay relationship or a nonadoptive parent. Persons with these statuses can provide support as full partners in parenting. If opting for conception, lesbian couples must determine which woman will bear the child. One will be the biological parent and the other the co-parent, or what some researchers call the social parent. Research affirms that the quality of the parent-child relationship is the strongest predictor of outcomes in a child's development (Bennett, 2003; Bos, Van Balen, & Van Den Boom, 2004a, 2004b; Vanfraussen, Ponjaert-Kristoffersen, & Brewaeys, 2003; Wainright, Russell, & Patterson, 2004). Bennett (2003) also contends that it is the quality of care, more than legal or biological status, that most saliently contributes to a child's connection to a parent. Vanfraussen et al. (2003) found that time spent with a child was the most significant factor in bonding; biological relationships rated second. Similarly, there is no difference between biological and social mothers in lesbian families with respect to the quality of parent-child interactions. Also, there are no significant differences between biological and social mothers in how they emotionally experience parenthood (Bos et al., 2004b). However, support for co-mothers from family may be variable (Appleby & Anastas, 1998).

Another issue is that the biological parent may not treat the co-parent as an equal parent (Mallon, 2000; Reimann, 1997), which results in an unequal balance of power (Rutter & Schwartz, 1996). Even with second-parent adoption, some lesbian co-parents continue to feel that the birth mother's bond with the child is stronger (Chambers & Polikoff, 1999). The family of a biological mother might also undermine the nonbiological mother's relationship to the child, perceiving her as "less" of a mother. The biological mother's family may also give excessive support to their family member and her child. The family's involvement and frequent presence may cause conflict between partners (Goldberg & Sayer, 2006).

Other concerns for the co-parent include managing invisibility. For example, in most jurisdictions, children in lesbian and gay families have only one legal parent. The co-parent has no legal rights regarding the child. The co-parent's name rarely appears on the child's birth certificate, and the co-parent rarely wins the right to adopt the child (Burke, 1993; Segal-Sklar, 1996). Without any legal claim to the child, the co-parent also receives no recognition from social institutions such as schools or medical providers (Reimann, 1997).

If a lesbian couple wants to have more than one child, a solution to the co-parent dilemma is to take turns in childbearing (Appleby & Anastas, 1998). Another solution is for the co-parent to legally adopt a child born to or adopted by the partner (Benkov, 1994; Shernoff, 1996), if doing so is allowed in the state of residence. Second-parent adoption removes any vagueness about the status of the "other" mother and the emotional and legal jeopardy of the nonlegal parent. It can also help clarify a parent's status for a child (McClellan, 2001).

In her study of twenty gay parents who obtained second-parent adoptions, Connolly (2002) found that legal status increased confidence of the parents when dealing with schools, hospitals, insurance companies, and other institutions that require a legally defined family (Pawelski et al., 2006). Some couples move to a state that allows for second-parent adoption (Patterson, 2007) or joint adoption rights (Herek, 2006).

Some states encourage child-placement agencies to discriminate against lesbian and gay persons on a religious or moral basis, which can prevent second-parent adoption. However, courts usually determine parenting rights on a case-by-case basis (Cahill & Tobias, 2007).

The establishment of joint and second-parent adoption in some parts of the country was the greatest legal accomplishment for lesbian and gay parents in the 1990s (Sodomy laws in the U.S., 2011). But starting in the mid-1990s, the high profile of lesbian and gay families escalated efforts to prevent them from adopting children or being foster parents (Chambers & Polikoff, 1999).

Children of same-sex couples without second-parent adoption live with the economic and emotional insecurity of not having their relationship with their second mother or father recognized (Cahill, Ellen, et al., 2002). If a child of lesbian or gay parents becomes sick, the legal parent's partner may be unable to authorize medical treatment or may be denied hospital visitation. If the legally recognized parent dies, a child may be removed from the custody of his or her other parent. However, if the second parent has been designated the child's guardian in a will, that may provide some protection against this situation (Cahill & Tobias, 2007).

## Variable Support from Families and Others

Lesbian and gay persons raise children with varying levels of support from their families of origin and their communities. Even when one's family of origin accepts the couple, family members' reactions may become negative if the couple decides to raise children (Muzio, 1999). In contrast, having children sometimes brings the couple closer to their families of origin. Family members may rally to support the couple and be available for and attentive to the children (Garnets, Hancock, Cochran, Goodchilds, & Peplau, 1991; Hequembourg & Farrell, 1999). However, family members may also interfere with the couple and cause conflict between partners.

Lesbian and gay parents also tend to lack support from formalized support systems that assist heterosexual couples during parenthood (Patterson, 1994, 1995b). Few communities openly endorse lesbian and gay families, although some extend them less hostility and present fewer obstacles. Urban settings are more tolerant than rural ones (Friedman, 1997). Lesbian and gay families usually receive less support from their own communities than heterosexual families receive. Moreover, lesbian and gay communities are not as structured around children as heterosexual communities are (Stiglitz, 1990). In deBoer's (2009) study, a gay couple who adopted a child discovered that their gay community was highly ambivalent about children. In part, this was because of the rarity of gay male parenthood; social life in their gay community was not organized around having children, and children were not expected to come to community events. Even friendships may undergo significant changes for gay and lesbian parents when they have children (deBoer, 2009).

## Declining Satisfaction in Couples with Children

Several studies have investigated relationship satisfaction among lesbian couples with children. Some evidence exists that relationship satisfaction may decline shortly after the birth of a child. A recent longitudinal study followed lesbian couples from one month before the birth of a child to three months after the birth (Goldberg & Sayer, 2006). For both the biological and the nonbiological mother, feelings of love for the partner typically declined and conflict increased with the transition to parenthood. Being able to spend less time alone as a couple and the stress from broadening one's repertoire of roles to include that of parent are potential explanations for these changes (Goldberg & Sayer, 2006).

## Division of Labor with Children

Does the egalitarian division of household labor typically found among lesbian and gay couples without children hold for those with children? Available research indicates that parenthood does not change the general pattern of shared household responsibilities. This is particularly true for household chores and decision making (e.g., Patterson, 1995b; Patterson, Sutfin, & Fulcher, 2004). Some studies have found an equal division of child-care responsibilities. Others have found that lesbian couples with children endorse an egalitarian division of child care as their ideal (Chan, Raboy, & Patterson, 1998b; Patterson, 1995b; Patterson, Sutfin, et al., 2004). In a study of lesbian and heterosexual couples rearing young children, lesbian mothers each spent an average of about thirty-five hours per week in paid employment and reported sharing child care evenly (Patterson, Sutfin, et al., 2004). Similar findings have been reported for lesbian couples in other studies, as well as for gay couples (Kurdek, 1995c; Patterson, 2000, 2002; Peplau & Spalding, 2000).

Some studies, however, have reported that lesbian couples adopt a less-than-egalitarian division of child care (Ciano-Boyce & Shelley-Sireci, 2002; Patterson, 1995b). For example, among lesbian couples that have children through insemination, role status (the fact that one woman carries, bears, and often nurses the child) may shape work-family roles, at least in the beginning. This may violate one partner's value of equality and equal power. But others may accept the differentiated roles as an efficient and satisfactory way to divide labor (Goldberg, 2010). Many couples in a study by Goldberg and Perry-Jenkins (2007) used various strategies to compensate for the biological differential; for example, the partner who could not breast-feed might bottle-feed the baby or take responsibility for bathing the baby.

How do the division of labor and parental roles change when children get older? In a follow-up study of parents with three-year-old children, the birth mothers continued to do more of the child care while nonbiological mothers engaged in more hours of paid work. Couples often shared housework equally (Goldberg, Downing, & Sauck, 2008; Johnson & O'Connor, 2002), and lesbian adoptive couples shared child care more equally (Ciano-Boyce & Shelley-Sireci, 2002).

Other researchers found no evidence of labor divisions based on biology (Chan, Brooks, Raboy, & Patterson, 1998; Patterson, Sutfin, et al., 2004; Tasker & Golombok, 1998). Partners shared child-care tasks relatively equally, and nonbiological mothers did not work more hours outside the home than biological mothers. So there is variability among lesbian couples regarding labor arrangements.

Schacher, Auerback, and Silverstein (2005) studied twenty-one men who became fathers as openly gay men. They viewed themselves as sharing both the mothering and the fathering roles with their partners rather than taking on differentiated roles. Men may change their work commitment when they become parents, or they may manage their work time more efficiently to be able to devote time to their families (Mallon, 2004). However, Carrington (2002) observed that both lesbian and gay couples concealed how much housework and child care they accomplished as a way to protect the other partner and his or her workload with respect to housework and child care.

## Disclosures to Children

A major issue for lesbian and gay parents is how open to be with their children about their sexual identities. Some children figure out their parents' sexual identities on their own, but most do not. Negative outcomes can result from parents not being open. Concealing basic aspects of one's family can lead to isolation and stress and may create tension among family members (James, 2002; Lynch & Murray, 2000). Parents' secrecy with children blocks intimacy and openness in addressing family issues (Patterson & Chan, 1996; Rohrbaugh, 1992). It also limits general support from others (Matthews & Lease, 2000).

Because of the fear of losing custody and other potential harms, lesbian and gay parents may decide not to disclose their sexual identities to their children (Patterson & Chan, 1996). Fredriksen (1999) studied lesbians and gay men with children. Three-quarters of the sample reported harassment because of their sexual identity. The harassment was verbal (88 percent), emotional (50 percent), physical (9 percent), and sexual (9 percent). Lesbian and gay parents who do not live with or have custody of their biological children may also experience disclosure dilemmas. They may not make disclosures to placate the custodial parent or members of the child's extended family if those persons control the parent's continued contact with the child (Appleby & Anastas, 1998).

Even if parents never officially disclose to their children, many children experience an awakening about their parent's sexuality. But often they do not recall the single moment or event in which they learned of it. Instead, it comes as a gradually increasing awareness and understanding of their parent's sexual identity over time. Some children grasp their parent's sexual identity because of books on lesbian and gay issues in the home or through behavior, such as frequent outings with a "close" friend (Tasker & Golombok, 1997).

Children also find out about their parents' sexual identities when their parents tell them directly. If members of a couple decide to disclose their sexual identities to their children, they usually wait until the children are old enough to understand and ask questions (Scasta, 1998). The timing also depends on other factors, such as whether parents believe the child may find out from some one else, such as an ex-spouse, or whether they want to explain a particular event, such as a divorce or the beginning of a serious same-sex relationship (Barrett & Tasker, 2001; Lynch & Murray, 2000; R. West & Turner, 1995). Parents may also disclose indirectly, such as taking their children to a gay-pride parade (Bigner & Bozett, 1990).

Disclosure can involve a complex and delicate discussion of conception, such as donor sperm insemination or why the child does not have either a mom or a dad (Segal-Sklar, 1996). In terms of sperm donors, Vanfraussen, Ponjaert-Kristoffersen, and Brewaeys (2003) found that the majority of forty-five mothers preferred that donors remain unknown. More than half (54 percent) of the forty-one children also preferred donor anonymity, but many (46 percent) wanted to have knowledge about their donors. More boys than girls wanted to know the donor's identity and to meet the donor.

The reactions of children to a parent's disclosure are generally positive (Bigner, 1996; Lott-Whitehead & Tully, 1993). They may respond with protectiveness toward their parents (O'Connell, 1993), or they may indicate that the information makes no difference or that they already knew it (Turner, Scadden, & Harris, 1990). In interviews with ten gay fathers and eleven lesbian mothers, Turner et al. (1990) found that for six of eleven mothers, the children responded as if it were not a big deal to them. Four responded with confusion, and one responded with anger and shame. For gay fathers, most children reacted mildly, several were confused, and one expressed anger and shame. Slightly more than half of children had mild or neutral reactions. Some children worry after the parents' disclosures, such as wondering whether they will become gay, worrying about their peers' discovery and potential harassment (Bigner & Bozett, 1990), or worrying about what to do with the negative attitudes they might have about lesbians and gay men (which result from living in a heterosexist society). Some children are ambivalent: intellectually, they accept their parents, but they also have to deal with the stigma related to their parents (Goldberg, 2010). Most children will have questions and will need to have continued discussions about the disclosure (Patterson, 1992).

Most lesbian and gay parents report that openness with their children improves their relationships in the long term. Gay fathers, however, tend not to be as open as lesbian mothers. Fathers fear that disclosure will damage their relationships with their children. But Golombok (2000) found that children seldom reject their gay fathers. Gay fathers who are out in their family life experience better relationships with their partners; their children; their extended families; and if formerly in a heterosexual marriage, with the relatives of their former wives (Bozett, 1993).

Younger children are usually unaware of the associated stigma with being lesbian or gay (Patterson, 1992). In a study by Dundas and Kaufman (2000), children age 5–12 did not feel stigmatized because they had two mothers. They also seemed to understand that their mothers loved each other, which is why they lived together.

Adolescent children might have a more difficult time adjusting to disclosure than either younger or adult children. Adolescents are more likely aware of the stigma associated with same-sex identities and may react with distress, anxiety, anger, or sorrow. They may make deprecating statements to their parents (Appleby & Anastas, 1998) or worry that their peers will see them differently (Hargaden & Llewellin, 1996), especially if they know that their peers have prejudices about same-sex relationships. They may fear that their peers will taunt them or harm them (Scasta, 1998), or they may not bring friends or dates home (Matthews & Lease, 2000).

Children who find out that their parents are lesbian or gay have to negotiate whether and how to disclose to others about their families. Bigner and Bozett (1990) described strategies that children can use to protect themselves from stigma. Children might use boundary control; try to control the parent's behavior, such as behaving in ways that conceal parents' sexual identity; or ask their parents to not hold hands in public, not to wear gay-affirmative clothing (e.g., T-shirts or jewelry with rainbow colors), or to sleep in separate rooms when friends come over. Some parents, especially parents of adolescents, respect their children's preferences and accommodate them within reason (Lynch & Murray, 2000). Others may resist hiding aspects of themselves and strategize with their children about how best to face social pressures (James, 2002). Children might control their own behavior, such as by refusing to appear in public with their parents, or try to control others' behavior, such as by not inviting friends over. They might not disclose their parent's sexual identities to others, or they might use selective disclosure or controlled disclosure to selected persons. Children who grow up with openly lesbian and gay parents will have less choice about making disclosures. In a study of ten-year-olds, Gartrell, Deck, Rodas, Peyser, and Banks (2006) found that 57 percent of children reported that they were completely out about their parents to their peers; 39 percent, to some peers; and 4 percent, to no peers.

Some parents caution their children to keep their parents' sexual identities secret. But there are some situations that require disclosure. For example, parents may have to make disclosures to medical staff, child-care workers, or school officials. In addition, parents face the issue of whether to write "other mother" or "other father" or "parent-parent" on forms (Segal-Sklar, 1996). Parents also have to handle ordinary encounters and questions when they are out in the world, such as when grocery shopping with their children (Martin, 1993).

## How Children Fare

As noted already, opponents to lesbian and gay persons parenting children claim that the children will suffer social stigma, confusion about their sexual identities, and psychological trauma because of their parents' sexual identities. The research on children of lesbian and gay parents, however, has consistently disputed claims that children of lesbian and gay parents display aberrant behavior or psychological damage (e.g., Patterson, 1992, 2000; Perrin, 2002, Stacey & Biblarz, 2001; Wainright et al., 2004). The children do not show significant discrepancies in personality or in social, sexual, or emotional development (e.g., Eliason, 1996; Erich, Leung, Kindle, & Carter, 2005), and the vast number of them grow up to be heterosexual (Bailey, Bobrow, Wolfe, & Mikach, 1995, Tasker & Golombok, 1997).

In early studies, a number of researchers compared development among children of divorced lesbian mothers with that of children of divorced heterosexual mothers and found few significant differences (Stacey & Biblarz, 2001). In the 1990s, studies were done with children who had never lived with heterosexual parents. In the Bay Area Families Study, C. J. Patterson (1997) surveyed a group of children age 4–9 who had been born to or adopted early in life by lesbian mothers. The results revealed that levels of adjustment for both mothers and children fell within the normal range on all measures. The children's self-concepts and preferences for same-gender playmates and activities were similar to those of other children of the same age. In addition, the children scored in the normal range on measures of social competence and behavior problems.

In another study, a probability sample, in contrast to the more typical convenience sample, included adolescents with parents in lesbian couples (Wainright et al., 2004). The adolescents were drawn from a large, national school-based sample. The adolescents experienced the same personal, familial, and school adjustments whether they lived with heterosexual or same-sex parents. Another study conducted research on lesbian and heterosexual couples who used the Sperm Bank of California. In both groups, one parent was biologically related to the child and one was not. Children of lesbian and heterosexual parents showed similar, relatively high levels of social competence, as well as similar, relatively low levels of behavior problems. Teachers' evaluations of the children's adjustment were in agreement with parents' evaluations (Chan, Raboy, & Patterson, 1998; Fulcher, Sutfin, Chan, Scheib, & Patterson, 2005).

Studies on gay fathers are fewer in number than those on lesbian mothers (Bigner & Jacobsen, 1992). But that does not mean that gay men are less fit or able as parents than heterosexual men. Gay partners tend to devote more time and efforts to child care than typical heterosexual fathers, although they are somewhat less involved in child care than lesbian mothers are (Patterson, 1996). Gay fathers, relative to heterosexual fathers, do not differ in their intimacy with their children and show higher levels of warmth and responsiveness (Lambert, 2005). In comparison with heterosexual fathers, gay fathers report being firmer in setting appropriate standards for their children and employing more reasoning strategies with their children (Tasker, 2005).

Stacey and Biblarz's (2001) review of twenty-one studies of children raised by lesbian, gay, and heterosexual parents showed that children with lesbian or gay parents may develop fewer gender stereotypes than those raised with heterosexual parents. Parents' same-sex sexual identity also appears to be positively associated with children being more open to alternatives to heterosexual relationships. But the children are no more likely than children of heterosexual parents to self-identify as lesbian or gay (Patterson, 2006).

The National Longitudinal Study of Adolescent Health provided an opportunity to address a more ethnically diverse group of families and an older group of children (Wainright et al., 2004; Wainright & Patterson, 2006). The sample was also representative of American adolescents and their parents. More than twelve thousand adolescents and parents completed interviews. From that group, the sample included forty-four children age 12–18 who lived with parents involved in marriage or marriage-like relationships with same-sex partners. This group was compared with a matched group of adolescents living with heterosexual partners. Results showed few differences in adjustment between adolescents living with same-sex parents and those living with different-sex parents (Wainright et al., 2004; Wainright & Patterson, 2006). No significant differences occurred on self-reported assessments of psychological well-being (e.g., self-esteem, anxiety), measures of school outcomes (e.g., grade point average, trouble in school), or measures of family relationships (e.g., parental warmth, care from peers and other adults). No significant differences were shown in self-reported substance use, delinquency, or peer victimization. The only statistically reliable difference was that those adolescents with same-sex parents experienced more of a sense of connection to faculty at school (Wainright & Patterson, 2006). Perhaps the most important finding was that the qualities of family relationships rather than parents' sexual identities were consistently related to adolescent outcomes. When parents reported having close relationships with their adolescent children, their children reported better adjustment. Most studies of children of lesbian and gay parents have found that when parent-child relationships are warm and affectionate, the children are more likely to be developing well (Patterson, 2006).

The foregoing findings have been supported by results from many other studies in the United States and other countries. From an ongoing longitudinal study on seventeen-year-old daughters and sons of lesbian mothers, Gartrell and Bos (2010) found from mothers' reports that the children were significantly advanced in school and academics, social areas, and competence. They showed significantly fewer social problems, externalizing problem behaviors, aggression, and rule-breaking, than did others the same age in a normative sample of American youths. Golombok et al. (2003) reported similar results with a near-representative sample of children in the United Kingdom. A longitudinal study in the United Kingdom found that adults reared in lesbian-mother families functioned well in adult life (Tasker & Golombok, 1997, 1998).

Although children of lesbian and gay parents generally develop well, they also experience challenges, as do their parents, from heterosexism, which may take the form of castigation, ridicule, or ostracism among their peers (Stacey, 1998). A substantial minority of ten-year-old children born to lesbian mothers reported that they were subjected to antigay sentiments among their peers. When this happened, they were likely to report having felt angry, upset, or sad. They may also experience prejudice against their parents, which can be painful for them. Overall, though, there is no evidence that these experiences affect their overall adjustment (Gartrell, Deck, Rodas, Peyser, & Banks, 2005).

Resilience research focuses on relational processes that assist family survival and growth under unfavorable circumstances. Many lesbian and gay parents show strength and flexibility, through resilience, intentionality, and redefinition, which assists all the members of a family in meeting the challenges of adversity, including discrimination. Resilience includes both intentionality and redefinition. Intentionality involves behavioral strategies that sustain and legitimize relationships through rituals and legalization of families, as well as the creation of external supports to help the family manage. Redefinition includes symbolic and linguistic mechanisms created to affirm lesbian and gay familial networks, such as inclusive and politicized views of the family, the use of familial names to reinforce relational ties (e.g., referring to friends as brother or sister), and emphasis on the importance to the parents of their sexual identities (Oswald, 2002).

## Summary

Many lesbian and gay persons have children or want to have children. They become parents in various ways, such as having children from previous heterosexual marriages, traditional surrogacy, and donor insemination. When they have children, they experience difficulties that heterosexual couples do not, including heterosexism, fears of losing custody, variable support from families of origin, and disclosure of their sexual identity to their children. Many studies show, however, that the children of lesbian and gay parents develop well, adjust well, and have no more behavioral problems than children in heterosexual families. Younger children adapt better than adolescents, who fear their peers' views on being raised by lesbian or gay parents. However, gay and lesbian parents often show resilience, which helps everyone in the family manage. But the children may still experience ostracism and ridicule. Their parents may also be subject to antigay sentiments. This can be upsetting to the children, but it does not seem to affect their adjustment.

## Vignette

Twenty-nine-year-old Jim and thirty-two-year-old Larry had both been in hetero-sexual marriages before they began their relationship together. They both had children, but their wives had won custody of the children. Jim and Larry decided that they wanted children of their own, so they decided to find a surrogate to have a child for them. The surrogate lived with them and was paid for her serv-ices. The surrogate had a baby girl, Lucy, and Jim and Larry were delighted. They divided up child-care and housework tasks. Jim did not have to get to work as early as Larry did, so he bathed and dressed Lucy. He also took her every day to his mother's home, and his mother cared for her while both men worked. Larry picked her up and took her home in the evening. Lucy grew up loving her par-ents and was proud of them. She felt loved and cared for every day. She asked for a brother or sister a lot, so Jim and Larry decided to have another child with a surrogate. They later had a boy, Jody. They were a happy family. The parents prepared for when their children would enter public school, but they later found a private school with many children of lesbian and gay parents and enrolled their children there.

## Resources

### Online

**COLAGE: People with a Lesbian, Gay, Bisexual, Transgender, or Queer Parent**
The COLAGE Web site (http://www.colage.org) focuses on advocacy, activism, so-cial justice, and community building for children of LGBT and queer parents.
**PFLAG**
Parents, Families, and Friends of Lesbians and Gays (PFLAG, at http://www.pflag .org) is a national organization that helps parents of lesbian and gay children and promotes respect, dignity, and equality for gay men and lesbians.
**Gay Parent**
*Gay Parent* magazine (http://www.gayparentmag.com) is a resource for gay and lesbian parents and their families. The Web site also includes a nationwide di-rectory of support groups.

## For Further Reading

Benkov, L. (1994). *Reinventing the family: The emerging story of lesbian and gay partners*. New York: Crown.

Burns, K. (2005). *Gay and lesbian families*. Farmington Hills, MI: Greenhaven Press.

Curry, H., Clifford, D., & Hertz, F. (2004). *A legal guide for lesbian and gay couples*. Berkeley, CA: Nolo.

Espeio, R. (2009). *Gay and lesbian families*. Detroit: Greenhaven Press.

Goldberg, A. E. (2010). *Lesbian and gay parents and their children: Research on the family life cycle*. Washington, DC: American Psychological Association.

Martin, A. (1993). *The lesbian and gay parenting handbook: Creating and raising our families*. New York: HarperPerennial.

Patterson, C. J., & D'Augelli, A. R. (1998). *Lesbian, gay, and bisexual identities in families: Psychological perspectives*. New York: Oxford University Press.

Tasker, F. L., & Bigner, J. J. (Eds.). (2007). *Gay and lesbian parenting: New directions*. Binghamton, NY: Haworth Press.

Tasker, F. L., & Golombok, S. (1997). *Growing up in a lesbian family: Effects on child development*. New York: Guilford Press.

Weston, K. (1991). *Families we choose: Lesbians, gays, kinship*. New York: Columbia University Press.

# Satisfaction, Other Benefits, and Maintenance Behaviors

In what ways are lesbian and gay couples similar to heterosexual couples with respect to relationship satisfaction? In what ways are they different?

What kinds of rewards affect higher relationship satisfaction?

How are lesbian relationships different, in a positive way, from gay and heterosexual relationships?

How do the variables of power equity, fairness, affectivity, attachment, personal autonomy, and psychological intimacy play a role in satisfaction?

What are your conclusions about frequency of sex and sexual satisfaction in lesbian and gay couples?

For gay men, how does sexual nonmonogamy play a role in couples?

How might gender socialization affect some lesbians' sexuality?

What are the basic maintenance behaviors in lesbian and gay couples?

Is conflict behavior more effective in lesbian, gay, or heterosexual couples?

Lesbian and gay persons want relationships that are satisfying to them. They are as capable as heterosexual persons are in creating satisfying relationships (Alonzo, 2005). In other words, lesbian, gay, and heterosexual people all can experience satisfying relationships and in similar ways (Mackey, Diemer, & O'Brien, 2004; Metz, Rosser, & Strapko, 1994; Peplau & Fingerhut, 2007). Roisman, Clausell, Holland, Fortuna, and Elieff (2008) found that committed lesbian and gay persons neither are less satisfied with their relationships than heterosexuals nor report higher levels of the kinds of personal attributes that support the quality and longevity of adult relationships. In lab studies with lesbian, gay, and heterosexual participants, Roisman et al. also found that lesbians and gay men were among the most secure adults they interviewed. Ethnic and interracial lesbian and gay couples are also no more or less satisfied with their relationships than heterosexual couples (Peplau, Cochran, & Mays, 1997).

In some samples, same-sex relationships were more satisfying for older people. For example, Schreurs and Buunk (1996) found that the older the participants were in lesbian couples, the more satisfied they were in their relationship. Berger (1996) found that for gay men, having a lover or exclusive sex partner was highly related to satisfaction in old age.

Partnerships were also associated with physical and emotional benefits for older persons. Grossman, D'Augelli, and Hershberger (2000) reported that older lesbian, gay, and bisexual persons who lived with a partner reported less loneliness and better physical and emotional health. Gay men experienced less depression when in love partnerships (O'Brien, 1992). Having a partner in a monogamous relationship also is strongly associated with higher levels of psychosocial adaptation and self-esteem for older gay persons (Brown, Sarosy, Cook, & Quarto, 1997).

## Factors Associated with Positive Relationship Satisfaction in Couples

A number of factors result in satisfaction in lesbian and gay couples. Some have been shown to have the same result in heterosexual couples.

### High Rewards and Low Costs

In line with social exchange theory, happiness tends to be high when partners perceive many rewards and few costs in their relationships (e.g., Beals, Impett, Peplau, & Rose, 2002; Kurdek, 1991a, 1994c). As perceived costs decrease and perceived rewards and emotional investment increase, satisfaction with one's relationship also increases. Contentment with one's partner also grows with the rewards of (1) having a partner who is a source of support and comfort and is willing to express warmth and nurturance and (2) perceiving that few differences exist with the partner regarding satisfaction with social support and expressiveness (Kurdek, 1992, 1995a).

Peplau and Fingerhut (2007) also found that relationship satisfaction is associated with low costs and high rewards. In addition, they found that greater expectancy of positive interaction and greater empathy (i.e., both partners agree on the affective tone of their interaction) are related to greater relationship satisfaction. This suggests the benefit of studies that use subtler measures of relationship rewards and costs. Such measures more directly relate to the quality of emotional connection between partners. Moreover, they may be better indicators of the fate of the relationship than variables that measure only positive or negative levels of interaction.

In studies of lesbian and gay persons in relationships, positive affects, such as humor and affection, are also rewarding, and thus related to higher levels of relationship satisfaction. Contempt, disgust, and defensiveness are related to lower levels of relationship satisfaction. These results are consistent with those found in research on married heterosexual couples (e.g., Gottman, 1994; Gottman, Coan, Carrere, & Swanson, 1998; Gottman & Levenson, 1992).

## Equity and Fairness

Lesbian partners strongly value equity and tend to believe that partners should be equal in every way. They strive for fairness in decision making about roles, finances, and household responsibilities (Kurdek, 1998b; Reilly & Lynch, 1990). Schreurs and Buunk (1996) also found that, for lesbian couples, greater satisfaction is linked to perceptions of greater equity or fairness in their relationships. Several studies of both lesbian and gay persons have found that satisfaction is greater when partners believe that they are relatively equal in terms of power and decision making (Peplau & Spalding, 2000). Wanting equity and fairness, however, may not necessarily mean attaining them. Although most lesbian and gay couples hold equity and fairness as important values, only a minority of partners reported that those values actually characterize their relationships (Reilly & Lynch, 1990). For example, two men in a couple may both want to play the dominant role in decision making (James & Murphy, 1998).

## Power Equity

Power in close relationships is usually assessed in terms of dominance, or whether one partner is more influential than the other (Peplau & Fingerhut, 2007). In a study by Kurdek (1995a), lesbians scored significantly higher on the value of power equity than did gay persons. Many partners, however, do not believe that their partnership are "exactly equal" in this area (Peplau & Cochran, 1990). Even when a couple values power equity, some partners will have more power. Social exchange theory predicts that the partner who has greater power has relatively greater personal resources, such as education, money, or social standing. For lesbians, research results are less clear cut, although some studies found that income is significantly related to power in their relationships (Reilly & Lynch, 1990).

## Affectivity

Positive and negative affectivity correlate positively and negatively, respectively, with lesbian and gay couples' relationship satisfaction (Todosijevic, Rothblum, & Soloman, 2005). Same-sex couples who show negative affectivity (e.g., depression, anxiety, fear, anger, guilt, neuroticism, sadness) may hang on to those attributes. They also are likely to amplify the significance of negative events in their relationships. In contrast, partners who show more positive affectivity (e.g., interest, excitement, strength, pride) help maintain each other's well-being by providing support and by minimizing the frequency of unresolved relationship conflict (Kurdek, 2003).

## Attachment

Individuals' differences in attachment are also associated with satisfaction in lesbian and gay relationships. A person is high in attachment to the extent that he or she desires shared activities, spending time with a partner, long-term commitment, and sexual exclusivity. Lesbian and gay persons who strongly value attachment in relationships report significantly higher satisfaction, closeness, and love for their partners than do persons who score lower on this variable (Eldridge & Gilbert, 1990).

## Personal Autonomy

Lesbians and gay men can also differ in the degree to which they desire personal autonomy, which is defined as wanting to have separate friends and activities, apart from one's primary relationship. Lower levels of love and satisfaction have been associated with high personal autonomy, and lower scores on this variable have been associated with higher levels of love and satisfaction (Eldridge & Gilbert, 1990).

## Psychological Intimacy and Intimate Communication

Psychological openness is the same as psychologically intimate communication. Open and honest communication is crucial in nurturing and sustaining the link between two persons. When people feel safe enough to be themselves with their partners and to reveal inner thoughts and feelings that are not customarily part of other relationships, such as those with friends and parents, a sense of psychological intimacy develops. Being connected in a close relationship that includes having one's inner thoughts and feelings accepted may contribute to deeper satisfaction (Mackey, Diemer, et al., 2004).

In a study by Mackey, Diemer, et al. (2004), lesbian, gay, and heterosexual respondents frequently used openness and honesty to convey psychological intimacy and what their relationships meant to them. More lesbian partners reported that their recent relationships were psychologically intimate than did gay and heterosexual partners. A similar trend was found in reports of psychological intimacy in lesbian and gay relationships that had lasted more than fifteen years (Mackey, O'Brien, & Mackey, 1997).

Other factors associated with psychological intimacy include minimal levels of relational conflict; a sense of equity or fairness about the relationship; and physical affection between the partners, such as touching and hugging. Effective communication or openness and honesty between partners may help hold conflict to manageable levels. With ineffective communication, unspoken differences may cause resentment, thus leading to major conflict (Mackey, Diemer, et al., 2004).

## Sexual Relations and Intimacy

Sexual relations are another aspect of intimacy considered here. The following sections focus on sexual frequency and satisfaction with sex.

***Frequency of sex.***   Among same-sex and heterosexual couples, wide variability exists in the frequency of sex. What is not variable is a general decline in sexual frequency over time. In the early stages of a relationship, gay couples have sex more often than other couples. Heterosexual couples have more sex than lesbian couples (Rosenzweig & Lebow, 1992).

The lower frequency of sex reported by lesbians may reflect broader issues about female sexuality (Fassinger & Morrow, 1995; Peplau & Garnets, 2000). For example, gender socialization may lead women to repress and ignore their sexual feelings. This effect is likely magnified in a relationship with two female partners. Women may also have difficulty initiating sexual activities with a partner (Rothblum, 2000). These factors may be potential issues for some lesbians, but most of the research on frequency of sex among lesbians suffers from methodological and conceptual problems. For example, the research is rooted in the definition of *sex* as genital contact and vaginal penetration, which is based on a male-centered definition of sex (Iasenza, 1995, 2002). This definition, however, may not be the most valid one for sexual behavior in lesbian couples. Compared with other groups of couples, many lesbian couples engage in less genital sex but participate in more nongenital sexual behaviors, such as hugging, cuddling, and kissing (James & Murphy, 1998). Lesbian couples tend to value emotional intimacy as an integral part of their sexual expression (Downey & Friedman, 1995). In studies, researchers have asked the wrong questions about the sexuality of lesbians. A better question would be what "having sex" means to them (James & Murphy, 1998; Rothblum, 2000).

A number of studies have countered the findings of less frequent sex for lesbian couples. Meana, Rakipi, Weeks, and Lykins (2006) studied one hundred women in a primary lesbian relationship and reported frequencies of sexual activity no lower than those of heterosexual or gay couples. A study of African Americans found no difference between lesbian couples and gay couples in the reported frequency of sex (Peplau, Cochran, & Mays, 1997). The most epidemiologically sound data from the National Health and Social Life Survey failed to find a significant difference among lesbian, gay, and heterosexual groups in the mean frequency of sex per month in the previous year (Laumann, Gagon, Michael, & Michaels, 1994). Matthews, Hughes, and Tartaro (2006) reported that lesbian and heterosexual women did not differ on frequency of sexual activity. Although differences were not statistically significant, heterosexual women were more likely to report an absence of sexual activity in their current or most recent relationships. Other studies have found that lesbians are more sexually arousable, sexually assertive, and verbally and nonverbally communicative about sexual needs, desires, pleasures, and distractions (Iasenza, 1999). They have higher levels of satisfaction with their sexual lives than do heterosexual women (Iasenza, 1991).

***Sexual satisfaction.***    Sexual satisfaction is associated with global measures of relationship satisfaction in lesbians and gay men, as well as in heterosexual couples (e.g., Bryant & Demian, 1994; Eldridge & Gilbert, 1990; Peplau et al., 1997). African American lesbians and gay men report high levels of sexual satisfaction with their partners (e.g., Peplau et al., 1997). Most older gay persons rated their current sex lives as satisfactory. For example, in a sample of gay persons age 40–77, Pope and Schulz (1990) found that most older gay respondents reported that their levels of sexual satisfaction had remained high since young adulthood.

With few exceptions, most studies have found that lesbians report high levels of sexual satisfaction, comparable, if not higher than, those of heterosexual couples (Haas, 2003; Meana et al., 2006; Rosenzweig & Lebow, 1992; Schreurs, 1993). Lesbians are also more satisfied than heterosexual women with the quality of their sexual lives (Iasenza, 1999). The existence of fewer sexual problems in lesbian couples also increases sexual satisfaction, and a much lower number of partnered lesbians report sexual problems than do married, heterosexual women. Also, unlike heterosexual and gay persons, lesbians did not report more sexual problems related to their performance or to that of their partner (Meana et al., 2006).

## Sexual Monogamy versus Openness

Research shows differences among lesbian, gay, and heterosexual couples in sexual exclusiveness versus openness. Major differences also occur in actual behaviors (Bryant & Demian, 1994). Kurdek (1991a) found that sexual fidelity was positively related to relationship satisfaction for lesbian and heterosexual couples but not for gay couples. The findings on gay couples may reflect the norms of the gay community and the fact that some gay couples have agreements that nonmonogamous sex is acceptable for them (Hickson et al., 1992). Bonello and Cross (2010) reviewed the theoretical and empirical literature on gay monogamy and nonmonogamy. Findings suggested that most gay couples that established nonmonogamous relationships did so for sexual variety. These couples had relationships that were as equally adjusted and functional as those of their monogamous counterparts.

LaSala (2004) studied sixty-five gay couples. Most of the men in sexually exclusive couples preferred their arrangement over others because they perceived monogamy as associated with commitment and intimacy. Other reasons for this preference included avoidance of jealousy and fear of HIV. Still, nineteen of the men were not monogamous and engaged in outside sex. Nonmonogamous couples did not view sex as always connected with intimacy and commitment. They valued their own freedom and that of their partner, and they did not believe that one partner could satisfy all of their sexual needs. Twelve of the nonmonogamous men reported that the impact of outside sex on their relationships was positive. Some said that outside sex had both positive and negative impacts on their relationship. Two men saw the effects on their relationships as mostly negative. The downside was most always related to jealousy. All of the nonmonogamous couples set guidelines prohibiting ongoing emotional involvement with outside partners. All but two men agreed to engage only in safe sex with outside partners. As indicated earlier, lesbians value monogamy and romantic love more highly than gay couples do (Downey & Friedman, 1995). Both heterosexual women and lesbians have reported being less interested in casual sex (Bailey, Gaulin, Agyei, & Glaude, 1994).

## Positives for Lesbian Couples

As noted already, lesbians experience more psychological intimacy than gay men in their relationships. In general, they also report high sexual satisfaction. And, as discussed subsequently, they show positive ways of resolving conflict. Other studies have reported more positive aspects of lesbian relationships. In their study of couples, Bryant and Demian (1994) reported that more lesbians (47 percent) than gay men (36 percent) rated the quality of their relationship at the highest level. They also experienced stronger liking of their partners, more trust, and more equality than did gay men in relationships (Kurdek, 2003). Kurdek (2008) reported from information obtained from lesbian, gay, and heterosexual couples over the first ten years of cohabitation. Lesbian partners had the highest levels of relationship quality on all assessments in the study. Gay partners also showed relatively high levels of relationship quality averaged over all assessments, but only relative to partners from heterosexual couples with children.

Other researchers have found that lesbian couples reported higher levels of cohesion, adaptability, equality, and satisfaction than heterosexual couples did (e.g., Metz et al., 1994; Rosenbluth & Steil, 1995). Schumm, Akagi, and Bosch (2008) found that lesbians scored higher on relationship satisfaction than did heterosexual women. Happy lesbian couples experience a high degree of closeness (Schreurs & Buunk, 1996), and closeness or emotional intimacy is the strongest contributor to couple satisfaction for lesbians (Eldridge & Gilbert, 1990).

## Maintenance Behaviors

Relationship maintenance involves purposive and intentional strategies to prevent relationship dissolution (Canary & Stafford, 1992; Haas & Stafford, 2005; Stafford & Canary, 1991). The goal is to sustain satisfaction levels as couples cope with the ebb and flow of everyday relating (Cutrona & Suhr, 1994; Prager, 1995; Stafford, Dainton, & Haas, 2000). Five primary relationship maintenance strategies have been identified (Canary & Stafford, 1992; Stafford & Canary, 1991). They include positivity (e.g., cheerfulness, positive comments), openness (e.g., self-disclosure, meta-relational communication), assurances (e.g., verbal and nonverbal expressions of love and comfort), shared tasks (e.g., performing household duties, relational responsibilities), and social networks (e.g., communicating with mutual friends and kinship ties).

Haas and Stafford (1998) carried out a study of heterosexual and same-sex couples. Participants included thirty women, fifteen of whom were heterosexual and fifteen lesbian, and thirty men, fifteen of whom were heterosexual and fifteen gay. The average age of the lesbian and gay group was thirty-four years and three months; for the heterosexual group, it was thirty-four years and five months. All participants reported that they were in committed relationships. Haas and Stafford found that same-sex couples used relationship maintenance behaviors comparable to those of heterosexual couples. The three most often reported behaviors were shared tasks (70 percent), metarelational communication (e.g., discussing difficulties; 57 percent), and sharing time together (50 percent). Three behaviors tied for fourth place: reactive prosocial behaviors (47 percent), overt assurances (47 percent), and social networks (47 percent). Two social network subcategories, family and coworkers, were the next most often reported behaviors, both at 43 percent. The lesbian and gay couples in Haas and Stafford's study also sought out lesbian- and gay-supportive environments to live in, work in, and socialize in. Being "out as a couple" with one's network also seemed to function as a relationship strengthening behavior for the couples. Within the home, sharing in tasks such as household duties, home maintenance, and child care were significantly associated with maintenance, as was working to establish equity. Rostosky, Riggle, Dudley, and Wright (2006) suggested that for same-sex couples, investments that signified their commitment were also maintenance behaviors, such as moving in together, disclosing their relationship to their social ties, actively making plans for their future, and continuing efforts to communicate.

In their comparison of relationship maintenance behaviors in lesbian and gay couples and married heterosexual couples, Hass and Stafford (2005) found that sharing tasks was the most commonly reported maintenance behavior (83.3 percent for heterosexual couples, and 73.3 percent for lesbian and gay couples). In addition, both heterosexual women and men and lesbians and gay men reported sharing tasks fairly equally. Although partners did not share all tasks equally, across all groups, partners consistently reported a general balance of task distribution. Sharing tasks involves accomplishing relational duties that are the responsibility of both partners, and they are often duties that revolve around running a joint household (e.g., paying bills, cooking meals, cleaning, doing laundry, performing household maintenance). All of the couples reported these types of task-oriented behaviors as the most common way they maintained their intimate relationships.

## Conflict Resolution

Some of the maintenance behaviors mentioned herein, such as discussing difficulties, suggest that conflict resolution can also be a maintenance behavior.

Conflict is inevitable in any relationship. Lesbian, gay, and heterosexual couples are similar in reporting the frequency and intensity of arguments and conflict (Metz et al., 1994). All couples tend to disagree about similar issues: finances, affection, sex, criticism, and household tasks (Kurdek, 1994a, 2005, 2006; Metz et al., 1994). Lesbian and gay couples report fighting less about money management than do heterosexual couples. In general, though, Kurdek (2004) reported that differences were largely nonexistent on twenty issues.

Conflict resolution involves how conflict is handled rather than what the conflict is about. Available research indicates that the problem-solving skills of lesbian and gay couples are as good as or better than those of heterosexual couples. In a study of lesbian, gay, and heterosexual couples, Kurdek (1998b) found no differences in the frequency of using positive problem-solving styles such as negotiating or compromising. Nor were there differences among couples in the use of negative strategies, such as personal attacks, defensiveness, withdrawal from the interaction, or refusal to talk to the partner. Gottman, Levenson, et al. (2003), however, found differences between lesbian and gay couples and heterosexual couples. The authors videotaped partners from lesbian, gay, and married heterosexual couples discussing problems in their relationships. Participants were age 21–40 (average age of lesbians, 29.3 years; average age for gay men, 32.5 years; average age for heterosexual women, 28.7; average age for hetero-sexual men, 29.6) and had lived together in a committed relationship for at least two years. The researchers coded the emotions the partners expressed in the course of the discussions. Compared to heterosexual couples, lesbian and gay partners began their discussions more positively and were more likely to main-tain a positive tone throughout the course of the discussions. Kurdek (2004) also found that lesbian and gay couples resolved conflict more positively than part-ners from heterosexual married couples did. They argued more effectively, and they were less likely to use a style of conflict resolution in which one partner de-mands and the other partner withdraws. They were also more likely to suggest possible solutions and compromises. Gottman, Levenson, et al. speculated that lesbian and gay couples handle conflict more positively than partners from het-erosexual couples because they value equality more and have fewer differences in power and status between them.

Satisfied and happy partners are more likely to use positive problem-solving methods (Kurdek, 1991a, 1998b). Unhappy couples are more likely to use nega-tive behaviors such as criticism, contempt, blame, and stonewalling. These be-haviors are negatively correlated with couple satisfaction, whether lesbian, gay, or heterosexual (Kurdek, 1991a, 1993).

Julien, Arellano, and Turgeon (1997) and Julien, Pizzamiglio, Chartrand, and Bégin (1995) studied hostile-withdrawal, withdrawal-withdrawal, and hostile-hostile behaviors. These behaviors occur across lesbian, gay, and heterosexual couples and are more intense in distressed couples. Yet the researchers also found differences across groups of couples. For example, hostile-withdrawal re-sponses are much stronger in the heterosexual group than in the gay group; les-bians are less hostile and withdraw less than do gay and heterosexual persons. Heterosexual wives are the most confronting and hostile. Arellano (1993) re-ported that, among partners in lesbian and gay couples, those who are "femi-nine" also display the highest levels of negative conflict behaviors, including hos-tility and confrontation.

In a study by Metz et al. (1994), lesbian couples showed a more positive pat-tern of conflict management than did gay or heterosexual couples. They felt greater optimism about conflict resolution, made a greater effort to resolve con-flict, and engaged in assertion more than physical aggression. Rutter and

Schwartz (1996) found that lesbians tried to minimize conflict and avoid power tactics. Roisman et al. (2008) found that lesbians seem to be particularly skilled at working harmoniously with their partners.

Mackey, O'Brien, et al. (1997) found that lesbian partners (age 40–60) tended to avoid face-to-face discussions about interpersonal difficulties early in their relationships. But later they reported both a substantial improvement in their abilities to discuss differences and increased relationship satisfaction. Connolly and Sicola (2005) studied ten lesbian couples (age 34–60) in relationships ranging from ten to twenty-four years, with an average length of eighteen years. Over time, the couples learned or grew to understand the importance of productive (versus nonproductive) conversation to successfully maintain their relationships.

The pattern of identifying and dealing with relational conflict over the years was different for gay partners. Both lesbian and gay partners reported progress in developing problem-solving skills by the later years of their relationships. But a greater percentage of gay men than lesbians reported continuing avoidant styles of conflict management. They tended to avoid discussing their thoughts and feelings about conflict unless difficulties threatened the viability of their relationships (Mackey, O'Brien, et al., 1997).

## Summary

Lesbians and gay men, regardless of age, establish satisfying relationships. Older lesbian and gay couples are often more satisfied with their relationships than younger couples. However, younger couples have satisfying relationships based on equity and fairness, positive affectivity, satisfying sex, maintenance behaviors, and positive conflict-resolution strategies. Lesbians report having more satisfying relationships than gay men, and they are better at conflict resolution. Lesbian and gay couples are like heterosexual couples in that they want satisfying relationships, but they are different from heterosexual couples in that they want equality in power and in decision making in their relationships. Lesbian relationships tend to include other more positive aspects than gay or heterosexual relationships, such as liking of the partner, more trust, and more closeness. Lesbians also handle conflict in a more positive way than do heterosexual couples.

## Vignette

Sally and Sue are a couple, and Mark and John are a couple. They are friends and live near one another. They frequently have dinner together and discuss their lives. They have intimate discussions about their couplehood. Recently, Mark decided to have sex outside of his relationship with John. John seemed to be OK with this. They told Sally and Sue, who were upset about this behavior, because they would not consider doing anything similar. Sally said that she could not trust Sue if she were to have sex outside their relationship, and Sue concurred. Both Sally and Sue agreed that they would probably break up in such circumstances. John and Mark tried to explain how gay men were different from lesbians in this regard, but they did not convince Sally and Sue of the merit of nonmonogamous sex. They all decided that monogamy versus nonmonogamy is not something for them to discuss in the future. They remained friends, but Sally and Sue realized that they were different from Mark and John with respect to monogamy but not with respect to wanting equality in their relationships or resolving conflicts positively. They all decided to emphasize these similarities and positives in future conversations about their relationships.

## Resources

### Online

**This Emotional Life**
The Web site to the PBS television series *This Emotional Life* (http://www.pbs.org/thisemotionallife/topic/relationships/same-sex-couples) features information and links to further resources on same-sex relationships, commitment and satisfaction, stability and discrimination, and marriage.

### For Further Reading

Appleby, G. A., & Anastas, J. W. (1998). *Not just a passing phase: Social work with gay, lesbian, and bisexual people*. New York: Columbia University Press.

Garnets, L., & Kimmel, D. C. (2003). *Psychological perspectives on lesbian, gay, and bisexual experiences*. New York: Columbia University Press.

Gottman, J. M., Levenson, R. W., Gross, J., Frederickson, B. L., McCoy, K., Rosenthal, L., et al. (2003). Correlates of gay and lesbian couples' relationship satisfaction and relationship dissolution. *Journal of Homosexuality, 45*, 23–43.

Kurdek, L. A. (1992). Relationship stability and relationship satisfaction in cohabitating gay and lesbian couples: A prospective longitudinal test of the contextual and interdependence models. *Journal of Social and Personal Relationships, 9*, 125–142.

Mackey, R. A., O'Brien, B. A., & Mackey, E. F. (1997). *Gay and lesbian couples: Voices from lasting relationships*. Westport, CT: Praeger.

Rose, S. (Ed.). (2002). *Lesbian love and relationships*. New York: Harrington
    Park Press.
Silverstein, C. (Ed.). (1991). *Gays, lesbians, and their therapists: Studies in
    psychotherapy*. New York: Norton.
Weeks, J., Heaphy, B., & Donovan, C. (2001). *Same sex intimacies: Families of
    choice and other life experiments*. New York: Routledge.

# Downturns in Couple Satisfaction and Breakups

What are the three factors that contribute to relationship commitment and longevity?

What are some of the negative factors that affect couple members and their interactions?

Does having children play a role in breakups?

How does internalized heterosexism affect a lesbian or gay couple in negative ways?

Is there a difference in breakup rates of those with civil unions and registered partnerships?

In breakups, do heterosexuals have different emotions than lesbians or gay men, or are lesbian and gay couples alike or different from heterosexual couples?

What do you think are the main reasons lesbian and gay couples break up?

What options do lesbian and gay couples have in negotiating a breakup?

Longitudinal studies on the course of satisfaction in lesbian and gay couples are rare. But Kurdek's work (e.g., 1992, 1995b, 1998b, 2000, 2008) assessed satisfaction in a sample of lesbian and gay couples over time. In Kurdek's studies, most participants were young adults—many lesbians and gay men in the studies were in their thirties and some in their forties. During the course of one year, Kurdek (1989) found that satisfaction and love for one's partner decreased for gay couples but not for lesbian couples. This study included 74 gay and 45 lesbian couples. In another study of five annual assessments, Kurdek (1998b) compared the trajectory of change in relationship satisfaction and relationship stability in lesbian and gay couples and heterosexual married couples. Controlling for age, education, income, and years together, the couples did not differ in relationship satisfaction at initial testing. Nor did they differ over the five years of this study. All types of couples tended to experience a decrease in relationship satisfaction, and no differences were found in the rate of change in satisfaction (Kurdek, 2001, 2005; Mackey, Diemer, & O'Brien, 2000; Peplau & Fingerhut, 2007; Peplau & Spalding, 2000).

## Factors That Prevent Breakups

Three factors challenge all couples and contribute to partners' psychological commitment to each other and to the longevity of their relationships (Kurdek, 2000; Peplau & Spalding, 2000).

First, there are positive attractions, associated with the partner and the relationship, such as love or satisfaction. Positive attractions make partners want to stay together. Lesbian and gay couples and married heterosexual couples generally do not differ in the level of attraction toward their partner (see chapter 3). When satisfaction with a relationship is high, partners are likely to perceive intrinsic rewards, such as enjoyable companionship, as reasons for not leaving the relationship. Expressiveness is another reward that seems to provide stability for lesbian and gay partners and to contribute to positive relationship quality (Miller, Caughlin, & Huston, 2003). Lesbians appear to use expressiveness to resolve relationship conflict (Gottman, Levenson, et al., 2003). When satisfaction with the relationship is low, members of a couple are likely to perceive reasons external to the relationship as reasons for not leaving it. For example, someone might not leave one's relationship because of the fear of upsetting friends and family members. Thus, the reasons for remaining in a relationship shift from rewards, which make it easy to stay, to barriers, which make it difficult to leave (Kurdek, 2007).

In another report of partners who had been together for more than ten years, Kurdek (2008) conjectured that most stable lesbian and gay partners are likely to be fairly happy with their relationships, which are regulated more by attractions than by barriers, or to stay in long-lasting relationships because they are satisfying (Kurdek, 2006).

A second factor involves barriers that make termination of the relationship costly. These barriers include the psychological, emotional, and financial costs of ending a relationship, as well as moral or religious feelings of obligation or duty to one's partner (Kurdek, 1998b, 2000; Peplau & Fingerhut, 2007). In addition, Kurdek (2007) obtained data from heterosexual dating partners and lesbian and gay cohabiting partners to examine the importance of an additional possible barrier to leaving a relationship—avoidance motivation. Avoidance motivation is the incentive to stay in a relationship to avoid the unpleasant consequences associated with ending the relationship. The negative consequences associated with ending a relationship are diverse. Negative consequences that participants noted in this study were dealing with external pressures to stay together, experiencing distress if the relationship were to end, and dealing with unpleasant practical consequences of a breakup (e.g., dividing material resources). These barriers can motivate couples to work toward improving declining relationships rather than ending them.

The third factor is the availability of alternatives—usually a more desirable partner—to the current relationship. Partners with few alternatives are less likely to leave a relationship (Peplau & Fingerhut, 2007). The three factors noted here apply to all couples, whether lesbian, gay, or heterosexual.

## Factors That Decrease Couple Satisfaction

Other factors may affect couples and cause them to experience downturns in satisfaction. There are three categories of such factors: (1) negative factors characterizing couple interactions, (2) negative factors characterizing couple members, and (3) negative factors external to the couple but affecting couple members. For example, negative factors characterizing couple interactions include the following: mismatches between partners (Rutter & Schwartz, 1996); absence of shared values and common interests, or lack of emotional compatibility (Weinberg, Williams, & Pryor, 1994); few similarities in emotional expressions and behaviors (Julien, Arellano, et al., 1997); display of more rigid sex-role stereotypical behaviors (Julien, Arellano, et al., 1997); boundary struggles (Rutter & Schwartz, 1996);

unequal power (Kurdek, 1993); sexual incompatibility (Kurdek, 1991b); arguments about sex (Kurdek, 1991c); decline in frequency of sexual activity (Otis, Rostosky, Riggle, & Hamrin, 2006); escalation of relationship conflicts (Kurdek, 1996); lack of basic communication skills for managing differences (Julien, Arellano, et al., 1997); and communication problems such as lack of open communication and not talking things out (Alexander, 1997).

Negative factors characterizing couple members include the following: immaturity (Weinberg et al., 1994); neuroticism (Kurdek, 1997b); fear of intimacy (Greenfield & Thelen, 1997); lack of trust, love, and respect; lack of the desire to share, or lack of willingness to make adjustments (Weinberg et al., 1994); unrealistic standards (Kurdek, 1997b); unfulfilled expectations (Rutter & Schwartz, 1996); rating one's relationship as costly (Kurdek, 1997b); dissatisfaction with sex (Kurdek, 1991c); low endorsement of monogamy as a relationship value (Andrews, 1990); negative affectivity (e.g., depression, anxiety, anger, sadness; Todosijevic, Rothblum, & Solomon, 2005); drug or alcohol addiction (Kurdek, 1991b); experiencing thoughts about the partner or the relationship but not expressing them (Alexander, 1997); mental cruelty (Kurdek, 1991b); nonresponsiveness (e.g., no communication or support); emotional distance; placement of high value on personal autonomy (Kurdek, 1991a, 1992); use of destructive conflict resolution methods (Kurdek, 1997b); display of contempt, disgust, and defensiveness; decrease in humor and affection (Gottman, Levenson, et al., 2003); ambitiousness in work; and frequent absences (Kurdek, 1991c).

Much of what is known about the negative factors or why and how same-sex couples break up has come from Kurdek's research. One study obtained data from seven lesbian and six gay couples (92 percent white) who had separated during the course of a longitudinal study (Kurdek, 1991c). The top two reasons for breakups were nonresponsiveness (73 percent; e.g., "there was no communication between us") and partner problems (50 percent; e.g., one or the other partner had a drug or alcohol problem). Other reasons for breakups included frequent absence, sexual incompatibility, and mental cruelty.

Kurdek (1992) compared twenty-two couples that had separated (twelve lesbian and ten gay; 94 percent white) with ninety-two couples (sixty-one gay and thirty-one lesbian) whose relationship had remained intact over the four years of the study. At year 1, gay couples cohabited for a mean of seven years, whereas lesbian couples cohabited for a mean of five years. Partners in separated couples differed in six ways from partners in intact couples: they reported (1) more negative emotions, (2) less relationship satisfaction, (3) fewer pooled finances, (4) less emotional commitment, (5) less invested time in the relationship, and (6) higher value on personal autonomy. Kurdek reported that the findings showed remarkable similarity to research on relationship dissolution of heterosexual couples.

Kurdek (1996) also traced the predictors associated with relationship dissolution in cohabitating lesbian and gay couples over a period of five years. Compared with couples that remained together, same-sex couples that separated reported a decrease in positivity and an increase in relationship conflict and personal autonomy.

## Breaking Up after Civil Unions and Registered Partnerships

Some states provide for civil unions for gay and lesbian couples. Civil unions provide state benefits only, whereas marriage also provides federal benefits. In a study of all couples who obtained civil unions in Vermont the first year that they became available, Solomon, Rothblum, and Balsam (2004) found that 1 percent had separated after one year. In a three-year follow-up, same-sex couples in Vermont who were not in civil unions were more likely to break up than same-sex couples in civil unions or heterosexual married couples in Vermont (Balsam, Beauchaine, Rothblum, & Solomon, 2008).

Differences in the dissolution rates of lesbian and gay registered partnerships also have been studied in Norway and in Sweden (Andersson, Noack, Seierstad, & Weedom-Fekjaer, 2004). Registered partnerships were first made available in Norway in 1993 and in Sweden in 1995. Dissolution rates were significantly higher for lesbian couples than for gay couples. In Norway, 56 of 497 lesbian partnerships were dissolved (11.26 percent), compared with 62 of 769 gay partnerships (7.78 percent). In Sweden, 117 of 584 lesbian partnerships were dissolved (20.03 percent), compared with 135 of 942 gay partnerships (14.33 percent). The percentage of dissolved heterosexual marriages in Sweden was 8 percent. For both Norway and Sweden, the higher rate of dissolution for lesbian couples than for gay couples persisted even when statistical analyses controlled for length of the partnership. However, the researchers concluded that the data were too scant to warrant any conclusions about the stability of lesbian and gay couples' relationships.

## What Happens When Children Are Involved?

In a longitudinal study of the transition to lesbian parenthood, Gartrell, Banks, et al. (2000) collected data in one interview with each of 224 participants (including 150 birth mothers and co-mothers and 74 children), either in person or by telephone. Close to one-third (31 percent) of the co-parenting couples had been together for a mean of eight years and had separated by the time their children were five years old. Those who separated had been together for significantly less time than those who remained a couple. Turteltaub (2002) interviewed ten mothers and their seven children (four sons and three daughters). All children were conceived through donor insemination. Most lived in the San Francisco Bay area. All mothers were white and had college degrees; the mean age was forty-five years. The mothers had been separated from their partner for a mean of nine years after being together for a mean of eight years. The current mean age of the children was thirteen, and on average, children were four years old when their mothers separated. In each family, only the biological mother was legally recognized as a parent. Seven couples shared custody equally, whereas three biological mothers had sole custody and their former partners had none.

Mothers reported in the Gartrell, Banks, et al. (2000) study that their relationships ended because they disagreed about how to parent and how to manage money. Furthermore, they had weak couple communication, which the demands of parenting exacerbated. Couple conflict worsened when extended family members failed to provide acceptance or support. Barriers to the nonlegal parents becoming legal parents also contributed to the parents' conflict with each other. Despite the fact that these challenges existed before separation, all mothers said that they tried to shield the children from their relationship problems. They consulted with psychologists, mediators, and therapists. They also received support during the breakup from their local lesbian community. Like children who experience heterosexual divorce, however, the children in this study found it difficult to adjust to the reorganization that comes from parental separation. All mothers recognized that their children found it hard to adjust to their relationship evolution, especially when the mothers were living in two different houses.

Co-mothers who lacked legal parental rights were fearful of losing all contact with their children. During the dissolution process, co-mothers felt coerced into cooperating with the biological mother for that reason. In the study by

Gartrell, Banks, et al. (2000), mothers equally shared custody after separation only when the nonbiological mother had legal rights. The mothering identities of co-mothers intensified after the breakup, perhaps as a result of the increased negotiations needed to parent across households. In some cases, others who did not perceive co-mothers as legitimate parents when they were in the couple arrangement began to identify them as mothers because they continued to parent despite the breakup. As described in chapter 4, when children are involved, collaborative practice can be useful in reaching a solution that all can agree to.

## The Toll of Internalizing Negative Beliefs and Images on Lesbian and Gay Couples

As noted in the introduction to this book and in other chapters, because of pervasive heterosexism, lesbians and gay men grow up internalizing negative attitudes and fears about their same-sex attractions and the dangers of discrimination (Mills et al., 2004). They experience daily assaults on their sense of self, and they are vigilant in their interactions with others.

Heterosexism takes a toll on intimate relationships (Murray, Brown, Brody, Cutrona, & Simons, 2001). Internalized heterosexism is negatively related to relationship-promoting behaviors (Downey & Friedman, 1995; Dupras, 1994; Shildo, 1994). This involves negative attitudes toward oneself, toward same-sex attractions in general, toward other lesbian and gay persons, and toward disclosure or others knowing about one's same-sex attraction (Gaines et al., 2005). Self, others, and disclosure measures tend to be positively intercorrelated. Attitudes toward oneself, however, have the closest association with the concept of internalized heterosexism (Shildo, 1994). Hyperawareness and preparedness for potential threats elevates stress levels, independent of any specific experience of discrimination (Meyer, 1995). Lesbian and gay couples have a high rate of internally and externally generated stressors that they must manage. And often they receive no support from families of origin or their larger community (Peplau, 1993; Weston, 1997).

Research by Otis et al. (2006) examined the association between same-sex couples' perception of the quality of their relationships and internalized heterosexism and perceived discrimination. Stress was significantly associated with experiences of internalized heterosexism and perceived discrimination. Also, the perceived discrimination that one partner experiences had a strong impact on the stress level of the other partner. Perceived stress had a significant impact on perceptions of relationship quality. An increase in either partner's reported level of internalized heterosexism was also negatively associated with reported relationship quality. Acceptance of society's negative attitudes can also lead to guilt, fear, self-hatred, or hatred of the partner (B. C. Murphy, 1994). Feelings of negativity elevated by internalized heterosexism (Crocker, Major, & Steele, 1998; Lewis, Derlega, Berndt, Morris, & Rose, 2001) can lead to devaluation of the relationship (Herdt & Koff, 2000). Lesbian and gay persons may conjecture that they cannot form enduring, happy relationships or that their relationships do not compare favorably with heterosexual relationships (Bryant & Demian, 1994). Same-sex couples may play out these negative perceptions in decreased satisfaction in their relationships and painful endings (B. C. Murphy, 1994).

## Hiding

Many same-sex couples grapple with issues of whether to make disclosures as individuals and as a couple, and when, where, and how to do so. Many couples decide to make no public disclosures because they anticipate hostile responses. When not out and when isolated from other lesbian and gay persons, however, couples have no observable models for alternative and possibly more satisfying couple and maintenance behaviors. Partners can also experience a sense of unreality about being a couple because their relationship is real only to them. When "invisible," some partners may intensify their dependency on each other (Patterson & Schwartz, 1994).

Partners can also disagree about disclosures. One partner may want to be secretive with work associates, parents, and children, but the other partner may want to make disclosures because he or she is in more liberal environments or because of a political commitment to openness (Rutter & Schwartz, 1996). The more open partner may also want involvement with the other partner's family, especially if he or she is alienated from one's own family (Okun, 1996). When there is disagreement within a couple about disclosures, negotiations are likely to be difficult and to provoke anxiety (Martin, 1993, 1998; Patterson, 1994, 2007). This disagreement can also cause considerable conflict. Couple members may also have conflicts in terms of where to live, such as in an obvious or not obvious gay neighborhood, or whether to bring a partner to work-related social events (Todosijevic et al., 2005). Although some couples have difficulties around disclosure, fear of disclosure is not the issue it used to be in earlier decades.

# Breakups

Studies of lesbian and gay couples show that many remain in relationships. In the 2004 study by Kurdek, for example, more than two-thirds of the lesbian and gay couples were still together (81 percent of gay couples and 76 percent of lesbian couples). But some lesbian and gay couples did break up.

As do most other people, lesbian and gay persons begin their relationships with high hopes for a lifetime of love and closeness. Little is known about the longevity of most same-sex relationships, as few studies have followed such relationships over a long time (Peplau, 1993). But no one in the beginning expects a breakup, and not many studies have addressed breakups among lesbian and gay couples.

Whether the various factors identified in this chapter will actually lead to breakups is an open question. If, however, such challenges arise and go unresolved, they may, at the least, decrease satisfaction. Satisfaction is a key factor in the attraction to being in a relationship. The challenges are probably more troublesome for couples in their second and third years. During the first year together, when couples are in love, they may overlook issues that can be problems later. When couple members are not as much in love, they notice differences more. In other words, they fall out of love. They make more adjustments and compromises. If the partners are comfortable with resolutions, they could regain satisfaction in the following years. Some couples, however, do not make it that far. And as noted already, heterosexism and internalized heterosexism can devastate a lesbian or gay couple.

# Breakup Rates

Kurdek (1992) found a 19 percent dissolution rate during a four-year study of same-sex cohabitants. Dissolution typically occurred after six to eleven years of cohabitation. In a five-year prospective study, Kurdek (1998b) reported a breakup rate of 7 percent for married heterosexual couples, 14 percent for cohabiting gay couples, and 16 percent for cohabiting lesbian couples. Controlling for demographic variables, cohabiting lesbian and gay couples were significantly more likely than married heterosexuals to break up. Kurdek (2004) reported that for 126 gay couples and 101 lesbian couples assessed annually up to twelve times, 24 of the gay couples (19 percent) and 24 of the lesbian couples (24 percent) dissolved their relationships. With controls for demographic variables (e.g., length of cohabitation), the difference in the rate of dissolution for lesbian and gay couples was not significant. Over a comparable period of eleven annual assessments, 70 of 483 heterosexual married couples (15 percent) ended their relationships. With controls for demographic variables, the dissolution rate for the heterosexual couples was significantly lower than that for either lesbian or gay couples.

The average length of time together for the sample of lesbian and gay couples in Haas and Stafford's (1998) study was five and a half years. Same-sex couples that had been together between zero and ten years had a breakup rate of 21 percent. Fewer lesbian couples (4 percent) broke up in this time period than gay couples (16 percent). Longevity in itself might lead to the continued longevity of relationships. Some lesbian and gay couples have been together ten years or longer (e.g., Bryant & Demian, 1994). Kurdek (2005) reported that between 8 percent and 21 percent of lesbian couples and between 18 percent and 28 percent of gay couples have lived together for ten years or more. In anecdotal accounts, older lesbian and gay persons reported that relationships of twenty years' duration or longer were usual (e.g., Clunis & Green, 1993).

As noted in chapter 3, lesbian couples experience more relationship satisfaction than other couples, but most studies have found that lesbians break up more often than other couples. They may be at greater risk of their relationship ending because many are isolated from family and community, and they may lack necessary resources and information about the unique nature of lesbian couples. They often interpret stresses and brief periods of conflict as serious problems rather than normal developmental transitions inherent to all couples (Toder, 1992). In addition, lesbian couples face not only the burdens of heterosexism, as do gay couples, but also the additional stressors associated with navigating a sexist culture (L. S. Brown, 1995).

## Divorce and Other Options

Some states allow same-sex divorce for married lesbian and gay couples, but the laws that apply to married heterosexual couples do not apply to lesbian and gay couples in most states. Unmarried couples are not required to take court action to end their relationships, and marital property rules usually do not apply.

A person who is in a civil union and later wants a divorce must follow the law in the state where he or she attained the civil union. In most states, to file for divorce, one of the partners must be a resident of the state for six months; to obtain a divorce, one has to have been a resident for one year before the final hearing. The court also has the authority to equitably divide property and award spousal support if needed (Grossman, 2010).

An option for unmarried couples is to use mediation to resolve conflicts and reach solutions. Mediators can be lawyers, social workers, therapists, or other professionals. Lawyers are usually, but not always, mediators. A benefit of working with a lawyer as mediator is that he or she can explain any laws that might affect the couple members. Mediation is a form of negotiation that involves a neutral facilitator, the mediator, who does not make rulings or decisions but helps the partners talk with each other and reach an agreement. Mediation is particularly appropriate for same-sex couples, and it is best for couples with children or who co-own property. It does require remaining calm and being able to articulate one's concerns (Hertz & Doskow, 2009). Both partners have to agree on the resolution. It is best if the mediator has worked with unmarried lesbian or gay couples before (Clifford, Hertz, & Doskow, 2007).

Another option is collaborative practice, or collaborative divorce, which is available to both unmarried and married same-sex couples. Collaborative practice has some elements of negotiation and mediation (Hertz & Doskow, 2009), and the process focuses on communication and cooperation. It emphasizes respect; mutual agreement; and soothing the painful disentanglement of lives, children, and assets. It allows for a solution that fits each person and the children. Both persons hire an attorney or someone else trained in collaborative practice, and all agree not to go to court. Other professionals can be hired if needed, such as accountants or custody experts. All persons involved can negotiate a solution. If an arrangement for custody of the children cannot be worked out, the issues can be heard in family court (Clifford et al., 2007).

Another option is arbitration, sometimes referred to as private court. Arbitration is similar to a court trial but takes place outside the courtroom. Each partner presents his or her case to a neutral decision maker who the couple has selected. Often the arbitrator is a retired judge or an experienced attorney. Couple members agree to be bound by the arbitrator's decision. This process is useful especially if property is in dispute, but it is an expensive process and not recommended for small disputes (Clifford et al., 2007).

Another option, which is free, is that a person negotiates or talks out a resolution with his or her former partner. This requires clarity of one's position, an understanding of the other person's position, and openness to compromise. This can save a lot of money, but if the couple cannot negotiate, they can hire others to negotiate for them (Hertz & Doskow, 2009).

## Breakups and Emotions

The dissolution of an intimate relationship is usually difficult and emotionally upsetting. Kurdek (1997a) studied lesbian, gay, and heterosexual persons who had been separated from their partners for about six months. None of them showed any differences in distress after the ending of their relationships. Kurdek (1991c) asked former partners in twenty-six lesbian and gay couples about the specific outcomes and problems they encountered after their relationships ended. The three most frequent outcomes included personal growth, loneliness, and relief from conflict (in that order). The three most frequently reported problems included the continuing relationship with the ex-partner, financial stress, and difficulties in becoming involved with someone else.

In a study of lesbian and heterosexual women, depression was a common experience for both groups when close relationships ended. Depression was especially likely for lesbians who were not connected to a lesbian social network and for whom their partner was their only confidant (Rothblum, 1990).

Certain factors associated with severe emotional reactions to breakup for both lesbian and gay persons included a long-term relationship, pooled finances, strong emphasis on attachment, and greater love for the partner than the partner has for the other person (Kurdek, 1991b). Some racial and ethnic lesbians may feel more hurt if the failed relationship involved someone from their own ethnic group instead of a white person (Greene, 1995).

After a breakup, some closeted lesbian and gay persons who are grieving their lost relationships disclose their sexual identity for the first time. The goal is to receive support from others in their community (Browning, Reynolds, & Dworkin, 1991). Often, however, they grieve the loss alone.

Over time, lesbian, gay, and heterosexual persons who experience severe emotional reactions to relationship dissolution are likely to experience more positive outcomes (Kurdek, 1991b). For others, addressing and preparing for a separation affected post-separation adjustment in a quicker, positive way (Lazarus &

Folkman, 1984). Kurdek (1997a) reported that the contemplation of separation decreased distress, perhaps because one starts to gather psychological and social resources to cope with the pending dissolution. When people feel a sense of self-efficacy and control, it is possible for them to contain the stress of separation. Partners who expected the breakup reported not only more positive emotional adjustment but also fewer post-separation problems. Managing well after the breakup was also associated with a higher level of education, having spent less time knowing and cohabitating with the ex-partner, maintenance of independent finances, low levels of love for and attachment to the partner, and less psychological distress. There were no significant differences in these results between lesbian and gay couples.

## Staying Friends

In comparison with heterosexual couples, lesbian and gay persons more frequently maintain post-breakup connections with their former partners. They might purposely handle breakups tactfully so as to remain friends (Weinstock & Rothblum, 1996). When a relationship is ending, partners fear the loss of the friendship they had. They want to remain friends because of the serious relationship they had when together (Harkless & Fowers, 2005). They are more likely than heterosexuals to report continued phone calls and social contacts with former partners (Nardi, 1999; Weinstock, 2004). They might even continue to consider a former partner as family (Nardi, 1999; Weston, 1997), or a former partner may act as a surrogate family member (e.g., grandparent) to one's children (Patterson, Hurt, & Mason, 1998).

Other factors that encourage same-sex former partners to remain friends include the small size of some lesbian and gay social networks, the norms of particular lesbian and gay communities, and the benefits of transforming ties with former partners into friendships (Nardi, 1999; Weinstock, 2004).

A heterosexual paradigm is not appropriate for analyzing breakups of lesbian and gay couples (L. S. Brown, 1995; Ossana, 2000), as many do not make the normative clean break. Some view ongoing attachments to former partners as enmeshment, codependency, or—worse—pathology, but this is not appropriate.

Legally recognized divorce may function for heterosexuals as a barrier to post-breakup relationship continuation, as it sanctions and sustains separation. This is particularly the case when lawyers and other outside parties foster contention between the two parties (Allen, 2007). This is rarely applicable to former lesbian and gay partners, as most are not in a legal marriage and do not have access to legal divorce proceedings.

## Summary

It is not common to think of breaking up at the start of a relationship. But because of internalized heterosexism, many lesbian and gay couples do expect to break up. Many of the other variables identified in this chapter affect both heterosexual and lesbian and gay couples. In certain couples, some of the variables can lead to a downturn in satisfaction. The areas in which lesbian and gay couples are different are heterosexism and internalized heterosexism. As suggested in this chapter, this could have more to do with lesbian and gay couple breakups than other variables. Some lesbians and gay men in marriages or civil unions have access to divorce proceedings. Options for other lesbians and gay men include mediation, collaborative practice, arbitration, or working things out between themselves. The emotions experienced during and after a breakup are no different from those that heterosexuals experience during breakups. Also, lesbians and gay men tend to remain friends with former partners, in contrast to heterosexuals.

## Vignette

Danny and Joe were very happy when they became a couple, but later in their relationship, they started growing apart. Danny thought that Joe's expectations of him were too high, and Joe thought Danny had unreasonable expectations too. They might have been able to resolve these and other difficulties, but what they could not resolve was the endless challenge of heterosexism. Their neighbors told them to leave the neighborhood after their dog was poisoned (discrimination and hate crimes result from heterosexism). They moved and decided not to tell anyone in their new neighborhood about their sexual identities. But they did not meet any other gay people in the area because they were hiding their sexual identities. Joe also had difficulty accepting his sexual identity and would often tell Danny that he wished he were heterosexual and normal. This endlessly troubled Danny, and he feared that Joe would break up with him. Eventually Joe did break up with Danny, and Joe told Danny that he did not want to be friends with him because he was gay. Danny wanted to remain friends but could not. He was depressed over the breakup for a long time.

# Resources

## For Further Reading

Alexander, C. J. (1997). Factors contributing to the termination of long-term gay male relationships. *Journal of Gay and Lesbian Social Services, 7*, 1–12.

Conant, E. (2010). The right to love—and loss. *Newsweek*, April 14. Retrieved from http://www.newsweek.com/2010/04/13/the-right-to-love-and-loss .html.

Demian. (2003). Relationship breakup: How to cope. Retrieved from Partners Task Force for Lesbian and Gay Couples Web site: http://www.buddybuddy .com/t-break.html.

Rose, S. (Ed.). (2002). *Lesbian love relationships*. New York: Harrington Park Press.

# Part Two

## Micro-level Practice with Lesbian and Gay Couples

# Requirements for Micro-level Practice with Lesbian and Gay Couples

What might practitioners lack when working with lesbian and gay clients?

What are some of the mistakes practitioners make with lesbian and gay clients?

Why is there no "typical" lesbian or gay client?

What are some clues that a practitioner is biased against lesbian and gay clients?

What should biased practitioners do if they want to work with lesbian and gay clients?

What are some unhelpful and helpful practitioner behaviors?

What are the most important prerequisites for working with lesbian and gay couples?

What does a "good working alliance" mean?

Because human service professionals will likely encounter same-sex couples as clients, it is essential that they provide them with competent practice. But practitioners may not be able to provide competent or effective service to lesbian and gay couples for two reasons. First is the lack of information about issues associated with being lesbian or gay. The second is bias against same-sex attractions and behaviors (Eubanks-Carter, Burckell, & Goldfried, 2005).

Nevertheless, many lesbian and gay couples whom Bryant and Demian (1994) surveyed reported that they had sought professional services for couple issues. Almost all (93 percent) experienced assistance from at least one professional. More lesbian couples (45 percent) than gay couples (27 percent) sought assistance. Modcrin and Wyers (1990) asked lesbian and gay persons, "If you experienced a serious problem in your relationship, would you seek professional help to solve that problem?" Most women (86 percent) reported that they would seek help, compared with 60 percent of men. Couples who had been together more than ten years sought assistance less often (48 percent) than did couples who had been together less than one year (64 percent) or between one and ten years (67 percent).

## Required Knowledge

Practitioners must have accurate knowledge about lesbian and gay couples, as there are numerous misconceptions and stereotypes about them. Practitioners also must acknowledge their own exposure to inaccurate and negative information. Many practitioners probably lack important information about aspects of lesbian and gay identity development and other life experiences (Eubanks-Carter et al., 2005). Some might assume that they can apply the same knowledge and skills from their work with heterosexual clients or think that the treatment needs for gay men and lesbians are the same as for heterosexual clients. Instead, humility about the limits of one's training, personal experience, and expert knowledge are necessary (Green & Mitchell, 2002).

Earlier chapters established that same-sex couples share many similarities with heterosexual couples, but they also have many differences from them. Many same-sex couples seek assistance for problems identical to those of heterosexual couples, such as attachment issues, communication patterns, conflict negotiation, sexuality, power, or a balance of closeness and independence (Bigner, 2000). Practitioners, therefore, do not need a whole new theory of practice to work effectively with same-sex couples (Green, 2007). Although practitioners can use the major models of couple and sexuality practice (Gurman, 2008), there are differences between lesbian and gay couples and heterosexual couples that make application of those models not always fit. Lesbian and gay persons face unique social and psychological obstacles in their relationships as a result of heterosexism (see the introduction to this book, as well as chapters 4–6 and chapter 8). There are also differences because lesbian and gay persons face coming out and making disclosures, and because of the fact that they are in relationships with a person with a similar gender socialization as their own (L. M. Markowitz, 1991b; B. C. Murphy, 1994; Peplau, 1993). They may seek assistance for other unique challenges, such as in developing adequate social supports or a family of choice. Many couples also seek assistance in dealing with specifically lesbian and gay issues, such as conflicts over heterosexism in one partner's or both partners' family of origin. Others come to practitioners with psychiatric symptoms, such as depression in a partner that seems to be compounded by heterosexism (Green, 2002).

Practitioners should also remember that, just like in any other population, there is no "typical" lesbian or gay couple (Peplau, 1993). Each couple is unique and may be affected by factors such as age, socioeconomic levels, occupations, financial status, whether they are parents, influences of family of origin, former marital status, geography (e.g., rural, urban), race, ethnicity, whether they are in an interracial relationship, personal health, able-bodied status, level of participation in lesbian and gay communities, disclosure (openness versus closeted), and HIV status (L. S. Brown, 1996; Cabaj & Klinger, 1996; B. C. Murphy, 1994; Peplau, 1993). Practitioners must undertake careful assessment to guide their work with particular couples (Green, 2002).

## Overcoming Bias

No matter what their education and training, the cultural heterosexism in our society influences practitioners, as it does everyone else. Practitioners are also influenced by the history of lesbian and gay persons as having pathology in the American Psychiatric Association's *Diagnostic and Statistical Manual of Mental Disorders*. The *DSM* no longer lists lesbian and gay persons—in 1987, all references to "homosexuality" were finally removed (American Psychiatric Association, 1980, 1987)—but the legacy of that pathological view continues to have an impact. In a survey of more than 2,500 psychologists, more than half (58 percent) knew of incidents when lesbian and gay clients received biased or inappropriate service from a practitioner (Garnets, Hancock, Cochran, Goodchilds, & Peplau, 1991). In another survey of clinical psychologists, although 79 percent reported that they viewed being lesbian or gay as acceptable, 12.9 percent reported that they viewed gays and lesbians as having a disorder, and 5 percent described them as having a personality disorder. Some respondents (5.8 percent) supported the use of aversion therapy to change the client's sexual identity, and 11 percent supported the use of other methods, such as psychoanalysis, for the same purpose (Jordan & Deluty, 1995).

Practitioners must deal with bias. Heterocentric stereotypes persist even after practitioners presumably know the basic information about lesbian and gay issues (Garnets et al., 1991; Johnson, Brems, & Alford-Keating, 1997). Didactic information does not override the heterosexism that one has acquired over a lifetime.

Bias is clearly an obstacle to practitioners who are working with lesbian and gay clients. If practitioners are not aware of their own biases and of the subtle ways in which they communicate them to clients, they risk colluding with their clients' internalized heterosexism. They will not be of help to these clients as they will pick up on the practitioners' heterosexism. Heterosexist practitioners perpetuate rather than alleviate their client's problems (McHenry & Johnson, 1993).

What are the clues of bias among practitioners? In general, the signs tend to be subtle. They consist of feelings of discomfort, ambivalence, pessimism, anxiety, or appearing expert on lesbian and gay persons. Practitioners should also keep in mind that lesbian and gay persons have years of experience in developing a heightened sensitivity to signs or indications of not being accepted, discomfort about them, or intolerance. When there is any sign of this from a practitioner, a lesbian or gay client is likely to discontinue treatment and may or may not decide to pursue work with another practitioner (Green & Mitchell, 2002).

Bias also comes through when practitioners think that the way heterosexual persons or couples do things is superior to the way lesbian and gay persons do things. Or practitioners might try to identify one partner as more masculine and the other as more feminine, according to their stereotypes of roles in lesbian and gay couples. Lesbian and gay clients respond to this view in disbelief. Practitioners may focus on the couple's sexual relationships, neglecting other areas that the couple wants to address (Dworkin & Gutiérrez, 1992; Garnets & Kimmel, 1991; Gonsiorek & Weinrich, 1991; L. M. Markowitz, 1991b). Some practitioners may be uncomfortable with the idea of lesbian and gay adults serving as role models for children (Green & Mitchell, 2002).

Even worse, some practitioners do not support the maintenance of lesbian and gay couples, and some even encourage dissolution. They might not value the commitment to each other from each member of the couple. They might tell a couple to view their problems as insurmountable (Garnets et al., 1991), and they might view the couple as a poor substitute for the "real thing" (L. S. Brown, 1996). They might not provide or recommend any services for them. Some practitioners even viciously attack same-sex sexual identities (Dworkin & Gutiérrez, 1992; Garnets & Kimmel, 1991; Gonsiorek & Weinrich, 1991; L. M. Markowitz, 1991a).

Heterosexual practitioners also ignore lesbian and gay clients by assuming that all of their clients are heterosexual. They express this assumption in subtle ways, such as by giving clients forms that ask about spouses rather than partners. When inquiring about a client's romantic life, they ask how they get along with heterosexual persons. If a client mentions having a significant other, they use different-sex pronouns to inquire further about that person. This assumption of heterosexuality sends a message about how closed practitioners are to working with lesbian and gay clients. Even if practitioners want to work with these clients, if the same clients detect heterocentric assumptions, they are not likely to return (McAllan & Ditillo, 1994). Some lesbian and gay persons may try to protect themselves from anticipated practitioner bias by concealing their sexual identity. Practitioners may support this attempt by viewing them as if they were not lesbian or gay.

When practitioners start working with lesbian and gay clients, critical attitudes and behaviors—even subtle ones—have been demonstrated to reduce the likelihood of success. Henry, Schacht, and Strupp (1990) found that unsuccessful practitioners exhibit higher levels of "blaming and belittling" behaviors and lower levels of "helping and protecting" behaviors than those who are more successful (p. 770). The researchers concluded that the presence of even subtle levels of negative practitioner behaviors prevents client change. Of even greater concern is the possibility that practitioners might not just hinder therapeutic progress but also cause their lesbian and gay clients harm.

Other unhelpful behaviors include viewing being lesbian or gay as a disorder, attributing all presenting concerns to sexual identity, and expressing demeaning beliefs about lesbian and gay persons (Bartlett, King, & Phillips, 2001; Garnets et al., 1991; Hayes & Gelso, 1993). In one study, the client experienced the practitioner as judgmental, indifferent, cold, or disaffirming in almost half of the unhelpful situations (Israel, Gorcheva, Walther, Sulzner, & Cohen, 2008).

The goal for practitioners is to make heterocentric assumptions conscious, examine them in light of existing knowledge and professional ethics such as regarding persons as having worth and dignity, and root them out (Green & Mitchell, 2002). The practice climate must be one in which lesbian and gay persons can feel safe and not exposed to the hurtful presence of heterosexist attitudes of the practitioner.

Practitioners' social contact with lesbian and gay persons can also help reduce bias (Bernstein, 2000; Green & Bobele, 1994; Siegel & Walker, 1996). In general, heterosexuals who have more interaction with lesbian and gay persons as personal friends, colleagues, family members, and clients report significantly fewer heterosexist attitudes. It is also helpful to experience high levels of immersion in lesbian and gay culture or to work against heterosexism in one's own families, friendships, professional settings, and communities. On the political level, practitioners can participate in local chapters of Parents, Families, and Friends of Lesbians and Gays (PFLAG). Working toward the elimination of heterosexism in a practitioner's own social networks and community institutions is good preparation for practice with lesbian and gay couples (Green & Mitchell, 2002).

Practitioners should also seek expert consultation if they are not knowledgeable about working with lesbian and gay couples, and especially if progress with such couples is slower than desirable. In addition, they should discuss all assessment results, treatment goals, and therapeutic plans in a collaborative manner with clients, soliciting the partners' active input. The key is for practitioners to guard against making unwarranted assumptions and to check out perceptions about lesbian and gay issues with the clients themselves. Effective work with lesbian and gay couples also requires that practitioners be familiar with the unique norms of the lesbian and gay community and refuse making pathological what may be normative behavior for couples in that community (Green & Mitchell, 2002).

The single most important prerequisite for helping same-sex couples is the practitioner's personal comfort with love and sexuality between two women or two men. This requires familiarity with lesbian and gay culture, the ability to empathetically identify with lesbian and gay clients, and genuine personal ease when dealing with lesbian and gay people's feelings for their partners. It also requires an ability to ask and talk about sex in explicit terms with couples who are having sexual difficulties (Green & Mitchell, 2002).

Changing attitudes and behaviors will take time, and practitioners may never be able to completely unlearn their negative biases. But practitioners can learn to recognize their biases and can take steps to enhance their effectiveness with lesbian and gay clients. Given that those who work with lesbian and gay clients have the necessary knowledge, have rooted out biases, and perform exemplary practice, they can address micro-issues that lesbian and gay couples may face, some of which are identified in the next several chapters.

What is required further of those working with lesbian and gay clients is a good working alliance (Israel et al., 2008). A good working relationship is characterized by the practitioner's respect for the client (Bachelor, 1995); the client's perception of the practitioner as caring and skillful (Hersoug, Hoglend, Monsen, & Havik, 2001); the client's high ratings of practitioner understanding, clarity, and supportive attitude (Price & Jones, 1998); and the practitioner's warmth and friendliness (Mohl, Martinez, Ticknor, & Huang, 1991). Even though some of the practitioners in unhelpful situations established adequate working relationships with their clients, the working alliance in those situations was never as strong or as positive as it was in the helpful situations. A poor working alliance occurred exclusively in the unhelpful situations (Bartlett et al., 2001; Garnets et al., 1991).

## Summary

Practitioners should have accurate knowledge and assumptions about lesbian and gay couples, such as, they can have relationships as good as any heterosexual person can have. More difficult is recognizing their biases and getting rid of them. They should seek help if they want to work with these clients but are not yet prepared. Without preparation, practitioners could harm lesbian and gay clients. Social contact with lesbian and gay persons, their communities, and organizations can also help practitioners. They should also know about the unique issues that lesbian and gay couples deal with, such as heterosexism, making disclosures, and rejection by families and others. They should feel comfortable with lesbian and gay relationships and establish a good working alliance with lesbian and gay couples.

## Vignette

Mary and Jackie were having some difficulties in their relationship and sought out a practitioner. They immediately felt uncomfortable with the practitioner because he wanted to know which one played the male role and which one the female role. In addition, he said that he thought each person should become in-volved with an opposite-sex person. Mary and Jackie got up and left. They de-cided to never go back to the practitioner or to recommend him to any other les-bian or gay couples. They told some friends about their experience and got a recommendation to see someone else who was not biased against lesbian and gay couples. This practitioner was a delight to them because she wanted to know their story and was happy about their relationship. She had posters in her office of lesbian and gay couples and books about them. She noted that she had gone to a gay-pride parade and had a wonderful time. Mary and Jackie relaxed with this practitioner and developed a working alliance with her. They trusted her and were able to work out their difficulties. They highly recommended this practi-tioner to their friends.

## Resources

### For Further Reading

Croteau, J. M. (2005). *Deconstructing heterosexism in the counseling professions: A narrative approach*. Thousand Oaks, CA: Sage.

Garnets, L., & Kimmel, D. C. (Eds.). (2003). *Psychological perspectives on lesbian, gay, and bisexual experiences*. New York: Columbia University Press, 2003.

Geier, P. (2011). *Relationship tip sheet: Couples therapy for lesbians and gay men—The basics*. Retrieved from http://www.helpstartshere.org/tip-sheets/couples-therapy-for-lesbians-and-gay-men.html.

Mallon, G. P. (Ed.). (1998). *Foundations of social work practice with lesbian and gay persons*. New York: Haworth Press.

# Micro-level Issues and Practice with Lesbian and Gay Couples

How can a practitioner determine whether heterosexism is a foreground issue for clients?

How can a practitioner determine whether sexual identity is an issue for clients?

What does it mean for a practitioner to be informed but not a knower?

How can practitioners make the practice environment affirmative?

What are some of the therapies that practitioners can use with lesbian and gay clients?

What are possible gender issues in gay and lesbian couples?

Is the fact that some lesbians are socialized to be nurturing and close an issue practitioners should deal with?

What are some behaviors of lesbian and gay persons who batter their partners?

What are interventions practitioners can use when working with the victim of a batterer?

What is problematic of a support group for lesbian or gay batterers?

What are some macro-level interventions for battering?

Lesbians and gay men face many life issues that heterosexual women and men also face. Nevertheless, they are more likely than the population in general to use therapy at some stage of their lives (Herman, 1994; Hughes, Haas, & Avery, 1997; Morgan, 1997). As noted earlier, the proportions of gay men who use therapy is lower than for lesbians, although the rates for gay men are still higher than for the general population (Jones & Gabriel, 1999).

Heterosexism affects all issues for lesbians and gay men, but sometimes it is more in the background than the foreground. Practitioners must, therefore, assess the extent to which heterosexism is a foreground issue and needs to be addressed, or whether other issues are more at the forefront. In addition, not every lesbian and gay client's concerns center around identity as a sexual minority. This is not always the pressing concern. Having a practitioner who focuses on sexual identity when it is not relevant can be just as frustrating as having one who ignores it when it is relevant. Jones and Gabriel (1999) found in their sample of six hundred lesbian and gay clients that only about one-third sought assistance for issues related to their sexual identity, such as difficulties with coming out or with making disclosures. Although practitioners clearly need to be prepared to help clients with issues specific to their sexual identity, they should not assume that these issues are always what clients want assistance with.

Laird (1999) recommended that practitioners who work with lesbian clients become "informed not [a] knower" (p. 74). This approach also applies to gay clients and to gay and lesbian couples. Practitioners should ascertain how each couple member individually and together with his or her partner makes sense of their experiences. In addition, practitioners should ask both couple members to define themselves and the couple. This allows the couple to indicate what is important to them that the practitioner may otherwise miss (Malley & Tasker, 1999).

In addition, the environment for lesbian and gay clients should be affirmative. This includes having other categories than single, married, or divorced on admission forms (practitioners should instead ask who clients view as their family); having visible statements in the waiting room, such as lesbian and gay magazines or an affirmative poster on the wall; and the practitioner having knowledge about community resources for lesbian and gay clients (Croteau & Theil, 1994). Practitioners should use gender-neutral language, such as "relationship status" instead of "marital status" and "partner" versus "spouse" (Gruskin, 1999; Kelly, 1998). Also, practitioners should ask open-ended and neutral questions, such as, "What persons are essential in your life?" and "Can you tell me about them?"

Cabaj and Klinger (1996) recommended some specific therapies for work with lesbian and gay clients, such as systems and family therapy. Systems theory views couples as part of multiple interacting systems. Family therapy with the couple and one's family of origin, children, or both is indicated for some couples. This approach can help couples deal with blended family issues when children live with them, deal with families of origin, and help couples with children negotiate visitation and custody issues (Cabaj & Klinger, 1996). When interactions between couple members are an issue, marital therapy approaches are useful, especially if the issues are unrelated to sexual identity. Fassinger (2000) reviewed the benefits and limitations of four practice approaches for lesbian, gay, and bisexual persons: humanistic, cognitive behavioral, psychodynamic, and systems cultural. More specific treatment is indicated if a partner is suicidal or if there is domestic violence (Cabaj & Klinger, 1996).

The rest of this chapter and the following chapters suggest other approaches to the issues discussed herein.

## Gender Role Issues

Most lesbians and gay men grow up anticipating primarily heterosexual relationships in adolescence and adulthood and relationships with different gender socialization between partners (L. S. Brown, 1996). Instead, in adulthood, they end up with a partner who has the same gender socialization (L. M. Markowitz, 1991b). The probability is high that lesbians and gay men have many values, attitudes, and cognitive and/or emotional frameworks that are typical for their gender, such as attitudes about reciprocity, division of labor, negotiation of power, patterns of communication, cooperation and competition, and initiation of sexual activity (Bepko & Johnson, 2000). Two members of the same sex must create patterns that work for them rather than trying to adhere to traditional male-female roles. Such a task, however, can create tension and confusion. Gender role socialization can also create guilt and shame, as some partners experience anxiety and depression around violating learned social norms for their gender (Bepko & Johnson, 2000).

Scrivner and Eldridge (1995) focused on three of the themes affected by gender role socialization: emotional intimacy, sexuality, and power. First, when approaching emotional intimacy, women are socialized to care and nurture. Men are more likely to value expressing their autonomous and separate selves. Second, men generally are socialized to express sexual desire before emotional desire, whereas women prefer affection before initiating the sexual aspect, as noted in chapter 1. Third, another issue in couples is equality versus power (Johnson & Colucci, 1999). Lesbians tend to put a higher value on power equity than gay men do (Kurdek, 1995a). Socialization affects how one lines up on these three themes as gendered males and females, although there are variations and exceptions (Young & Long, 1998). The first and third themes are discussed further here, as they may especially be issues for practitioners to work on.

## Gender Role Issues for Gay Couples

### Overseparation

Western culture seems to forbid overt male-to-male intimacy, sexual or emotional. Gay men are subject to the same cultural conditioning as heterosexual men (e.g., difficulty in expressing feelings, maintaining emotional connection, and being vulnerable). They may be even more sensitive about exhibiting emotional vulnerability to other men. Many gay men report shaming experiences from being taunted as young boys by male peers and their fathers when they displayed emotional sensitivity or exhibited other nonconforming gender role behavior. To cope, many gay youths develop a false self and manage an impression as heterosexual for others. They appear as "masculine" as possible to stay above suspicion. The creation of a false self, however, creates a distance between oneself and others, and especially with other males. This may contribute later to gay men not acknowledging their emotional needs, as well as to emotional distance, isolation, separateness, and creation of physical distance (e.g., avoidance of affectionate behavior, excessive travel; Colgan, 1988). Social expectations for men reinforce this situation by emphasizing independence and differentiation of themselves or separation from other men (Cabaj & Klinger, 1996).

Instead of the overattachment that may characterize some lesbian relationships, gay men are said to experience overseparation in their relationships (Colgan, 1988). The goal of overseparation is to preserve independence, but this makes it difficult to form and maintain intimate bonds (Cabaj & Klinger, 1996). Once sexual attraction fades, couple members may be at a loss as to how to proceed (L. S. Brown, 1996).

Some studies challenge the notion of gay couples' disengagement. They found that gay couples had higher ratings of couple cohesion than did heterosexual couples (Bepko & Johnson, 2000). Similarly, other studies comparing lesbian, gay, and heterosexual couples found no significant differences among the groups in various aspects of relationship closeness and satisfaction (Peplau, 1991). Wester, Pionke, and Vogel (2005) found that gay couples do not lack the interpersonal skills needed for relationship success. Although socialized like all men into the male sex role, the impact of socialization may be lessened in gay relationships.

Research by Green, Bettinger, and Zacks (1996) found that some male couples are disengaged and others are enmeshed. It is more common, however, to find a pursuer-distance arrangement, as in many heterosexual couples. The dynamics for male couples, however, are much more complex, because the man who voices the need for connectedness may reexperience shame about his desire for emotional closeness with a man (Greenan & Tunnell, 2003). He may feel that he is not masculine or is worthless when distance renders him lonely or depressed. A perpetual double bind with no comfortable solution can cause havoc in one's relationship (Johnson & Keren, 1996). Emotional distancing and impaired communication may result in a person not openly identifying relationship issues. When a person does finally address those issues, an explosion of pent up negative feelings can erupt (Rutter & Schwartz, 1996). Marital therapy is appropriate in aiding clients to express feelings and vulnerability. Professional practice can become an arena for each man in a gay couple to have novel experiences in trusting another man with his feelings and to develop new ways to create boundaries. To defuse the constriction that stereotypes create, direct conversation about the effects of traditional gender biases is often a helpful intervention (MacDonald, 1998). This might involve exploring the gender narrative in each partner's family of origin and searching for exceptions to this and more unique outcomes (White & Epston, 1990).

## Power and Influence

Men in Western cultures are socialized to equate their personal value with power, prestige, and income (L. S. Brown, 1996). Conflicts in gay couples can occur over perceived inequities in these areas or over the degree of influence that each partner holds over the other (L. S. Brown, 1994, 1996; McVinney, 1998). The partner with more personal assets usually has more influence (Reilly & Lynch, 1990).

Gay men may consider their partner a competitor or an enemy with respect to status and power. This may occur when one partner is in an occupation with greater power, prestige, or income than the other partner (L. S. Brown, 1996). If there is insecurity about the relationship, each may try to prove that he is worthy of love (MacDonald, 1998). This may be hard to attain, however, as competitive partners may devalue and insult each other (L. S. Brown, 1996; MacDonald, 1998).

Members of gay couples may expect the partner with the lower status or lower income to do more of the homemaking tasks. In a heterosexual partnership, the woman usually does the homemaking tasks because she is typically of lower status. Heterosexual men also have learned to be a stereotypical husband or to be in control, to be competitive, to express anger, and to garner power and territory. It is important for the practitioner to probe for the impact of occupational and income differences on gay clients and to explore symbolic meanings and cultural messages regarding money, status, and power. This helps partners comprehend why one of them may feel demeaned or "losing" in the competition, even if he experiences no overt desire to compete in the partnership (L. S. Brown, 1996).

Exposure of the patterns that gay men may follow and the reasons for those patterns may help gay couples reduce or eliminate the power struggles they experience (MacDonald, 1998). But couples have to work especially hard to give up ingrained assumptions about stereotypical masculine behaviors (e.g., aggression, competitiveness) and to develop the collaborative communication and negotiating skills required for more satisfying relationships (Okun, 1996).

## Gender Role Issues for Lesbian Couples

Whereas men use shared activities to establish intimacy and sexual activity, women share feelings, secrets, and insights to establish intimacy (Wood & Inman, 1993). These "feminine" behaviors, however, are not generally valued by society and members of society. L. S. Brown (1996) emphasized that, for practitioners to work well with lesbian couples, it is necessary for them to attain a thorough grounding in women's adult development within a sexist cultural context (e.g., J. V. Jordan, Kaplan, Miller, Stiver, & Surrey, 1991). Growing up in a sexist context, women learn to place little value on stereotypically feminine behaviors, such as nurturance, empathy, and relational identity, and on themselves as women. This devaluation of women may lead women in couples to devalue each other. In contrast, they may set standards of perfection for their partner to make up for the perceived deficiency of not being a man (L. S. Brown, 1996).

Female partners are expected to be nurturers with no shortcomings: endlessly available, always listening, and always interested. At the same time, female partners are supposed to be independent, individuated, and able to take care of their own needs. This is a double bind. The practitioner must challenge each woman to overcome the devaluation of women so that she values her partner and reduces expectations of perfection (L. S. Brown, 1996).

Perhaps neither partner in lesbian couples learned that it was acceptable to express anger or to be aggressive in sex. A woman may feel shame and guilt about such behaviors (L. S. Brown, 1996). It can be helpful for these partners to explore gender role socialization and how that influenced negative outcomes. Just as with gay men, they have to learn to overcome the socialization that causes difficulties in their relationships.

It is important that there is not one partner following a feminine sex role and the other partner a masculine sex role, because doing so increases negative behaviors. The negative effects of the feminine-masculine pair are strongest in lesbian couples. When two women are together, each may expect from the other nurturing and emotional support. If one of the partners, however, subscribes to a traditionally masculine sex-role identity, she may not provide satisfactory levels of the behaviors that her partner desires; she may pull away if the other partner pushes for nurturance and emotional support, thus escalating a demand-withdrawal pattern. Feminine-masculine pairs also experience the highest levels of destructive communication and conflict management, the lowest levels of constructive conflict management, the lowest levels of satisfaction with their relationship and relationship efficacy, and the highest levels of "problem" intensity and verbal and physical aggression (Julien, Arellano, & Turgeon, 1997).

Couples who are comparable in sex roles may better understand and communicate with each other, but they must also balance their similarities (Rutter & Schwartz, 1996). For example, if high levels of emotionality become claustrophobic in lesbian couples, this may lead to avoidance behaviors (Gottman, 1994). A high level of emotionality, however, is not always an issue in lesbian couples.

## Attachment and Autonomy

Attachment puts an emphasis on emotional closeness, spending time together, shared activities, sexual exclusivity, long-term commitment, and security in a relationship with another person. Autonomy puts an emphasis on independence, separation, or boundaries between partners. Some partners prefer a combination of both high attachment and high autonomy, whereas other partners emphasize one identity and not the other. For example, some partners want to maintain a high degree of personal independence, including separate interests and friends. Other partners do everything together and develop few boundaries between them; they may seek no outside interests and activities (Peplau, 1993).

The stereotype of lesbian partners is that they want to blend and merge. Many studies have reported that lesbian couples put more emphasis on attachment than on autonomy (e.g., Burch, 1997; Toder, 1992). They may experience overattachment primarily as a result of their expectations from gender socialization (Cabaj & Klinger, 1996), which leads them to seek connection rather than autonomy and relational distance (Kirkpatrick, 1991; Krestan & Bepko, 1980). The nurturance and empathy that women learn from childhood facilitates the development of intimacy through talking and expressing feelings, but it may also predispose them to problems with maintaining autonomy in their relationships (MacDonald, 1998). Writers on this topic use terms such as *fusion* (Bowen, 1996), which implies a sense of oneness (Burch, 1986), to describe this phenomenon. Many researchers have concluded that too much closeness underlies both intimacy and conflict in lesbian relationships (e.g., Greene, Causby, & Miller, 1999).

Others believe that closeness in lesbian couples is wrongly labeled in pejorative terms. Moreover, generalization from clinical to nonclinical groups is problematic (Green et al., 1996). Therefore, it is necessary to question whether too much closeness poses difficulty for lesbian couples (Kitzinger & Perkins, 1993). It may not even exist in some lesbian couples. No good evidence supports the notion that female socialization makes women predisposed to too much closeness in relationships (Green et al., 1996). Kurdek (1991c) did not find this phenomenon in nonclinical samples of lesbian couples. Spencer and Brown (2007) also found that fusion may not result between two women in a couple. Several other researchers found that lesbian respondents did not think that too much closeness characterized their relationships, nor did they desire it. They wanted both attachment and autonomy in their partnerships (Hill, 1999; Mackey, Diemer, & Mackey, 1997). Probably an accurate description of lesbian couples in general is that they are close instead of merged, or as Surrey (1985) suggested, that they are both exceedingly close and exceedingly differentiated.

## Interventions When Too Much Closeness Is Problematic

It can be helpful to distinguish between different forms of closeness. High time fusion, or spending large amounts of time together, is not problematic. High levels of sharing fusion, however, interfere with one's sense of personal autonomy.

Sharing fusion includes sharing personal possessions, such as clothing and cars. These personal items may reflect one's sense of individuality, and a person may prefer to keep clearer boundaries around these items (Causby, Lockhart, White, & Greene, 1995).

It can help for the practitioner to view closeness not as negative and devalued but as normative. Closeness represents strength, and independence and emotional autonomy exist along with closeness (Greene et al., 1999). Other terms can be useful, especially those following the feminist emphasis on empowerment in naming and renaming terms. Instead of negative terms such as *merger* or *fusion*, for example, terms such as *connection* or *commitment* are more accurate (Greene et al., 1999).

Rather than viewing closeness as characteristic of lesbian couples, it is better for practitioners to present it as a learned way of relating to others. This kind of assessment leaves out preconceived notions about intimacy and distance in lesbian couples. It also is based on extensive research and can be assessed with validated self-report questionnaires (Hindy & Schwarz, 1994).

Some lesbian couples may want more distance regulation and boundary maintenance, and they may attempt to achieve this through fighting or triangulation of a third person, such as an ex-partner (Elise, 1996). Another strategy is to withdraw from sexual contact. But there are more constructive ways to accomplish the goal of creating distance.

The most typical prescription for modifying excessive closeness involves methods that can increase distance and differentiation between the partners. This can help the partners achieve both intimacy and independence while maintaining strong boundaries (Cabaj & Klinger, 1996). Partners learn to clearly state their desires and expectations (Igartua, 1998). Matteson (1996) recommended interventions to assist clients develop a fuller sense of self and more autonomous expression, such as teaching them to speak from the first-person position of "I." These couples may need help communicating their views directly and clearly. The couple members may report that they are afraid to directly ask for what they desire (Cabaj & Klinger, 1996). They can benefit from role-playing more direct requests and from reading books that emphasize more autonomy.

A group process helps couples find support and encouragement from other couples who have experienced similar relationship issues and to establish pride in their identities. A group experience also offers the members of a couple safety for open expressions with each other in the group. Couple members can learn to identify and express their own needs with group support (Kleinberg & Zorn, 1995).

Practitioners can also help couple members with a dialogue. Kleinberg and Zorn (1995) proposed the use of two roles (sender and receiver). Each member of the couple role-plays one of the roles, and then they reverse the roles. The dialogue also involves the three processes of mirroring, validation, and empathy. Mirroring requires the partner who is the receiver to be receptive to the other partner's (the sender's) spoken message. The receiver reflects back what the other partner (the sender) said. He or she can paraphrase the message or repeat it word for word. This process goes back and forth until the sender feels that she has been heard. Validation requires temporary suspension of the receiver's point of view and allows the sender to state one's own reality with no judgment of it. This step highlights the fact that there are always two points of view operating. When practicing empathy, the receiver expresses the feelings that one's partner is experiencing because of a painful situation the partner is describing. The receiver does not have to agree with the feelings, feel them, or deny her own self. Instead, the goal is to understand the partner's feelings and tell the partner that one understands them.

The activities suggested here may be useful for helping clients with aspects of too much closeness, but another important element to address is fear that the relationship will not last. The goal here is to assist partners in moving toward a more secure relationship by reducing the fear that it could end at any time. If desired, changes can also be made using effective empirically validated therapy methods (Feeney, Noller, & Hanrahan, 1994; Griffen & Bartholomew, 1994), such as emotionally focused couple therapy (Johnson & Greenberg, 1995).

Some professionals may think that the closeness in lesbian couples is immature. It is important, however, for practitioners not to impose their ideas of an appropriate balance between autonomy and intimacy. It is also important not to impose male-biased theories or the overly individualist bias of Western culture (Matteson, 1996). Also, what practitioners may consider immature, lesbians may consider an advantage. Given that satisfaction is high in lesbian couples, their closeness may not be distressing. In addition, there is no definitive research that delineates what levels of closeness or differentiation may be normative for couples in general or for lesbian couples in particular (Zacks, Green, & Morrow,

1988). The negotiation of intimacy and independence goes on continually, whether in lesbian, gay, or heterosexual couples (Elise, 1996).

## Violence in Lesbian and Gay Couples

Some of the variables discussed here, such as a desire for power, can result in intimate partner violence (IPV), a pattern of behavior in which one partner coerces, dominates, and isolates the other partner. The desire is of one partner to maintain power and control over the other partner (National Coalition of Anti-Violence Programs, 2005). Abusive behaviors include but are not limited to verbal abuse, emotional manipulation, restricted access to finances, physical assaults, and sexual assault or rape.

The term *sexual violence* encompasses any type of unwanted sexual activity, including touching of the body, kissing, vaginal penetration by objects or fingers, oral sex, anal sex, and forcing a person to do things to his or her own body (Girshick, 2002). Sexual abuse also involves forcing the partner to perform uncomfortable sexual acts, having affairs, accusing the partner of having affairs, criticizing the partner's sexual performance, and withholding affection. Physical abuse includes such actions as punching, shoving, slapping, biting, kicking, using a weapon, throwing items, pulling hair, and restraining the partner. Emotional and/or verbal abuse involves putting the partner down, calling the partner names, criticizing the partner, playing mind games, using humiliation, making the partner feel guilty, telling the partner he or she asked for the abuse, telling the partner what to wear, and reinforcing internalized heterosexism. Financial dependency involves keeping the partner from getting a job, getting the partner fired, making the partner ask for money or taking the partner's money, and expecting the partner to support oneself. Social isolation involves controlling who the partner sees and talks to and where the partner goes, as well as limiting the partner's involvement in a lesbian or gay community. Coercion, threats, and intimidation involve making the partner afraid by looks or gestures; destroying property; hurting pets; displaying weapons; threatening to leave; taking the children; threatening to commit suicide or committing suicide; and threatening to reveal that the partner is lesbian or gay to community members and/or his or her employer, family, or ex-spouse (Peterman & Dixon, 2003).

Some victims experience severe aggression, including beatings and assaults with weapons. Same-sex violence also tends to occur multiple times within a couple, and the severity of the abuse increases over time (Lockhart, White, Causby, & Isaac, 1994).

Intimate partner violence has been correlated with a mix of variables, such as internalized heterosexism (Renzetti, 1997); violence in one's family of origin (Renzetti, 1992); substance abuse (e.g., alcohol; Coleman, 1990; Schilit, Lie, & Montagne, 1990); dependency and autonomy conflicts (Renzetti, 1992); power imbalances (Renzetti, 1992), as well as unemployment, finances, household responsibilities, and sexual behavior (Lockhart et al., 1994; Schilit et al., 1990). Because the cause of IPV is not clear, more important to practitioners are scales that assess partner abuse. McClennen, Summers, and Daley (2002) developed a lesbian partner abuse scale that practitioners can use.

Although many similarities exist with IPV in heterosexual couples, there are important differences in lesbian and gay couples, including heterosexist control, the HIV status of one or both partners, and the myth of mutual battering. The abuse of heterosexist control or threatening to expose one's sexual identity to parents and others is common in same-sex couples. Renzetti (1992) studied one hundred victims of lesbian battering; 21 percent reported that their partners threatened to out them or to reveal their sexual identity without permission. Outing a partner's sexual identity to family, friends, employers, or the general community is a unique option available to perpetrators of same-sex IPV. They use it to keep victims from reporting acts of violence and to force them to remain in an abusive relationship (Aulivola, 2004).

Some gay men and lesbians are HIV positive (Letellier, 1996). A batterer with HIV may threaten to infect the partner or may use his or her failing health to make the partner feel guilty about wanting to leave the relationship. If the victim is HIV positive, the partner may withhold medical care or reveal the HIV status to others, which could result in loss of insurance benefits and loss of income. Heintz and Melendez (2006) found that many abused partners felt unsafe in asking their abusive partners to use protection for safe sex. Many experienced sexual, physical, and/or verbal abuse as a consequence of asking their partner to use protection. Some reported being raped with no protection.

Some studies suggest that the violence in same-sex relationships is mutual (e.g. Lie, Schilit, Bush, Montagne, & Reyes, 1991). But many lesbians say their aggressive behavior is self-defense (Renzetti, 1992). Batterers also may claim mutual abuse to deny their responsibility for abuse (Farley, 1992). Minimizing or denying involves making light of abuse, saying it did not happen or that it was mutual, and blaming the partner for the abuse (Peterman & Dixon, 2003).

## Prevalence of Violence

According to the National Coalition of Anti-Violence Programs (1998), at least one in four lesbian and gay partners will experience domestic violence in their lifetime. Another report indicates that between 25 percent and 33 percent of lesbians and gay men are abused by their partners (LAMBDA, 2004). These data are comparable to reported rates in heterosexual relationships (Greenwood et al., 2002; National Coalition of Anti-Violence Programs, 2005). In lesbian relationships, between 41 percent and 68 percent of women experience IPV at the hands of a same-sex partner at some time in their lives (Burke, Jordan, & Owen, 2002; National Coalition of Anti-Violence Programs, 2002). In a review of research studies on IPV in lesbian partnerships, West (2002) found that approximately 30–40 percent of lesbian women have been involved in at least one, if not more, physically abusive relationships. The most commonly reported forms of physical abuse were slapping, pushing, and shoving. Physical beatings and assaults with weapons also occurred, but less often. Sexual violence that included coerced kissing and fondling, as well as vaginal, anal, and oral penetration, ranged widely from 7 percent to 55 percent. By far, the most common types of partner abuse were verbal and psychological, with a reported rate higher than 80 percent. In addition, Renzetti (1992) found instances of child abuse and pet abuse. Perpetrators abused the partner's children in almost 30 percent of cases, and pets in about 38 percent of cases. Renzetti also noted abuse of lesbian women with disabilities, such as being left by a partner in high-risk or dangerous circumstances without help or means to escape. A diabetic victim reported being forced to ingest sugar, thus significantly increasing her risk of a medical crisis. The rates reported here are probably underestimations because of fears of censure or safety when reporting, lack of uniform legal definitions across states, and variability in mandatory arrest policies.

In their review of the literature on IPV, Johnson and Ferraro (2000) declared that more was known about lesbian battering than about violence in gay men's relationships. This is in part because of the role of the women's movement in generating research on domestic violence against women. However, Island and Letellier (1991), in their groundbreaking book *Men Who Beat the Men Who Love*

*Them*, extrapolated from the rates of relationship violence and the number of gay men in the United States to provide the first prevalence estimate of gay male IPV. They concluded that IPV occurs in 11–20 percent of all gay male relationships. With no national database to measure the rate of IPV among gay men, Island and Letellier (1991) estimated that between 350,000 and 650,000 gay men in the United States have been victims of IPV—or roughly one in five gay men will experience IPV in their lifetime.

In her survey of 499 lesbians and gay men in the Houston area, Turell (2000) found that of the 53 percent of gay and bisexual men in her sample, 83 percent reported emotional abuse, 44 percent reported physical violence, and 13 percent reported sexual abuse while in a relationship with a male partner. In a non-probability sample of fifty-one HIV-positive gay men currently or recently in a relationship (within one year), 39 percent reported perpetrating physical assault on their partner, whereas 45 percent reported being a victim of physical violence by their partner (Craft & Serovich, 2005). Greenwood et al. (2002) used a probability-based sample of 2,881 men who reported having sex with men to measure three types of partner violence: physical, sexual, and psychological and/or symbolic. They found that 39 percent experienced at least one type of partner violence in the previous five years and 18 percent experienced multiple forms of battering (34 percent, psychological and/or symbolic; 22 percent, physical; and 5 percent, sexual violence).

Despite these studies, the vast majority of estimates regarding same-sex IPV should be interpreted with great caution. Most studies lack probability and representative sampling.

## Help

The rates of help seeking by lesbian and gay victims of violence are low. The first behavior among most abused women is to call the police. However, the expectation of help is not consistently realized. For example, police responses are hostile or inadequate in many cases (Rose, 2003). In some cases, police refuse to take complaints and arrest both victims and offenders (Kuehnle & Sullivan, 2003). Social service agencies also are inconsistent with their resources and interventions. Even agencies serving lesbian, gay, bisexual, and transgender communities are not always sources of help, and most agencies help victims of hate crimes more than victims of partner abuse (Burke et al., 2002). In Renzetti's (1992) study of one hundred abused lesbians, fewer than twenty sought help from legal authorities, religious leaders, shelters, or physicians. Fifty-eight sought help from counselors.

Island and Letellier (1991) found that gay victims were reluctant to seek help from legal and social service agencies. This may result from feelings of shame and fear of retaliation. They may also have concerns about revealing their sexual identity or fear of heterosexism and discriminatory practices. These fears are not unfounded (Renzetti, 1996).

Practitioners must provide crisis intervention to victims of IPV. They also must help the victim assess the danger that exists in his or her relationship (Peterman & Dixon, 2003). Indicators of danger include the abuser's "ownership" of the partner, threats of homicide or suicide, fantasies of homicide or suicide, obsessions about partner or family, one's life being focused on the partner, mental health problems, use of weapons, drug and alcohol consumption, pet abuse, and prior criminal history (Center against Spouse Abuse [CASA], 2000). The number of items observed and the intensity can help the practitioner and victim estimate the probability of another attack (Peterman & Dixon, 2003).

A safety plan is an essential part of crisis intervention, no matter whether the victim decides to stay or leave. If she or he wants to stay, it is necessary to identify a safe place in the home with an exit and no weapons; to observe if the abuser is tracing incoming and outgoing phone calls; to develop a support system of trusted family members, friends, and coworkers; to call the police if in danger; and to prepare an emergency bag if a quick escape is necessary. The emergency bag should include important papers (e.g., birth certificate, social security card, driver's license); medications; a change of clothing; and important phone numbers, including that of a local shelter when possible and numbers for legal protection and assistance from other agencies. A person who leaves an abusive relationship must keep in mind that doing so may escalate the danger of the situation, and so he or she should call the police if in danger and vary routines of work, school, shopping, and so on, as the abuser may be looking for the victim (CASA, 2000). In a crisis situation, victims need a caring practitioner and the opportunity to express themselves and to feel heard and understood. They need respect, genuineness, and support from the practitioner.

It is essential that practitioners know of shelters or safe houses for victims of abusive relationships. They have to make a quick assessment of imminent danger (Roberts, 2000). Locating resources that cater to lesbians and gay men or that are "gay friendly" is essential in encouraging individuals to follow through with treatment. Those experiencing violence may need both LGBT-specific resources (e.g., support group, advocacy) and general services (e.g., financial, housing) to assist them. Lesbians experiencing domestic violence and needing temporary shelter may be able to seek shelter at a heterosexually oriented women's shelter solely on the basis of their gender. However, a gay man experiencing violence may not have that same alternative (McKenry, Servovich, Mason, & Mosack, 2006). If shelters are unavailable, seeking safe haven with family members or friends may be an option.

If there is no risk of imminent danger, the practitioner should assess both partners but separately (Istar, 1996). Listening to both can reveal relational roles, boundaries, level of fusion, balance of power, and the types of abuse occurring.

Other interventions for battered lesbians and gay men can be at the individual, community, or society levels (Hamberger, 1996). Some recommend counseling on an individual basis; some recommend couples counseling, although that is controversial and many practitioners will not see the victim and batterer together. Other interventions include support groups and systemic interventions (Coleman, 1990; Dutton, 1994), which may be the most helpful approaches. Support groups are recommended for both lesbian and gay victims of IPV. They provide an opportunity to focus on issues that all members have in common, to strategize ways to cope, and to manage new situations. They also empower members to recover from abuse (for information on developing such groups, see Johnson, 1999).

It is important in support groups to provide safety. For example, the group can be held in a confidential location with agreement among members not to disclose the location, in order to prevent batterers from showing up. The groups usually meet for twelve to fourteen weeks for ninety minutes at each meeting. The groups combine process and discussion with psychosocial education (for topics to cover in each session, see the appendix in Johnson, 1999).

Support groups can also reduce isolation for ethnic minority women if they experience community ostracism. An exception might be Asians, who may have cultural concerns about revealing family affairs to outsiders. Practitioners should discuss such concerns with clients before deciding on appropriate interventions (West, 1998).

Less acculturated or immigrant women may need more direction in negotiating resources (Franco, 1996). Therapists should respect these women's culture and how it affects them in seeking help. Some women might want to consult with community elders or healers. For ethnic or racial batterers such as African American males, group therapy can used for treatment (West, 1998).

Cayouette (1999) describes the negative aspects of group therapy for lesbian batterers. The groups are problematic in that batterers may use the group as a way to get back with the partner or to convince the partner to give the batterer another chance. A total end to abuse is rare, and changes resulting from the group will be limited. If batterers are referred from a court or probation officers, they may attend but not work toward any changes. Another problem is that batterers may learn about how other batterers controlled their partners, and then use that against their own partners. The partner should be prepared for these consequences of the batterer's group participation. The focus of these groups should be on safety and advocacy for the battered person. Batterers should be held accountable, and excuses and justifications not accepted. Three things can get in the way of batterers' progress: denial or refusal to admit they battered their partner; minimizing of or underplaying the full extent of the violence; and sidetracking or saying something like, "I hit her because of stress at work."

## Macro-system Practice

Practitioners who work with lesbian and gay persons who have been battered should also address macro systems, including cultural norms; patriarchal institutions; and community values that limit or enhance access to legal, medical, and shelter services. Victims often say that fear of heterosexism is a barrier to seeking services (Balsam, 2001). Fear of disclosure and possible negative consequences also prevent them from reporting to law enforcement. Renzetti (1996) surveyed domestic violence programs for battered women in the United States. She found that most programs (96 percent) said that they welcomed lesbians as clients, but only 10 percent provided services related to lesbian battering.

Rose (2003), the cofounder and director of the St. Louis Lesbian and Gay Anti-Violence Project, described ways to work with community agencies that may come in contact with lesbian and gay victims of abuse. The ideas of that project are also applicable in other cities. The first community intervention is to work closely with key officials in the police department and to improve relations between the police and the lesbian and gay community. Having a police liaison for local lesbian and gay communities is also helpful.

The second community intervention is to work with victims' services agencies to make them more aware of lesbian and gay issues. Victims' services volunteers and staff are trained to enact two improvements. The first concerns intake and treatment at agencies. Volunteers and staff are sensitized as to how to be alert to possible lesbian and gay domestic violence. In addition, practitioners can work with selected agencies to identify staff who can serve as specialists in domestic violence. If agencies do not have available staff for this, they can be encouraged to refer victims of abuse to other agencies for supportive counseling. Victims' services agencies also can improve by focusing on increasing the accuracy of reporting of domestic violence.

The third community intervention is aimed at legislators. The former absence of protective hate crime legislation encompassing same-sex sexual identity at the federal level was a barrier to effective police and criminal justice intervention, but a hate crimes bill protecting LGBT persons has since passed Congress. A lack of protection at the state level is equally a problem, so practitioners must also work at that level (for more details on interventions, see Rose, 2003).

## Summary

Lesbians and gay men use therapy more than the general population. Issues particular to gay men and lesbians include heterosexism, gender role issues, and too much closeness in some lesbian relationships. Other issues, just as common among heterosexuals, include balancing attachment and autonomy, as well as intimate partner violence. Heterosexism affects nearly all issues for lesbians and gay men.

## Vignette

Susy and Jan were happy when they were first together, but Jan seemed possessive of Susy and became upset if Susy saw friends or went to dinner with work colleagues. One evening when Susy came home late after an evening out with her coworkers, Jan was pacing the floor and angry. She said she never wanted Susy to go out with coworkers again. Susy did not accept this and said she would continue to see her friends from work. Jan became more agitated and hit Susy in the face and threw her up against a wall. She hit her again and gave her a black eye. Susy was able to get out of the house with her car keys and left as fast as she could—Jan ran after her and banged on the car window. Susy first went to friends but was afraid Jan would find her there. The friends called Susy's therapist, who met her at her office even though it was late at night. The therapist decided that Susy was in danger because of the obsessive and controlling tactics of Jan and took her to a shelter. The therapist helped Susy with her decision to leave the relationship because Jan's behavior would most likely not change. Susy moved out of the area, taking nothing with her because she was afraid to go to the house and get clothes and other items. She went to a shelter in another city that her therapist had recommended. The staff there gave her some clothes and helped her find a job so she could support herself. Jan never found her but made abusive calls to the therapist, thinking that she probably helped Susy, and threatened to come after her and hurt her. The therapist had Jan arrested. She denied ever harming Susy or wanting to harm the therapist, but the therapist knew that neither story was true. Jan never bothered the therapist again because she did not want to be arrested again. She became involved with another woman, and the same controlling behavior took place in that relationship. Her new partner also was able to escape, but with many bruises and a broken arm. Eventually, Jan's reputation as an abuser spread around the lesbian community, and no one else would get involved with her. She, too, left the area but continued her controlling behavior until others found out about it. Jan refused to get any help, saying that she did not need it, as she never abused anyone.

## Resources

### Online

#### *Sydney Gay Counselling*

Sydney Gay Counselling (http://sydneygaycounselling.com/gay-couples) is based in Australia, but the Web site offers a wealth of resources for gay and lesbian couples who are considering couples' therapy, as well as a blog about healthy gay and lesbian relationships.

### For Further Reading

Dworkin, S. H., & Gutiérrez, F. J. (Eds.). (1992). *Counseling gay men and lesbians: Journey to the end of the rainbow.* Alexandria, VA: American Association for Counseling and Development.

Girshick, L. B. (2002). *Woman-to-woman sexual violence: Does she call it rape?* Boston: Northeastern University Press.

Hamberger, L. K., & Renzetti, C. M. (1996). *Domestic partner abuse.* New York: Springer.

Laird, J., & Green, R. J. (1996). *Lesbians and gays in couples and families: A handbook for therapists*. San Francisco: Jossey-Bass.

Lundy, S. E., & Leventhal, B. (Eds.). (1999). *Same-sex domestic violence: Strategies for change*. Thousand Oaks, CA: Sage.

Mallon, G. P. (Ed.). (1998). *Foundations of social work practice with lesbian and gay persons*. New York: Haworth Press.

McClennen, J. C., & Gunther, J. J. (Eds.). (1999). *A professional's guide to understanding gay and lesbian domestic violence: Understanding practice interventions*. Lewiston, NY: Mellen.

Renzetti, C. M. (1992). *Violent betrayal: Partner abuse in lesbian relationships*. Newbury Park, CA: Sage.

Ritter, K., & Terndrup, A. I. (2002). *Handbook of affirmative psychotherapy with lesbians and gay men*. New York: Guilford Press.

Rose, S. (Ed.). (2002). *Lesbian love and relationships*. New York: Harrington Park Press.

# Additional Micro-level Issues and Practice

How can practitioners help couples handle relationship ambiguity?

How can practitioners help with gender role rigidity if a problem for some couples?

How can practitioners help deal with stage discrepancy?

How can practitioners help interracial couples with their specific difficulties?

What are the best ways to deal with couples' conflicts over disclosure?

What are some of the sexual issues that lesbian and gay couples might have?

How can practitioners help a nonmonogamous gay couple?

What are the three most important areas of safe-sex awareness to protect against HIV/AIDS?

How does HIV/AIDS in one member of a couple affect a gay couple?

# Relationship Ambiguity

Relationship ambiguity results when members of couples are not clear about important things in their relationship. In general, all couples tend to function best when they meet ambiguities with clear agreements about commitment and boundaries. Lesbian and gay relationships, however, do not look like heterosexual marriages, which settle many uncertainties by law and tradition. Especially because most lesbian and gay persons are not legally married, they are vulnerable to relationship ambiguity (Green & Mitchell, 2002), although heterosexual couples might sometimes experience relationship ambiguity.

To counter relationship ambiguity, Green and Mitchell (2002) suggested that practitioners address the following items with lesbian and gay couples:

- Definition of a couple or what it means to be a couple
- Their history of being a couple
- How being a couple affects relationships with others, such as family members, friends, their lesbian and gay community, and others in the heterosexual community
- Rules about monogamy and, if one partner has sex outside the relationship, rules for safe-sex practices
- Agreements about financial matters such as monthly finances, current or future debts, pooling versus separation of financial resources, ownership of joint property, and other financial planning matters
- Assignments of household tasks and decision-making process, and whether the division or sharing of those tasks is satisfactory
- Commitment to caring for each other in illness, injury, or disability

Partners also need to clarify whether each partner feels that there is a lifetime commitment and allegiance between the partners. Clarifying the extent of a couple's emotional commitment is central to practitioners' work with couples in the early stages of a relationship. Sometimes this necessitates resolving partners' conflicts of allegiance between the couple relationship and other family members, friends, or ex-partners. It may also involve the promises and reassurances that each partner is willing to give to the other (e.g., care giving, time, monogamy) (Green & Mitchell, 2002).

Practitioners might give "homework" assignments or in-session exercises that involve negotiations, and sometimes putting relationship vows in writing can be useful. Such vows (in addition to legal contracts) require that the partners address the issues they have concerns about and come up with behavioral agreements for the future. Interventions that help the partners clarify expectations and agreements in contested areas or areas that they have not discussed (e.g., finances, monogamy) will help reduce relationship ambiguity and thus increase partners' feelings of secure attachment and belief in the permanence of their union (Green & Mitchell, 2002).

If they desire, practitioners can support lesbian and gay partners in having a commitment ceremony and a formal exchange of vows, which can cover some of the issues discussed here. A couple can also draw up legal documents (especially health-care power of attorney and wills and trusts; Green & Mitchell, 2002; for details about legal documents, see Burda, 2004, 2008). Resolving the issues discussed above and reinforcing relationship vows increase the partners' security and the durability or potential longevity of the relationship (Green & Mitchell, 2002).

## Gender Role Rigidity

Many partners in couples find themselves carrying out patterns that are similar to those that parents displayed. Parental relationships serve as the primary and internalized model for how a couple functions. Sometimes, however, the internalized model of one partner is not acceptable to the other partner (Cabaj & Klinger, 1996).

Other patterns come from gender role traits or rigidity in gender roles. Assessment of the gender role traits of each partner is useful for practitioners because differences may predict difficulties in communicating and in handling conflicts (Julien, Arellano, & Turgeon, 1997; Stein & Cabaj, 1996). Practitioners can teach couple members the skills associated with beneficial gender traits that they do not exhibit (Julien, Arellano, et al., 1997). For example, increasing empathy with one's partner may result in conflicts being handled in a more constructive way (Okun, 1996). It is important to note that gender role rigidity is an issue only if a couple sees it that way or if only one member of the couple plays out a specific gender role and the other member has an issue with it. Some couples may prefer to have strict gender role definitions.

## Stage Discrepancy

Discrepancy in stages may be a key to conflict in lesbian and gay relationships. For example, one person may be more at an individualistic stage while the other wants more blending of their lives (Cabaj & Klinger, 1996). There can be considerable relief when couples are presented with the discrepancy concept. They can reframe their difficulties as part of the developmental progression of couples rather than as flaws in themselves and their partners. This allows couples to reduce stress by removing anxiety and blame from within the couple. The discrepancy concept also can help couples to normalize the problems they face. Difficulties may seem less threatening when couples view them as characteristic hurdles within an overall picture of relationship progression (MacDonald, 1998). Couples can recognize that differences are typically correctable or manageable by recognizing what is going on (McWhirter & Mattison, 1996).

## Issues in Interracial Couples

Data on interracial issues in lesbian and gay couples are minimal, but cross-cultural and mixed-race lesbian and gay couples deal with racism, misunderstanding, miscommunication, and possibly loss of support from families or racial and ethnic communities (Browning, Reynolds, & Dworkin, 1991; Greene, 2000). Furthermore, they may be targets of harassment and violence.

A white partner may not recognize racist subtleties and think that his or her partner's anger is inappropriate. In contrast, if the white partner recognizes such a situation, he or she may be upset because the other does not react to it. This partner may also take on the role of rescuer, or because of feelings of guilt about racism, may attempt to compensate the partner for it. Because success in this is not possible, this partner may end up feeling angry and frustrated.

A white partner cannot understand what the experience of racism is like for his or her partner. The ethnic or racial partner may never completely feel that the white partner is free from racism and may experience feelings of jealousy or resentment about the partner's privileged status in both the mainstream and/or their lesbian and gay community (Clunis & Green, 2000; Greene, 1994b, 1995).

The groups to which partners in interracial couples belong may perceive them as lacking in loyalty to their group. Both partners may experience shame about their involvement with a person who is not of their culture or race (Clunis & Green, 2000; Falco, 1991; Greene, 1994a, 1995).

Rostosky, Riggle, Savage, Roberts, and Singletary (2008) studied a small sample of interracial same-sex couples. The sample had five female and eight male couples; the average age of each couple member was thirty-four years, and the mean length of the relationship was 6.5 years, with a range of one to thirteen years. Nine couples consisted of one African American couple member and one European American couple member; one couple consisted of an Asian American and a European American; one couple was South Asian–American Indian and European American. Of the thirteen couples, eleven reported race-related stress, including hearing racist language, experiencing isolation or rejection from their communities, and feeling anxious about the stability of their relationship. They also experienced double-minority stress, in that they were both in a same-sex relationship and interracial. The study found that the couples used five types of coping strategies: social support seeking, meaning making, humor, problem-solving actions, and avoidance. They sought social support from each other and from others. Meaning making involved reframing negative experiences to give them a positive meaning. Humor also helped reframe stressful situations, reduce tension, instill hope, and help couples cope with stresses they experience. Problem solving included confrontation and assertion, having a commitment ceremony to validate their relationship, and acting in ways to disprove negative stereotypes. Avoidance included distancing themselves from family members and community members from whom they anticipated rejection and avoiding discussion of sensitive issues and topics with each other.

It is important that practitioners have awareness of how race, sexual identity, and other aspects of identity may or may not matter in helping interracial couples. Some couples are isolated because they lack a social network or community that accepts and validates their relationships. They can be rejected by both the local lesbian, gay, bisexual, and transgender communities and ethnic or racial communities. Practitioners can provide support groups for interracial same-sex couples and assess other sources for social support. Sometimes, because of internalized heterosexism couples distance themselves from others like them. Some couples avoid talking directly with each other about the issues they are dealing with. However, relationships require engaging each other about issues that create anxieties or insecurities about the relationship. To facilitate intimacy and relational development, practitioners can help couples state their anxieties and respect their own and their partner's similar and different perspectives instead of disconnecting or withdrawing from each other. Practitioners can also assess psychological strengths and resources available to the couples. They can help couples develop flexibility, read nonverbal cues, reframe negative experiences, make obstacles become opportunities, subvert oppressive social institutions, and create safe spaces for themselves. Practitioners can also encourage clients to speak out about racism in their LGBT communities and heterosexism in their ethnic or racial communities (Rostosky et al., 2008).

## Identity Development

Issues of identity development include stages of coming out for each person in a couple (for a comprehensive view of coming-out stages, see Cass, 1996). Basically, one moves from self-awareness to comfort with that awareness and then to disclosure (Cabaj & Klinger, 1996). Practitioners assessing disclosure might ask the following: How out is each partner? How out is the couple? Who are they out to? Who are they not out to? In what contexts are they out or not out as a couple?

Some partners seek to avoid discrimination by disclosing their sexual identities only in certain contexts (Alonzo, 2005). Being out in some situations and not in others is a reasonable approach when it could be harmful for the couple to be out in certain circumstances.

Other couples make no disclosures. They never express affection outside of their homes. They learn to be discreet, unnoticeable, and in hiding (Slater, 1995). It is helpful for practitioners working with closeted couples to examine the reasons they have chosen not to come out (MacDonald, 1998). Practitioners can address with couples the costs and benefits of both remaining closeted and of disclosing. For example, a benefit of disclosing one's sexual identity is that it can foster the development of a cohesive self-identity. Relationship quality is higher when both partners are open about their same-sex relationship, especially with their families of origin. Family actions such as asking the partner to come to family events and accepting affection between the partners have a positive effect on couple satisfaction (Caron & Ulin, 1997). Hiding such an important part of one's life requires constant vigilance and can result in distant and awkward communications with others (Slater, 1995). Invisibility can also perpetuate stigma and shame and undermine a sense of morale and well-being (Cohler & Galatzer-Levy, 2000). Being "in the closet," or being invisible, limits potential social support from one's family and from friends and work associates (Cohler & Galatzer-Levy, 2000).

All couples want positive relationship quality, but there are some contradictory research findings in terms of disclosure and relationship quality. Jordan and Deluty (2000) investigated the correlation between being out and relationship quality in 305 lesbians who were in committed relationships. The results indicated that the degree of openness regarding sexual identity was positively correlated with relationship satisfaction but that discrepancy between the partners in being out was negatively correlated with relationship satisfaction. In contrast, Beals and Peplau (2001) found no association between extent of disclosure and relationship satisfaction in a sample of 784 lesbian couples. Other researchers, however, have found that the stress associated with concealing one's sexual identity can be harmful to couple satisfaction (Berger, 1990b; Caron & Ulin, 1997). The practitioner can examine together with clients which of these findings fits best with them. If they think that making no disclosure is harmful, then they may be open to experimenting with disclosure to selected persons or to other couples, which may result in new friendships. If they think that making no disclosure has no effect or minimal effect on their relationship quality, then they can stay with that.

For some couples, one partner wants to make disclosures and the other partner does not. For example, in lesbian couples, one partner may have identified as lesbian since adolescence but the other partner identified as heterosexual, married, bore children, and did not identify as lesbian until later adulthood. The couple members may be at the same chronological age but have quite different experiences with a lesbian identity and with being out or not. The partner who has been out for a longer time may be patient and tolerant or impatient and frustrated at her partner's slowness to progress through the coming-out stages. Practitioners can provide each person with a clearer view of the other's own unique experiences and many other variables that may affect each person's views on disclosure (L. S. Brown, 1996). A partner who wants to be more open must understand the other's fear of losing friends, family, and job. People's choice not to disclose their sexual identity has nothing to do with ambivalence about the relationship, nor is it related to the love one feels for his or her partner; the closet can be a safe place. Practitioners can help the partners to see the big picture of their developmental needs so that they reduce the blame they place on each other (MacDonald, 1998).

It helps if members of a couple see costs and benefits of disclosure in the same terms, and it helps if their respective work and other social environments provide incentives for openness or obstacles to it. Then they are likely to reach similar decisions about disclosure (Patterson, 2000; Patterson, Fulcher, & Wainright, 2002). The problem is that family and work environments, for example, can vary widely in their treatment of lesbians and gay men following disclosure (D'Augelli & Garnets, 1995). In some employment settings, lesbians and gay men may be subject to job discrimination or even loss of employment if they are open about their sexual identity (Badgett, 2001, 2003). In other employment settings, it may feel much safer for them to make disclosures. One person's parents may be tolerant, whereas another person's parents cannot accept lesbian or gay identities. If disclosure places existing child-custody or visitation arrangements at risk, then it can be especially laden with emotions (Martin, 1993, 1998; Patterson, 1994, 2007).

Practitioners can ask couples to evaluate whether the psychological costs of hiding or concealing their identity outweigh the potential benefits of disclosing a relationship (Harper & Schneider, 2003). Even with the positives that can result from disclosure, however, it is important for practitioners not to impose a normative template on clients. They are not to expect or prescribe the coming-out process in a particular, predictable fashion (Long & Pietsch, 2004). Practitioners should also be careful not to broadcast their bias one way or another regarding disclosure. Only the couple can make the choice of disclosing their couple status or remaining closeted. The task for practitioners is to help the couple make an informed choice and cope with the consequences of that choice (MacDonald, 1998).

Disclosures by lesbians and gay men are much more frequent today than in the past. This is a generational change; in previous generations, disclosure was much more dangerous. Still, some lesbians and gay men in the current generation are wary of making disclosures.

## Sexual Issues

Lesbian and gay couples can experience issues related to sex that are similar to those that heterosexual couples experience: frequency of sex, discrepancies in the partner's level of sexual desire, and sexual behavior preferences. For example, a lesbian couple can be happy and satisfied even with limited genital contact, as lesbian couples often value nongenital contact such as kissing and touching more than genital sex (MacDonald, 1998).

When lesbian couples discuss their sex lives with a practitioner, the practitioner must understand that sexuality for them is highly individual to each member of the couple (Iasenza, 1999). For some lesbians sex may not be as genitally focused as it is for heterosexuals. If practitioners define sex as genital acts leading to orgasm, then they are adhering to sexist and heterosexist assumptions.

Two women together are able to enjoy many ways of relating sexually that may not fit traditional notions of intercourse, penetration, and climax (Iasenza, 1999). Not all lesbian partners, however, are happy about a nontraditional sexual situation, and members of a couple may have complaints about either discrepancies in the couple's sexual desire or low sexual desire (Nichols, 1995).

Tracy and Junginger (2007) reported that lesbians in committed partnerships experienced less desire for sexual activity but greater sexual satisfaction during sexual activity than did unpartnered lesbians. Also, in committed partnerships, higher relationship satisfaction was associated with greater arousal during sex, sexual pleasure, sexual satisfaction, and better overall sexual functioning. The quality of the couple's relationship has positive effects on the nature and quality of the couple's sexual interactions, including arousal, pleasure, and satisfaction. Younger lesbians reported more optimal sexual functioning than older lesbians. Age does not affect sexual satisfaction or responsiveness or enjoyment of sexual activity, but it is associated with decreased sexual desire and sexual arousal, greater difficulty with lubrication during sexual activity, and lower overall sexual functioning. Matthews, Hughes, and Tartaro (2006) reported from a study of lesbians and heterosexual women that 40 percent reported at least one symptom of sexual dysfunction. Pain was the symptom that heterosexual women reported most frequently (34 percent). Low frequency of orgasm was the symptom that lesbians most frequently reported (20 percent). But both groups of women reported positive feelings about sexual activity with their partners and did not differ on frequency of sexual activity.

Meana, Rakipi, Weeks, and Lykins (2006) found that the frequency of sexual activity and levels of sexual satisfaction for lesbians were equivalent to those of heterosexual and gay couples. Lesbians also reported fewer and different types of sexual problems than did heterosexual women. Sexual dysfunctions that lesbians reported included difficulty getting excited, difficulty maintaining excitement, reaching orgasm too quickly, difficulty reaching orgasm, and inability to reach orgasm. Considerably less than half the sample of one hundred lesbians reported these difficulties. More than half reported no dysfunctions. So, practitioners should not assume that all lesbians have sexual problems. The best resources for practitioners to learn about lesbian sex and gay sex are *The New Lesbian Sex Book* (Caster, 2008) and *The Joy of Gay Sex* (Silverstein & Picano, 2003). Practitioners can also recommend these resources for lesbian and gay clients. Practitioners can also recommend online bulletin boards and clubs devoted to sexual activities of particular variations (Silverstein & Picano, 2003).

## Monogamy versus Nonmonogamy

In general, lesbian couples are likely to be monogamous, although this is not always the case (Bryant & Demian, 1994; Peplau, Cochran, & Mays, 1997). Monogamy is not as frequent in gay couples (James & Murphy, 1998). For nonmonogamous gay couples, there can be complicated rules, jealousies, and hurt feelings (McWhirter & Mattison, 1996). A partner who remains monogamous in a couple may fear losing the nonmonogamous partner. Couples can reduce conflicts associated with sexual nonexclusivity if they negotiate a mutually agreeable arrangement (Cabaj & Klinger, 1996; McVinney, 1998). Some gay couples can work out agreements that do not harm their commitment to each other (McWhirter & Mattison, 1996).

The focus of practice is to strengthen the primary partnership and reduce the threats (e.g., losing the partner) experienced by the monogamous partner. The practitioner can explore what nonmonogamous gay partners can do to clarify their commitment to the primary relationship (Matteson, 1996). Couples should also commit to safe-sex practices with a written agreement that details specific practices (Granvold & Martin, 1999). There are many safe-sex programs, videos, and books for lesbian and gay couples that encourage more open and direct discussion about sexuality—much of this is also available on the Internet.

## HIV/AIDS

Many gay men are likely to know others who are HIV positive and to know someone who died of AIDS. When in a dating process, gay persons struggle with questions of when to test, whom to date, when to disclose one's HIV status, and how to have sex. These can also be issues for lesbians who are HIV positive or have AIDS (Wapenyi, 2010).

Practitioners should make sure that they know, and that all sexually active clients—male or female; gay, lesbian, heterosexual, bisexual, or transgender—know the specifics about safe sex and openly discuss their knowledge of it (Paul, 1992). Counseling about safe sex, however, requires specialized training. Practitioners should explore with every couple in empathic and nonjudgmental ways the realities of HIV, its effects on their relationship, and whether the couple should consider an open relationship (Grossman, D'Augelli, & O'Connell, 2001; Stokes & Damon, 1995). Monogamy as a method of reducing the risk of becoming infected with HIV, however, is not always a viable option for some people, particularly gay and bisexual persons.

Practitioners should be up to date on HIV/AIDS treatments. For gay men, in the 1980s and early 1990s, having sex put them at high risk of contracting HIV, which would develop into AIDS. But gay life dramatically changed in 1995 when the first effective treatment against the HIV virus was introduced: the cocktail. The cocktail is officially called highly active anti-retroviral therapy (HAART). The deaths from AIDS dropped dramatically, and AIDS became a more manageable, if still incurable, disease. Since then, death rates have continued to dramatically lower. However, HAART is not a cure. It provides longer life but at the cost of being sick some or much of the time because of the toxicity of the drugs. Those diagnosed with AIDS may deal with more long-term side effects of medications than opportunistic infections. A person with AIDS today may not die from it but from something else that AIDS causes such as wasting.

It is impossible to know the HIV status of every person one has sex with. Lesbian and gay persons should assume that their sex partner is HIV positive, which means everyone should have safe sex. For men, condoms are essential. Having sex without a condom is dangerous sex. For women, they should use a dental dam which is a thin square of latex that can be used to prevent the spread of sexually transmitted infections such as during oral sex. And everyone should be tested for HIV regularly. Rates of HIV infection have particularly risen among young men, who tend to have considerably more sex partners than other groups and are less likely to use condoms (Silverstein & Picano, 2003).

There are three sex categories for both lesbians and gay men to know about. Sexual behaviors that are safe include mutual masturbation, hugging, body rubbing, massage, dry kissing, sadomasochism without bleeding or bruising, and using sex toys only on oneself. Sexual behaviors that can be considered safer than unsafe behaviors include anal intercourse with a condom, wet kissing, oral sex that ends before climax, being urinated on during sex, and fisting (with latex gloves). Sexual behaviors considered unsafe include swallowing semen, anal intercourse without a condom, urinating in the mouth or on skin with sores, sharing enema equipment or sex toys, and using one's tongue on the anal rim of another (Silverstein & Picano, 2003).

## Other Issues Related to HIV/AIDS

Peplau et al. (1997) found no relationship between HIV status and overall relationship satisfaction. Couples affected by HIV, however, experience many challenges, such as a discordant diagnosis (e.g., one partner has HIV and the other partner does not), caregiving and its attendant losses of privacy and control, and preparing for possible death (Powell-Cope, 1995). Palmer and Bor (2001) studied ten gay couples (average age of 33.5 years), whose relationship length ranged from 6 to 132 months, with an average of 52.5 months. The length of time since diagnosis of HIV ranged from 12 to 108 months, with an average of 35.8 months. Diagnosis with HIV results in the possibility of keeping secrets from family members. Partners who had not disclosed their HIV status to family members wanted to protect them from the emotional consequences of such a disclosure. Secrets may cause difficulties and confusion in relationships, but partners felt that this was preferable to the alternative. Revelation could cause emotional pain and a shift in family dynamics (Palmer & Bor, 2001).

## Death of a Partner

Anyone can be in the position of losing a partner to cancer, HIV/AIDS, and other illnesses. No matter the cause of death or one's sexual identity, the death of a partner is difficult to navigate. Grief counseling or grief therapy may help when a partner has died. Hooyman and Kramer (2006) offer helpful information about grieving for a lost partner. To resolve grief, one must restore functioning and integrate the loss.

### Tasks and Stages of Grieving

The tasks thought to be necessary to restore functioning and integrate the loss of a partner include (1) accepting the reality of the loss, (2) experiencing the pain of grief, (3) adjusting to an environment in which the deceased is not there, and (4) withdrawing emotional energy from the past relationship and reinvesting it in other relationships (Worden, 2002).

Some researchers (Rando, 1993; Worden, 2002) suggest phases that people commonly go through after the death of a partner, including avoidance, shock, numbness, disbelief, and denial. These phases can be buffers from the painful reality, especially when one first learns of the loss. Others may experience fear, anxiety, dread, unreality, disorganization, and an inability to comprehend the situation. Some surround themselves with as many people as possible; others prefer to be alone. Other phases include confrontation and accommodation.

**Confrontation.**    In the confrontation phase, a person's grief is the most intense. One learns or hears that his or her loved one is gone. Common feelings are intense sadness, guilt, blaming others or oneself, helplessness, panic, confusion, powerlessness, anger, rage, despair, loss of faith, a sense of injustice, and disillusionment.

**Accommodation.**   In the accommodation phase, the bereaved person gradually reenters the everyday world, moves on, and learns to live with the loss. Losses are turning points that may become growth points, but only if the person works through the pain by releasing emotional grief. Even if one reaches accommodation or integration, one's painful feelings may persist for many years and perhaps for the rest of one's life (Granvold & Martin, 1999).

## Questions to Ask

When working with a grieving person, practitioners can ask different levels of questions: entry level, explanation, and elaboration (Neimeyer, 1998). Entry-level questions explore the experiential world of one's grieving. For example:

- What experiences of death or loss are you experiencing?
- What do you remember about how you responded to it?
- Did your feelings about it change over time?
- How did others in your life respond to the loss and your reactions to it?
- What was the most painful part of the experience to you?

Explanation-level questions extend the preliminary questions into greater concern over meaning. For example:

- How did you make sense of the death or loss?
- How do you interpret the loss now?
- What philosophical or spiritual beliefs contributed to your adjustments to this loss?

Elaboration-level questions promote taking a broader perspective regarding the loss. For example:

- How has this experience affected your sense of priorities?
- Has the experience affected your view of yourself or your world?
- What lessons about loving has this person or this loss taught you?
- How would your life be different if this person had lived or if this loss had not happened?
- Are there any steps you can take that would be helpful or healing now?

## Summary Model of Grief Reactions

The R model integrates much prior work on grief. In the R model, the first step is to acknowledge and accept that the person is gone and will not ever return. The second step is to react to, to experience, and to express the pain of separation or giving up control, giving way, and abandoning oneself to the feelings of chaos and the uncontrollable aspects of existence. For deliverance from the past, one must experience a confrontation with the loss through rage, anger, and honest expression of sorrow (Harvey, 1998). We cannot integrate grief at a cognitive level or in our head or by just thinking about it. Many people maintain their bonds with the deceased. The challenge is to maintain this connection but hope for new attachments and to love others. The third step is to readjust and reinvest in life. A person might never be able to accept the loss or resolve grief, but he or she can adapt to the changed situation.

# General Techniques and Interventions

Social support is critical for helping people who are grieving to adjust. The benefits of social support include feeling less alone by being able to share one's grief; feeling validated when others legitimize one's experiences; receiving information about loss; learning strategies for coping with loss; having role models who offer ways to solve problems; having opportunities to express feelings, thoughts, and grief responses, and even to help others (Lund, 1999; Pesek, 2002). Web-based support groups and online interventions also exist. They can provide emotional and informational support; convenience; and opportunities to gain knowledge, share experiences, help others, and minimize costs of therapy (Bacon, Condon, & Fernsler, 2000). Other forms of help include therapeutic bereavement groups, family-based interventions, healing rituals, and grief counseling and grief therapy. Grief counseling aims to facilitate "uncomplicated" grieving. The goal is to alleviate suffering and help bereaved persons adjust well (Stroebe, Hansson, Stroebe, & Schut, 2001). One-on-one, family, or group interventions support those seeking help for their bereavement-related distress and encourage the expression of feelings. Grief therapy is provided by highly trained professionals who use specialized techniques of intervention to address more traumatic, complicated, or chronic grief (Stroebe et al., 2001).

Complicated grief is the persistence of symptoms of separation distress and feelings of devastation and trauma from the death (Jacobs, 1999). A person might have obtrusive thoughts about the deceased; feelings of yearning and searching for the deceased; excessive loneliness; purposelessness or futility about the future; numbness, detachment, or absence of emotional responsiveness; difficulty acknowledging the death; feelings that life is empty, meaningless, or that part of oneself has died; harmful coping behaviors, such as excessive use of drugs and alcohol or violent behavior; or thoughts that one would be better off dead (Prigerson & Jacobs, 2001). Most social workers and other counselors offer grief counseling, not specialized grief therapy.

## Counseling Models

A variety of grief-counseling models exist, but few have been validated empirically. Worden's (2002) task-based model of grief counseling has been widely adopted:

- Help the bereaved actualize the loss or have a more complete awareness of it.
- Help one express one's feelings.
- Help one live without the lost person.
- Help one find meaning in the loss.
- Help one relocate the deceased so one can move forward with life and form new relationships.
- Provide time to grieve.
- Normalize the grieving process by comparing it with the normal behaviors of grieving.
- Note individual differences in grieving.
- Examine defenses and coping styles: certain forms of response to loss, such as excessive use of alcohol or drugs, may intensify grief and depression and impair the bereavement processes.
- Recognize difficulties that require special intervention and whether one should see a grief therapist.

## Additional Interventions

Practitioners can use various other intervention techniques with people who are grieving the loss of a partner, including the following (Corless, 2001; Neimeyer, 1998; Worden, 2002):

- The grieving person can write a letter to the deceased expressing his or her thoughts and feelings, or keep a journal or write poetry.

- The grieving person can imagine that the deceased is sitting in front of him or her in a chair (with or without a picture of the deceased) and express his or her feelings.
- Practitioners can use cognitive restructuring to help those in grief identify their thoughts and talk about them, and then put them to a "reality test" for overgeneralization or inaccuracy.
- Practitioners and the bereaved can role-play various situations that allow for building skills, addressing fears, reducing uncertainty about future situations the bereaved is preparing for, and expressing feelings to the deceased or others.
- The bereaved can draw pictures or paint or use other artistic expressions that reflects their feelings and promotes discussion.
- The grieving person can make a memory book including stories, photos, poems, drawings, and so on for reminiscence and as a concrete keepsake.
- The bereaved can share items that hold symbolic meaning, such as photos, letters, audio- and videotapes, or jewelry.
- Practitioners can encourage the bereaved to speak in metaphors to express their loss (e.g., "My partner reminded me of a daffodil, a delicate flower I love").
- Practitioners can help the bereaved reconstruct meaning by posing questions to elicit understanding of the loss and the meanings and interpretations of the loss from the bereaved's perspective.

## Loss of a Partner to AIDS

This section applies primarily to gay men, as rates of HIV/AIDS are higher among gay men than among lesbians. However, heterosexual persons and lesbians also may lose a partner to AIDS, and the information here applies to them as well. The loss of a partner to AIDS involves special aspects of grief, although it also shares many features with loss not related to AIDS. One dimension of bereaving the loss of a partner to AIDS is anticipatory grief, or the process of reacting and adjusting to anticipated loss, often in circumstances of protracted illness. Changes in close relationships and physical and mental deterioration are distressing and may accentuate the anticipated loss of a person before he or she dies. Other special features include survivors' grief, which social support can help ameliorate. But when outcomes (e.g., wasting) of AIDS are the cause of death, the bereaved may experience a lack of support because of the stigma associated with AIDS and gay sexual identity (Richmond & Ross, 2004). The lack of social support may in turn result in loneliness, disconnectedness, and isolation, along with anger, sadness, and ambivalence. There also could be other losses of friends from AIDS (Biller & Rice, 1990) that one is grieving.

If people who are potential sources of support deny the cause of death or deny the sexual identity of the dead person's partner or friends, this may inhibit survivors' grief and render them unable to focus on the loss, because its reality is denied. When the family of the deceased is overtly hostile toward the survivor, this exacerbates the survivor's distress. Finally, bereavement overload appears to be related to both the number of AIDS-related deaths one experiences and the span of time in which the deaths occur, as well as the lack of clear conclusions (whether the person will get better or worse), all of which make death an on-going rather than a past event (Richmond & Ross, 2004).

There are four significant ways that AIDS is different from other terminal illnesses: (1) the infection is not immediately terminal; (2) it usually affects people already stigmatized as members of minority groups; (3) its progression to terminal illness is completely unpredictable and, with today's drugs, may not even happen; and (4) the status of "cures," vaccines, and scientific breakthroughs often discussed in the media is uncertain (Richmond & Ross, 2004).

## Summary

Most of the issues in this chapter are applicable to lesbian, gay, and heterosexual couples, all of whom can experience relationship ambiguity, a rigid pattern of coupling although this can be acceptable to some couples, going through stages of coupling, dealing with discrepancies between the two partners, sexual difficulties, safe sex, HIV/AIDS, and the grief process following death of a partner.

## Vignette

Michael and David could not seem to work out some ambiguous areas in their relationship, so they saw a practitioner. The practitioner helped them with various questions, such as how they define what it means to be a couple and the rules they wanted to establish about having sex outside of their relationship. These seemed to be pressing issues for them. The practitioner also helped them come to agreements on how to deal with finances, debt, paying for things, and how to best assign household tasks. The practitioner also encouraged them to consider an issue that they had not thought about: caring for each other if one should become ill, injured, or disabled. The practitioner asked whether Michael and David felt a lifetime commitment to each other. This was important to their feelings of security and longevity as a couple. The practitioner asked them to put their agreements in writing and to think about other areas in which they could create agreements for the next session.

# Resources

## Online

### AIDS Arms
The AIDS Arms organization (http://aidsarms.org) works to improve the health and lives of people living with HIV/AIDS in various U.S. communities.
### HIV/AIDS
The Web site eMedicineHealth.com (http://www.emedicinehealth.com/hivaids/article_em.htm) provides full articles on HIV/AIDS transmission, symptoms, treatment, and more.

## For Further Reading

Bent, K., & Maglev, J. K. (2004). *When a partner dies: Lesbian widows.* Paper presented at "Issues in Palliative Care," 15th annual International Nursing Research Congress, Dublin. Retrieved from http://stti.confex.com/stti/inrc15/techprogram/paper_17756.htm.

Derlega, V. J., & Barbee, A. P. (1998). *HIV and social interaction.* Thousand Oaks, CA: Sage.

Emmers-Sommer, T. M., & Allen, M. (2005). *Safer sex in personal relationships: The role of sexual scripts in HIV infection and prevention.* Mahwah, NJ: Erlbaum.

Mayo Clinic. (2010). *HIV/Aids: Definition.* November 5. Retrieved from Mayo Clinic Web site: http://www.mayoclinic.com/health/hiv-aids/DS00005.

Shernoff, M. (1997). Gay marriage and gay widowhood. *Harvard Gay and Lesbian Review, 4.* Retrieved from http://www.gaypsychotherapy.com/hglrwidower.htm.

Shernoff, M. (Ed.). (1997). *Gay widowers: Life after the death of a partner.* New York: Haworth Press.

Silverstein, C. (Ed.). (1991). *Gays, lesbians, and their therapists: Studies in psychotherapy.* New York: Norton.

Walter, C. A. (2003). *The loss of a life partner: Narratives of the bereaved.* New York: Columbia University Press.

# Part Three

## Other Issues That Affect Lesbian and Gay Couples

# Coping with Heterosexism

What are the results of internalized heterosexism in lesbians and gay men? How can it affect them in couples?

What are the four different types of heterosexism?

Which type of heterosexism affects lesbians and gay men the most, and in what ways?

What is the difference between overt and covert heterosexism?

Should practitioners probe for internalized heterosexism when they see a lesbian or gay couple? If so, why?

How can a practitioner discover internalized heterosexism?

How can a practitioner help couples with internalized heterosexism?

What types of practice can diminish internalized heterosexism?

How does joining political groups help?

How does social support help?

This chapter and the next involve issues that operate both at the micro and macro levels. Those issues affect lesbians and gay men in a personal way, but oppressors and macro-level policies create difficulties or limitations for them also.

Most lesbians and gay men experience some degree of prejudice and fear of discrimination in their lives (Bepko & Johnson, 2000), and they often internalize the heterosexism that drives those experiences. Most of the issues that lesbian and gay clients see a practitioner about are influenced directly or indirectly by heterosexism. In general, society uses the heterosexist ideology to pathologize lesbians and gay men. As a result, lesbians and gay men are viewed as disturbed, immoral, laughable, tragic, dangerous, or despicable. Often, the narratives about them include a mixture of those attributes (Russell, 2000; Russell & Bohan, 2007).

In a study of lesbian couples by Rostosky, Riggle, Dudley, and Wright (2006), close to half of respondents made statements that revealed negative attitudes about same-sex relationships directed toward themselves or their relationship. Three themes captured their negative attitudes or internalized heterosexism. First, about one in four couples expressed low expectations for the longevity of their couple relationship. Second, nearly one in four couples discussed the ways that they defended or protected themselves, such as by creating distance from, avoiding, or rejecting other lesbians and gay men who were open about their sexual identity. Third, several couple members discussed their struggle to accept their sexual identity.

Some couples in Rostosky, Riggle, Dudley, et al.'s (2006) study expressed feelings of guilt about experiences of closeness with their partners, inhibitions about displays of affection with their partners, or fear of not being intimate or sexual with their partners. Difficulties expressing sexual desire or thoughts that a relationship is not permanent may result not only from guilt and inhibition but also from depression. Withdrawal may result from one or both partners feeling unworthy or ambivalent about committing to a lesbian or gay relationship (Green & Mitchell, 2002). Self-hatred can turn into criticism of the other partner (Israel & Selvidge, 2003). Sometimes inexplicable arguments result from displacing frustration onto the partner, from conflict over combining finances and household items, or from one partner claiming that there is no use in combining things because they will break up (L. S. Brown, 1996). Sometimes one partner may physically abuse the other partner (Israel & Selvidge, 2003). Partners might not only sabotage their relationships but also give up too quickly. Or they might not try to work through their difficulties or seek help to prevent abuse or a breakup (L.S. Brown, 1996).

## Probing for and Challenging Internalized Heterosexism

External heterosexism has to be differentiated from internalized heterosexism. External heterosexism pervades our culture and beliefs about lesbians and gay men. It stigmatizes anyone who does not comply with heterosexual norms. Yep (2002) developed four quadrants to represent different kinds of heterosexism. One quadrant is exterior-individual, or externalized heterosexism. This happens when heterosexuals call lesbians and gay men names and other derogatory terms. Other forms of this type of heterosexism can include avoidance, discrimination, and physical violence. Another quadrant is exterior-collective, or institutional violence; this quadrant shows how heterosexist thinking pervades our social and collective consciousness. Heterosexuals are viewed as normalized, whereas lesbians and gay men are viewed as disadvantaged and disempowered. Few institutions, for example, provide them domestic partnership benefits, but heterosexual couples take those benefits for granted.

Another quadrant is interior-individual, or internalized heterosexism. We all learn at a young age that being lesbian or gay is shameful and is stigmatized as deviant, immoral, and deficient, and that lesbians and gay men are outcasts. We learn this stigmatization of lesbians and gay men from many sources, such as family, friends, teachers, and the mass media, and we internalize that stigma. Another quadrant is interior-collective, or discursive violence. Lesbians and gay men are treated differently and talked about differently than are heterosexuals. The purpose of this is to degrade and pathologize them. Discursive violence also includes words, tone, and gestures that threaten lesbians and gay men. Lesbians and gay men often are asked questions that would hardly ever be asked of heterosexuals, such as, "What acts do you do in bed?" and "Are you the man or the woman in your relationship?"

Interior or internalized heterosexism affects everyone, as heterosexism is internalized in all of us. The difference with lesbians and gay men who internalize heterosexism is that they apply it to themselves (Meyer & Dean, 1998; Otis & Skinner, 1996; Ross & Rosser, 1996; Wagner, Brandolo, & Rabkhi, 1996).

High levels of internalized heterosexism have negative outcomes for lesbians and gay men. They experience decreased levels of self-acceptance and self-esteem, along with shame and self-hatred (Purcell, Camos, & Perrilla, 1996). They also may experience depression, demoralization, guilt, fear, suicidal ideation and behavior, sexual dysfunction, less involvement in intimate relationships, expectations of rejection by others, isolation, lack of connection to a lesbian and/or gay community, drug and/or alcohol abuse, and limited aspirations (Boatwright, Gilbert, Forrest, & Ketzenberger, 1996; Harris, Cook, & Kashubeck-West, 2008; Meyer & Dean, 1998; Otis & Skinner, 1996; Shildo & Schroeder, 2002; Wagner et al., 1996). In addition, they accept myths about themselves (Boatwright et al., 1996; Meyer & Dean, 1998; Otis & Skinner, 1996; Wagner et al., 1996), such as that they are abnormal, pathological, perverted, shameful, or evil.

There are two types of expression of internalized heterosexism in lesbians and gay men: overt and covert. The overt expression includes depreciating oneself as inferior or deviant. A person may not seek support because he or she thinks it is undeserved. Covert forms are more common. For example, one may appear to accept oneself and one's same-sex sexual identity but act in ways that sabotage oneself, such as by abandoning educational or career plans, tolerating abusive behavior from bigoted others, or setting oneself up for rejection with impulsive disclosures in situations where people are likely to react with hostile responses (Gonsiorek, 1993).

When lesbian and gay couples see practitioners, practitioners might consider reducing internalized heterosexism as a goal if they ask for it or complain about it (Green & Mitchell, 2002). Although practitioners might recognize that heterosexism affects the lives of lesbians and gay men, they might not recognize its subtler results (Russell & Bohan, 2007). Lesbian and gay couples may not help the situation, because a practitioner may perceive that on the surface they are affirmative about their sexual identities. Even a person with a positive self-image, however, cannot be totally shielded against heterosexism or its internalization. Because internalized heterosexism can manifest in subtle and unconscious ways (L. S. Brown, 1996), it is important for practitioners to not limit their thinking about heterosexism to only overt manifestations of it (American Psychological Association, Committee on Lesbian and Gay Concerns, 1991). Practitioners have to probe for the subtleness of internalized heterosexism because it may be central to a couple's difficulties (Israel & Selvidge, 2003) even though they are not aware of it.

Internalized heterosexism can be detected in various ways, including a client's coming-out stories, thoughts and feelings about being lesbian or gay, experiences of heterosexism in various institutions (e.g., school, family, church), and results of disclosure to others. Practitioners can also ask clients about stereotypes about LGBT persons they have heard about (Kashubeck-West, Szymanski, & Meyer, 2008; Szymanski, Kashubeck-West, & Meyer, 2008).

If couples identify internalized heterosexism as behind some of their difficulties and decide to explore it, practitioners can challenge the results of heterosexism. For example, they can challenge couples' expectations of failure (Okun, 1996), or they can help clients realize that the choice of a lesbian or gay partner is as natural as what heterosexuals do in selecting a partner (Igartua, 1998). Connecting couples with support groups can provide them with opportunities to meet others who have overcome internalized heterosexism. Support groups also help normalize the difficulties that couples experience. If such groups are not available, practitioners can provide educational materials, including books and videos (MacDonald, 1998).

Another important discussion to have with lesbian and gay clients is that they and all others are immersed in a homonegative environment. Without external heterosexism, internalized heterosexism would not exist. They are one in the same. Everyone lives in a social context that devalues any deviation from heterosexuality. We all participate in that social context, contribute to it, and are influenced by it (Russell, 2000; Russell & Bohan, 2007; Russell & Richards, 2003).

The ways that lesbians and gay men deal with heterosexism may take different directions. Some persons accept the dominant narrative, with its homonegative meanings. Others use compartmentalization. They may reject the dominant, homonegative narrative and claim a more gay-positive narrative. Other ways to more fully move away from internalized heterosexism are through liberation practice, feminist and pro-feminist practice, gay-affirmative practice, or some combination of those practices (Russell, 2000; Russell & Bohan, 2006; Russell & Richards, 2003).

## Practice to Diminish the Effects of Heterosexism on Lesbians and Gay Men

### Liberation Practice

Heterosexism can result in social and personal alienation, a sense of ill fit, and a sense of hopelessness for lesbians and gay men. Once internalized heterosexism is demystified, however, one is freed from its outcomes and self-hating beliefs (Russell, 2000; Russell & Richards, 2003).

Through liberation practice, clients work with their practitioner to question and deconstruct old understandings. Then they create new understandings and try them out in various different relationships and different settings, such as social and political arenas. Practitioners also ask clients to review the ways in which they personally participate in homonegativity, they encourage them to take responsibility for their own complicity, and they ask them to assume responsibility for their future attitudes and behaviors. The major goals are to demystify internalized heterosexism and not be complicit with it (Russell, 2000; Russell & Richards, 2003).

Russell and Bohan (2007) noted that liberation practice has much in common with liberation psychology, which emphasizes a macro-sociological understanding of the forces that frame the internalization of negative attitudes (e.g., Kashubeck-West et al., 2008; Martin-Baró, Aron, & Corne, 1994; Prilleltensky, 1994; Russell & Bohan, 2006). Remediation involves resistance to heterosexism by also investing oneself in political campaigns and public policies that have the goal of perpetuating heterosexism. These campaigns and policies can be considered expressions of broad cultural attitudes that are in need of change. Joining others in becoming change agents helps insulate a person against anti-gay politics. One also attains coping skills and some resilience. Activity directed toward social change that is relevant to one's life is also linked to personal well-being (Russell, 2000; Russell & Richards, 2003).

## Feminist and Pro-Feminist Practice

Feminist and pro-feminist theories of practice can help same-sex couples deal with internalized heterosexism through cultural resistance and subversion. Practitioners can counter oppressive messages about loving someone of the same sex by not only communicating that being lesbian or gay is a normal human variation but also providing enthusiastic support for same-sex couples. To try to subvert oppression and reduce heterosexism, becoming involved in political action is also part of this practice (Russell, 2000; Russell & Richards, 2003).

## Affirmative Practice

As for all practices mentioned here, central to affirmative practice is the practitioner's belief that a same-sex sexual identity is as normal, natural, and as healthy as any other sexual identity (Davies & Neal, 1996; D. C. Haldeman, 2000; Hitchings, 1994; Morrow, 2000; I. Young, 1995). Practitioners can affirm and celebrate their clients' efforts to build loving, giving relationships with their friends, families, and partners (Eubanks-Carter, Burckell, & Goldfried, 2005). Also, sexual identity is often not the cause of the difficulties that lesbian and gay clients present (Garnets, Hancock, Cochran, Goodchilds, & Peplau, 1991; Haslam, 2000; Milton & Coyle, 1998); instead, the cause is often society's prejudicial views. Gay-affirmative practice involves actively challenging society's negative attitudes toward lesbians and gay men. It helps lesbian and gay couples dispute society's prejudicial views rather than continuing to internalize them or to be limited by them. Gay-affirmative practice is similar to narrative practice in terms of externalizing the problem (or viewing heterosexism rather than one's sexual identity as the problem; White & Epston, 1990).

Affirmative practitioners also emphasize the benefits of being lesbian or gay. For example, many lesbians and gay men have reported that the experience of challenging societal norms by coming out led them to become more thoughtful, introspective, and resourceful (Morgan & Eliason, 1992). Lesbian and gay couples often report that their efforts to overcome biological and legal barriers to have children have made them more loving and appreciative parents (Johnson & O'Connor, 2002). Other benefits discovered in a study of lesbians and gay men by Riggle, Whitman, Olson, Rostosky, and Strong (2008) include belonging to a community with the commonality of experiences of being lesbian or gay; creating families of choice, including one's current partner, former partners, and friends, both LGBT and heterosexual; having strong connections with others, including partners and friends; serving as a positive role model at work or in social networks; and promoting social justice and being active in lesbian and gay rights. In addition, many lesbians and gay men feel freedom from societal definitions of roles related to gender and sexuality. They are freer to explore different expressions of sexuality and intimate relationships, and they have egalitarian relationships with their partner. They experience creative and authentic living, empathy, integrity, social intelligence, and citizenship. Practitioners can help lesbian and gay clients explore the positive ways in which their sexual identity affects their lives (Eubanks-Carter et al. 2005).

## Social Support

When lesbian and gay couples experience rejection by family, peers, and others, they may tighten their boundaries with the outside and become a closed system. But this puts considerable pressure on them as responsible for fulfilling most of their needs (McVinney, 1998). In couples in which hiding and concealment is pervasive, the cost may be inadequate social support for their relationships.

Social support helps lesbians and gay men develop a more positive narrative (Russell, 2000; Russell & Bohan, 2006; Russell & Richards, 2003). It includes persons who offer assistance and validation, among other supports. In addition, many of the couples in Rostosky, Riggle, Dudley, et al.'s (2006) study shared a longing for role models for their relationship. The invisibility of successful same-sex couples or the lack of access to that type of social support exacerbates a sense of isolation. In addition, an expectation of failure for lesbian and gay relationships results from no role models of long-term permanent relationships (Okun, 1996).

Social support is associated with the quality of relationships (Smith & Brown, 1997). Rostosky, Riggle, Dudley, et al. (2006) found that the role of social support has an important influence on same-sex couples' perceptions of their well-being. Social support is also associated with increased commitment (Smith & Brown, 1997). People in a couple's social network may encourage the couple to stay together through stressful times. Formal support groups can also provide opportunities for lesbian and gay couples to offer one another support. Practitioners can provide short-term support groups for same-sex couples within their practice settings (Laird, 1999). Resources provided by support groups such as Parents, Families, and Friends of Gays and Lesbians (PFLAG) are also useful.

In evaluating overall social support for a same-sex couple from both family and nonfamily sources, it frequently helps to do a family genogram and a sociogram to map out people in a couple's social network. In a genogram, one draws circles and squares with connecting lines to various people (Swainson & Tasker, 2005). In a sociogram, circles represent people in a group. A solid line with an arrow at the end represents that one person "likes" or feels close to another (there may be arrows at both ends if the feeling is mutual). A broken line represents a person who is "not liked" or is in conflict with a person. Sociograms show the relationships and subgroupings within the group, as well as the overall cohesion of a group (Hogan, Carrasco, & Wellman, 2007).

In working on social support, a practitioner should encourage a couple to take a proactive, deliberate stand on the goal of developing an ongoing social support system that consists of about eight to twelve people (Berger & Mallon, 1993).

In the Rostosky, Riggle, Dudley, et al. (2006) study, couples discussed four general types of coping strategies—including most of those discussed here—that they used to deal with the stresses of their stigmatized status. Self-acceptance as a sexual minority and positive views of the couple relationship were important aspects of coping for some couples. Several couples discussed the importance of ignoring, compartmentalizing, or externalizing the experiences of rejection that they encountered. Some couples used internal "subversive dialogues" to create positive self and relational concepts to replace the negative messages and stereotypes that they encountered (see L. S. Brown, 1994). Many couples discussed how they reframed their negative experiences as empowering rather than as immobilizing or diminishing them. Finally, couples coped by creating support systems composed of family members, friends, other lesbian and gay couples, and each other. These couples expressed deep appreciation for the affirmation and validation that they received (Rostosky, Riggle, Gray, & Hatton, 2007).

When working with lesbian and gay clients, all practitioners are charged to address not only questions of individual identity and psychological functioning but also matters of political power and social heterosexism. Internalized heterosexism is not a malady that lesbians and gay men have created alone. It results from the heterosexism that exists outside of them. This is the reality practitioners should have when working with gay and lesbian clients.

## Summary

This chapter focuses on heterosexism, its negative effects on couples and the members of couples, and how to cope with it. There are four main categories of heterosexism, including interior-individual and internalized heterosexism. Practitioners should challenge couples' negative view of themselves and of their relationship. They can also use one or all of several therapeutic approaches: liberation practice, feminist and pro-feminist practice, and affirmative practice. In addition to rooting out one's internalized heterosexism, practitioners can urge couples to join political groups to work against antigay politics and to develop social support groups, which can positively affect a couple's well-being and commitment.

## Vignette

Angela and Sheila were having considerable difficulties because they both did not like being in a lesbian relationship. They did not want to buy things together because they believed they would not have a lasting relationship. A friend recommended a practitioner to help them. The practitioner felt almost immediately that the underlying problem was internalized heterosexism. Angela and Sheila related to each other in such a negative way that the heterosexism was obvious to the practitioner. They also told her that they were pathological and shameful.

The practitioner told them that they were suffering from internalized hetero-sexism and that there was nothing wrong with their being together. They had in-ternalized negative perceptions and feelings about their relationship, and they had to do away with this. The practitioner started with liberation practice to help them replace old views of themselves with new ones. She also used affirmative practice to get across to them that they are as normal as anyone else and should celebrate their relationship. This helped Angela and Sheila rethink things about themselves, their beliefs, and their relationship. They decided to get rid of all their negative thinking and think more positive things about themselves and their relationship. They were happier and enjoying their relationship in a way they never did before.

# Resources

## Online

### Definitions

Professor Gregory M. Herek, of the University of California, Davis, provides a helpful site (http://psychology.ucdavis.edu/rainbow/html/prej_defn.html) with definitions of homophobia, heterosexism, and sexual prejudice.

## For Further Reading

Bieschke, K. J., & Perez, R. M. (2007). *Counseling and psychotherapy with lesbian, gay, bisexual, and transgender clients*. Washington, DC: American Psychological Association.

Chernin, J. N., & Johnson, M. R. (2003). *Affirmative psychotherapy and counseling for lesbians and gay men*. Thousand Oaks, CA: Sage.

Coyle, A., & Kitzinger, C. (2002). *Lesbian and gay psychology: New perspectives*. Oxford, UK: Blackwell.

Heldke, L. M., & Connor, P. (2004). *Oppression, privilege, and resistance: Theoretical perspectives on racism, sexism, and heterosexism*. Boston: McGraw-Hill, 2004.

Herek, G. M. (1998). *Stigma and sexual orientation: Understanding prejudice against lesbians, gay men, and bisexuals*. Thousand Oaks, CA: Sage.

Herek, G. M., & Berrill, K. (1992). *Hate crimes: Confronting violence against lesbians and gay men*. Newbury Park, CA: Sage.

James Madison University. (N.d.). *Fact and information sheet about heterosexism*. Retrieved from http://www.jmu.edu/safezone/wm_library/Heterosexism %20Fact%20Sheet.pdf.

National Coalition of Anti-Violence Programs (2008). *Hate violence against lesbian, gay, bisexual and transgender people in the United States.* New York: Author. Retrieved from http://ncavp.org/common/document_files/Reports/2008%20HV%20Report%20smaller%20file.pdf.

Rothblum, E. D., & Bond, L. A. (1996). *Preventing heterosexism and homophobia.* Thousand Oaks, CA: Sage.

Sears, J. T., & Williams, W. L. (1997). *Overcoming heterosexism and homophobia: Strategies that work.* New York: Columbia University Press.

Stewart, C. (1999). *Sexually stigmatized communities: Reducing heterosexism and homophobia: An awareness training manual.* Thousand Oaks, CA: Sage.

Wehbi, S. (2004). *Community organizing against homophobia and heterosexism: The world through rainbow-colored glasses.* New York: Harrington Park Press.

# The Marriage Issue

What advances have been made for lesbian and gay couples aside from marriage?

What is the general reaction in the United States to legal marriage for lesbian and gay couples?

In the gay community, what is the opposition to marriage?

Why do some lesbian and gay couples want marriage?

What are the benefits of marriage?

How are lesbians and gay men affected from being denied marriage?

How do heterosexuals' reactions to gay marriage instill heterosexism in lesbian and gay persons?

Before discussing the issue of marriage for lesbian and gay couples, there are some other important advances worth mentioning. For example, the U.S. Supreme Court's striking down of all remaining sodomy laws in 2003 (*Lawrence v. Texas*) ended the criminalization of lesbian and gay sex. This is the most important legal advance in recent times.

Moreover, for lesbians and gay men who want to become parents through adoption, most states do not discriminate against prospective adoptive or foster parents on the basis of sexual identity (Patterson, Fulcher, & Wainright, 2002). Only a few states restrict or prohibit foster or adoptive parenting by lesbians and gay men (National Gay and Lesbian Task Force, 2005a, 2005b). Second-parent adoption, which allows for legal ties to both parents, is not as prevalent. Although some states allow second-parent adoptions, others have appellate rulings that do not allow second-parent adoptions (National Gay and Lesbian Task Force, 2005b). In most jurisdictions, children of lesbian and gay parents do not have legal ties to both parents.

The custody situation is not as dire as it was when courts viewed lesbians and gay men as unfit to be parents. Such discrimination has declined, and today sexual identity is typically irrelevant to child custody (Patterson, Fulcher, et al., 2002).

A hate crimes bill passed at the federal level and was signed into law in October 2009 (Stout, 2009). The bill includes sexual identity, meaning that crimes against lesbians and gay men can be prosecuted. The Department of Justice can take over hate crimes cases no matter where they are committed, and as a result of the bill, more crimes against lesbians and gay men will be identified as hate crimes. In addition, the bill includes transgender persons, and the FBI will also track hate crimes against them.

Today marriage is the issue that is most in the foreground, and a few states have granted marriage rights to gay and lesbian couples. Those people opposed to gay marriage in their state, however, have tried to repeal the laws that grant it, as in California in a 2008 election (Proposition 8), and they try to vote out the judges who established the marriage laws in their state, as recently happened in Iowa. The rest of this chapter focuses on the marriage issue.

## Advances Outside of Legal Marriage for Lesbians and Gay Men

First, what advances have been made for lesbian and gay couples outside of legal marriage? Some foreign nations allow for legal registration of same-sex partnerships (Eskridge, 2001). In lesbian and gay communities in the United States, same-sex couples sometimes hold commitment ceremonies to celebrate their relationships, and some religious groups perform same-sex wedding cere-monies. In addition, increasing numbers of employers provide domestic partner benefits to same-sex partners (Human Rights Campaign Foundation, 2005a, 2005b), such as medical, dental, and vision care; accidental death and dismem-berment insurance; dependent life insurance; bereavement and sick leave; long-term-care insurance; relocation benefits; and survivor benefits from a partner's pension (Cahill et al., 2002).

On July 1, 2000, Vermont became the first state to legally recognize civil unions between same-sex couples, the result of a December 1999 state supreme court decision that denying lesbian and gay couples the benefits of marriage was unconstitutional discrimination. This groundbreaking law granted the same state benefits, civil rights, and protections to same-sex couples as those granted to married couples living in Vermont. Although Vermont civil unions are not legally equal to heterosexual marriage and are not recognized outside of the state, they are the same-sex institution that is closest to heterosexual marriage (D. L. Markowitz, 2000). Some other states also recognize some form of same-sex civil union. In general, though, the laws change frequently and vary widely from state to state.

What civil unions do not include are the General Accounting Office's (2004) estimated 1,138 federal rights that marriage provides. Some of the major federal rights include an individual's rights to inherit from a partner who dies without a will, to visit one's partner in government-run institutions (e.g., prisons, hospitals), to inherit a social security survivor's benefits, to have immunity from testifying against a partner in a criminal proceeding, to sponsor a partner from another country for U.S. immigration, to reduce tax liability by filing joint tax returns, and to take advantage of marital estate and gift deductions on taxes. In addition, those rights include the right of residency for a foreign partner of a U.S. citizen and the right of an employee to include a partner on health insurance coverage (Cahill & South, 2002; Zicklin, 1995).

In 1989, Denmark became the first nation in the world to legalize marriage for lesbian and gay couples (Soland, 1998). Since then, some other foreign coun-tries have legalized same-sex marriage. Efforts to legalize same-sex relationships in the United States, however, have met with considerable opposition (Arie, 2003; Collins, 2008; Herdt & Kertzner, 2007; Rothblum, 2006).

## Reactions in the United States to Same-sex Marriage

As soon as the first legal referendum took place for same-sex marriage, many U.S. states introduced legislation prohibiting the recognition of same-sex marriages formalized in other states. Conservatives in Congress introduced the Defense of Marriage Act (DOMA) in 1996, which defined marriage as a union between a man and a woman and stipulated that a partner should be defined only as "a person of the opposite sex who is a husband or a wife." The act ensured that federal benefits would be denied to same-sex couples if at some point in the future they should win the right to marry in any particular state. The act also enables states to ignore valid marriages that same-sex couples enter into in other states. The act took control over who could marry and effectively circumvented the traditional role of state governments over the matter (Cahill et al., 2002; Cahill & Tobias, 2007; Human Rights Campaign Foundation, 2006).

National poll data collected by the Pew Forum on Religion and Public Life (2003) indicated that a majority of Americans oppose allowing lesbian and gay couples to marry legally (53 percent in a 2003 survey and 55 percent in a 2007 survey; see also Herek, 2006). The 2007 survey found only 36 percent of respondents in favor of same-sex marriage, about equal to the proportion in favor of same-sex marriage in 2003. A Gallup Poll found that 39 percent of respondents felt that "marriages between same-sex persons should be recognized by the law as valid, with the same rights as traditional marriage" (Gallup Poll, 2006).

Despite opposition to same-sex marriage, 60 percent of voters support some form of legal recognition for same-sex couples (Kohut, 2004). In national surveys (e.g., Kaiser Family Foundation, 2001), more than two-thirds of Americans support providing inheritance rights, health insurance, and social security benefits to same-sex domestic partners. In 2010, Bajko reported a 50 percent majority of those polled in California favored permitting lesbians and gay men to enter into civil unions that would give them the same state rights as married couples.

## Debates in Lesbian and Gay Communities over Marriage

Lesbians and gay men disagree about whether same-sex marriage is an ideal situation for them. If given the opportunity to marry, not all same-sex couples would choose to do so (Kaiser Family Foundation, 2001).

### The Opposition

The developments of civil ceremonies and marriage go against the urging of the early gay liberation movement for lesbians and gay men to reject heterosexual norms of marriage and family. In this view, same-sex relationships should be unique and not mimic heterosexual norms (Yep, Lovaas, & Elia, 2003). Sanctioning marriage undermines and hides other ways of relating (Wintemute & Andenaes, 2001).

Some lesbians and gay men view marriage as an oppressive and heterocentric proprietary institution that is both inappropriate for and irrelevant to lesbians and gay men (S. Haldeman, 2007; Yep et al., 2003). It supports patriarchal domination of one partner over the other. In contrast, the lesbian and gay communities' alternative definitions of relationships are based on equality (Warner, 1999). Some do not want to marry because they want to make their own decisions about how to share their lives. They do not want to have to abide by state requirements, which is implied in legal regulation of same-sex relationships (Duclos, 1991).

The opponents are also not fond of the compromise position of civil union status. Civil unions ascribe second-class status to lesbian and gay couples, as they offer no federal benefits. Quasi-marital institutions restrict same-sex couples to a separate and inherently unequal status that perpetuates antigay stigma (S. Haldeman, 2007).

Many feminist lesbians oppose marriage because they view the institution of marriage as oppressing women. Heterosexual marriage can disadvantage women, so same-sex marriage should be examined separately for each gender. Others oppose it because it is a church-sanctioned institution (Parks & Humphreys, 2006). Some think the institution of marriage should be abolished altogether and that the state should stay out of private lives (Clifford, Hertz, & Doskow, 2007). In this case, marriage is viewed as an outdated, dysfunctional institution, one that should be replaced with civil marriage or registered partnerships that do not have the problems of marriage (Walters, 2000). For example, every married couple has joint liability for debts and potentially the obligation to pay alimony if they separate. Marriage and divorce records are also public, so there is no staying in the closet with respect to sexual identity. Divorce laws usually require a residency requirement. People who marry, register, or enter a civil union in a state other than the one they live in cannot legally divorce or separate in their state of residence. In most states, assets acquired during marriage must be divided equally if the marriage ends (Clifford et al., 2007). Card (2007) also argues for the abolition of marriage, stating that legally regulated marriage results in unjust distribution of benefits for the unmarried, and particularly those who are poor. Same-sex marriage could create a differentiation between wealth and poverty in the gay community. The emphasis instead should be on rights that would benefit all sexual minorities regardless of partnership status.

Books such as *That's Revolting! Queer Strategies for Resisting Assimilation* (Sycamore, 2004), *I Do, I Don't: Queers on Marriage* (Wharton & Phillips, 2004), and *Same-Sex Marriage: Pro and Con: A Reader* (Sullivan, 2004) argue that mainstream issues such as marriage have drained LGBT communities of power and cultural identity.

## The Position for Marriage

Lesbians and gay men who take an assimilationist position argue that everyone has the right to get married. They want marriage for lesbians and gay men to be legalized. The desire is for same-sex couples to have access to the same benefits as heterosexual couples (Kaiser Family Foundation, 2001; Wintemute & Andenaes, 2001). Marriage also validates one's primary relationship. Legal recognition allows the participants in a relationship to care for each other, particularly in the event of a health emergency or other crisis. It also provides more economic security. Many of the statutory advantages that married partners enjoy are financial, including those based in tax laws, employee benefits, death benefits, and entitlement programs. Without legal marriage, most lesbian and gay couples have few rights. Most states do not have laws that prohibit workplace or housing discrimination. Lesbian and gay couples also receive fewer job-related benefits than their married coworkers. Family-leave policies, health insurance, and pension plans, for example, typically include an employee's heterosexual partner but not a same-sex partner. Even when benefits such as health insurance coverage are extended to a same-sex partner, they are taxed as income, which is typically not the case when the same benefits are provided to heterosexual partners (L. S. Brown, 2000; Ross, Mirowsky, & Goldsteen, 1990; Stack & Eshleman, 1998). When a legally married couple separates or divorces, the relationship is legally terminated and the rights of both partners as individuals would be recognized (Sullivan, 1995).

## Benefits to Children

Government recognition of same-sex relationships will enhance the well-being of children, who benefit from having parents who are financially secure and who experience physical and psychological well-being (Chan, Brooks, Raboy, & Patterson, 1998; Patterson, 2001). Children born to same-sex couples do not automatically enjoy a legally defined relationship with both parents. Such legal clarity is especially important during times of crisis, ranging from school and medical emergencies involving the child to the incapacity or death of a parent (Amato & Keith, 1991). In the latter event, a legal bond with the surviving parent gives a child much-needed security and continuity and minimizes the likelihood of conflicting or competing claims from nonparents for the child's custody.

Moreover, in the absence of legal recognition for same-sex couples, the children born to such couples are accorded a status historically stigmatized as illegitimate (Witte, 2003). Although the social stigma attached to illegitimacy has declined in recent decades, being born to unmarried parents is still widely considered undesirable (Gallagher, 2004).

## Assistance during Breakups

Marriage and civil unions are structured to allow the courts to oversee the dissolution of relationships. The goal in part is to ensure the equitable division of property. Many same-sex couples with financial means have hired lawyers to draft contractual agreements governing the terms of their financial relationship. They regulate the division of their property in the event of separation. Most couples, however, do not have formal, written contracts governing separation and property agreements. A California court, however, opened the door to recognizing verbal and de facto agreements between unmarried opposite-sex partners in the case of *Marvin v. Marvin* (Moller, 2004). Some courts also have enforced oral agreements between same-sex partners.

## Consequences of Being Denied Legal Marriage

Direct assessment of the effects of not recognizing lesbian and gay relationships is not available, but it is not unreasonable to conclude that being denied the right to marry has negative consequences for the well-being of those who want legal marriage. It may also present obstacles to the success of their relationships (Herdt & Kertzner, 2007). For example, members of a same-sex couple may be excluded from their partner's medical care or denied access to the partner in a hospital setting if restricted to immediate family members, such as an emergency room or intensive care unit. With no protections when a partner dies, they must incur the considerable expense of creating legal protections through wills, trusts, and contracts for joint ownership of property (see Burda, 2004). But, even these measures do not always protect the partners if a decedent's biological relatives contest a will or other documents. When a member of a same-sex couple dies, the decedent's biological relatives may take control of the decedent's estate, thus completely excluding the surviving partner (Richards, Wrubel, & Folkman, 1999–2000). The surviving partner of a same-sex relationship is also likely to incur a substantial tax burden when taking sole legal possession of a home that the couple jointly owned (Badgett, 2001; see also Burda, 2004). A surviving heterosexual partner typically does not experience these barriers. They can make decisions about funeral and burial arrangements, and they have automatic rights to inheritance, death benefits, and bereavement leave. They also are more likely to receive social support and sympathy from others (Norris & Murrell, 1990).

## Consequences of Debates over Same-sex Marriage

The public debate over same-sex marriage can have a negative effect on lesbians and gay men. The ongoing national debate over granting lesbians and gay men the right to legally marry has resulted in a widely publicized, often heterosexist backlash from opponents of same-sex marriage. Initiatives such as the federal Defense of Marriage Act (DOMA) as well as individual state-level debates on same-sex marriage have heightened public antigay sentiment in recent years. The legalization of same-sex marriage in several states coupled with further attempts to enact a federal marriage amendment have also incited considerable antigay sentiment. Lesbians and gay men living in communities where same-sex marriage is being debated may also confront heterosexism in personal interactions. Those exposed to greater amounts of anti-same-sex marriage propaganda may be more likely to internalize heterosexist stereotypes. As same-sex marriage continues to be debated, the heterosexist propaganda that surrounds the issue will directly affect many more lesbian and gay communities (Seacat, 2005).

Anti-same-sex marriage campaigns commonly portray lesbians and gay men according to heterosexist beliefs as sexually deviant, promiscuous, and incapable of maintaining committed and loving relationships (Dailey, 2001). With regard to same-sex marriage, the internalization of those beliefs may serve to increase shame, self-loathing, and frustration among members of lesbian and gay communities (on the effects of internalized heterosexism, see also the introduction and chapters 4, 5, 6, and 8).

Stigma can also create a felt need among lesbians and gay men to conceal their sexual identity, which can have negative effects on their psychological and physical health (Cole, Kemeny, Taylor, & Visscher, 1996; Herek, 1996). Green and

Mitchell (2002) noted that discrimination and fear of discovery can undermine relationships if the partners do not have internal ways of countering the social stigma of their sexual identities or a social support system to buffer the stress associated with discrimination.

Practitioners need to be aware of laws and policies that may be relevant to their lesbian and gay clients. Do local laws provide for domestic partner registration, civil unions, or legal marriage? If clients are not well informed about these areas, practitioners can help by offering accurate information. Practitioners also need to be aware of the negative effects on lesbians and gay men from the debates about same-sex marriage. They may be called on to treat some of these persons for depression, suicidal ideation, and other difficulties.

## Summary

Some significant legal advances have been made in recent years for lesbians and gay men, starting with the Supreme Court's striking down of all remaining sodomy laws. Some states even grant lesbian and gay couples legal marriage, civil unions, or domestic partnership benefits. Legal marriage, the main topic of this chapter, is hotly debated by antigay groups but also within lesbian and gay communities. Those who want gay marriage see benefits not only for themselves but also for their children. As a result of the propaganda and negative messages of antigay groups, lesbians and gay men experience a backlash to the marriage issue and sometimes face-to-face confrontations. Those who want legal marriage may experience a lower sense of well-being because of the laws such as DOMA and antigay propaganda against gay marriage.

## Vignette

Mary and Barbara became a couple after Barbara went through a divorce and a year of depression. After they met, Barbara told Mary that she loved being married and wanted to marry her. Mary agreed, even though they would have to go to a different state to get married. They did so and feel that they are married, although their state does not recognize their marriage. In fact, their state is so against same-sex marriage that people have rejected lesbian and gay persons because of the marriage issue. The governor is also against same-sex marriage and talks about it in every speech he gives. Mary and Barbara had some difficulty in the face of antigay views, and Barbara took Mary to her practitioner for some help in dealing with them. The practitioner explained that it was easy for them to internalize the heterosexism associated with the marriage issue. She helped them realize what had happened and disassociate from this heterosexism. They became involved in a gay political movement, which also helped them. They are quite happy with their relationship and knowing they are married. They treasure this for themselves but keep it under wraps from any antigay persons. They laugh about this strategy, and it works for them.

## Resources

### For Further Reading

Bidstrup, S. (2009, June 3). Gay *marriage, the arguments and the motives*. Retrieved from http://www.bidstrup.com/marriage.htm.

Cabaj, R. P., & Purcell, D. W. (1997). *On the road to same-sex marriage: A supportive guide to psychological, political, and legal issues*. San Francisco: Jossey-Bass.

Eskridge, W. N. (1996). *The case for same-sex marriage: From sexual liberty to civilized commitment*. New York: Free Press.

Lewin, E. (1998). *Recognizing ourselves: Ceremonies of lesbian and gay commitment*. New York: Columbia University Press.

Mello, M. (2004). *Legalizing gay marriage*. Philadelphia: Temple University Press.

Pew Forum on Religion and Public Life. (2008). *An overview of the same-sex marriage debate*. Retrieved from http://pewforum.org/Gay-Marriage-and-Homosexuality/An-Overview-of-the-Same-Sex-Marriage-Debate.aspx.

Sherman, S. (1992). *Lesbian and gay marriage: Private commitments, public ceremonies*. Philadelphia: Temple University Press.

Sullivan, A. (1997). *Same-sex marriage, pro and con: A reader*. New York: Vintage Books.

# References

Alexander, C. (1997). Factors contributing to the termination of long-term gay male relationships. *Journal of Gay and Lesbian Social Services*, *7*, 1–12.

Allen, K. R. (2007). Ambiguous loss after lesbian couples with children breakup: A case for same-gender divorce. *Family Relations*, *56*, 175–183.

Alonzo, D. J. (2005). Working with same-sex couples. In M. Harway (Ed.), *Handbook of couples therapy* (pp. 370–385). Hoboken, NJ: Wiley.

Amato, P. R., & Keith, B. (1991). Parental divorce and the well-being of children: A meta-analysis. *Journal of Family Psychology*, *15*, 355–370.

American Psychiatric Association. (1980). *Diagnostic and statistical manual of mental disorders* (3rd ed.). Washington, DC: Author.

American Psychiatric Association. (1987). *Diagnostic and statistical manual of mental disorders* (3rd ed., text rev.). Washington, DC: Author.

American Psychological Association, Committee on Lesbian and Gay Concerns. (1991). Avoiding heterosexist bias in language. *American Psychologist*, *46*, 937–974.

Andersson, G., Noack, T., Seierstad A., & Weedom-Fekjaer, H. (2004). The demographics of same-sex marriages in Norway and Sweden. *Demography*, *43*, 79–98.

Andrews, J. (1990). Don't pass us by: Keeping lesbian and gay issues on the agenda. *Gender and Education*, *2*, 351–353.

Appleby, G. A., & Anastas, J. W. (1998). *Not just a passing phase: Social work with gay, lesbian, and bisexual people*. New York: Columbia University Press.

Arellano, C. M. (1993). *The role of gender in handling negative affect in same-sex couples* (Unpublished doctoral dissertation). University of Denver, Denver, Colorado.

Arie, S. (2003, September 25). Gay marriages to get European passports. *The Guardian*. Retrieved March 20, 2007, from http://www.buzzle.com/editorias/text9-25-2003-45838.asp.

Arnup, K. (1999). Out in the world: The social and legal context of gay and lesbian families. *Journal of Gay and Lesbian Social Services, 10*, 1–25.

Aulivola, M. (2004). Outing domestic violence: Affording appropriate protections to gay and lesbian victims. *Family Court Review, 42*, 162–177.

Bachelor, A. (1995). Client's perception of the therapeutic alliance: A qualitative analysis. *Journal of Counseling Psychology, 42*, 323–337.

Bacon, E. S., Condon, E. H., & Fernsler, J. I. (2000). Young widows? Experiences with an Internet self-help group. *Journal of Psychosocial Nursing and Mental Health Services, 38*, 24–33.

Badgett, M. V. L. (2001). *Money, myths, and change: The economic lives of lesbians and gay men.* Chicago: University of Chicago Press.

Badgett, M. V. L. (2003). Money, myths and change: The economic lives of lesbians and gay men. *Sexualities, 61*, 122–123.

Bailey, J. M., Bobrow, D., Wolfe, M., & Mikach, S. (1995). Sexual orientation of adult sons of gay fathers. *Developmental Psychology, 31*, 124–129.

Bailey, J. M., Gaulin, S., Agyei, Y., & Glaude, B.A. (1994). Effects of gender and sexual orientation on evolutionarily relevant aspects of human mating psychology. *Journal of Personality and Social Psychology, 66*, 1081–1093.

Bailey, J. M., Kim, P. Y., Hills, A., & Linsenmeir, J. A. W. (1997). Butch, femme, or straight acting? Partner preferences of gay men and lesbians. *Journal of Personality and Social Psychology, 73*, 960–973.

Bajko, M.S. (2010, March 25). CA poll shows 50% support for same-sex marriage. *Bay Area Reporter*. Retrieved from http://www.ebar.com/news/article.php?sec=news&article=4648 (reporting results of a study conducted by the Public Policy Institute of California).

Balsam, K. (2001). Nowhere to hide: Lesbian battering, homophobia, and minority stress. *Women and Therapy, 23*, 25–37.

Balsam, K. F., Beauchaine, T., Rothblum, E. D., & Solomon, S. E. (2008). Three-year follow-up of same-sex couples who had civil unions in Vermont, same-sex couples not in civil unions, and heterosexual married couples. *Developmental Psychology, 44*, 102–116.

Balsam, K. F., Rothblum, E. D., & Beauchaine, T. P. (2005). Victimization over the life span: A comparison of lesbian, gay, bisexual, and heterosexual siblings. *Journal of Consulting and Clinical Psychology, 73*, 477–487.

Balsam, K. F., & Szymanski, D. M. (2005). Relationship quality and domestic violence in women's same-sex relationships: The role of minority stress. *Psychology of Women Quarterly, 29*, 258–269.

Barrett, H., & Tasker, F. (2001). Growing up with a gay parent: Views of 101 gay fathers on their sons' and daughters' experiences. *Educational and Child Psychology, 18*, 62–77.

Bartlett, A., King, M., & Phillips, P. (2001). Straight talking: An investigation of the attitudes and practice of psychoanalysts and psychotherapists in relation to gays and lesbians. *British Journal of Psychiatry, 179*, 545–549.

Battle, J., Cohen, C. J., Warren, D., Fergerson, G., & Audam, S. (2002). *Say it loud: I'm black and I'm proud: Black Pride Survey 2000.* New York: Policy Institute of the National Gay and Lesbian Task Force.

Beals, K. P., Impett, E. A., Peplau, L. A., & Rose, S. M. (2002). Lesbians in love: Why some relationships endure and others end. *Journal of Lesbian Studies, 6*, 53–63.

Beals, K. P., & Peplau, L. A. (2001). Social involvement, disclosure of sexual orientation, and the quality of lesbian relationships. *Psychology of Women, 25*, 1–10.

Benkov, L. (1994). *Reinventing the family: The emerging story of lesbian and gay partners.* New York: Crown.

Bennett, L., & Gates, G. J. (2004, April 13). *The cost of marriage inequality to children and their same-sex parents.* Retrieved February 1, 2011, from Human Rights Campaign Foundation Web site: http://www.hrc.org/costkids.pdf.

Bennett, S. (2003). Is there a primary mom? Parental perceptions of attachment bond hierarchies within lesbian adoptive families. *Child and Adolescent Social Work Journal, 20*, 159–173.

Bepko, C., & Johnson, T. (2000). Gay and lesbian couples in therapy: Perspectives for the contemporary family therapist. *Journal of Marital and Family Therapy, 26*, 409–419.

Berger, R. M. (1990a). Men together: Understanding the gay couple. *Journal of Homosexuality, 19*, 31–49.

Berger, R. M. (1990b). Passing impact on the quality of same-sex couple relationships. *Social Work, 35*, 328–332.

Berger, R. M. (1996). *Gay and gray: The older homosexual man* (2nd ed.). Binghamton, NY: Haworth Press.

Berger, R. M., & Mallon, D. (1993). Social support networks of gay men. *Journal of Sociology and Social Welfare, 20*, 155–174.

Bernstein, B. E. (2000). Attitudes and issues of parents of gay men and lesbians and implications for therapy. *Journal of Gay and Lesbian Psychotherapy, 1,* 37–53.

Berrill, K. T. (1990). Anti-gay violence and victimization in the United States. *Journal of Interpersonal Violence, 5,* 274–294.

Berrill, K. T. (1992). Organizing against hate on campus: Strategies for activists. In G. M. Herek & L. T. Berrill (Eds.), *Hate crimes: Confronting violence against lesbians and gay men* (pp. 259–269). Newbury Park, CA: Sage.

Bigner, J. J. (1996). Working with gay fathers. In J. Laird & R. Green (Eds.), *Lesbians and gays in couples and families* (pp. 370–403). San Francisco: Jossey-Bass.

Bigner, J. J. (2000). Gay and lesbian families. In W. C. Nichols, M. A. Pace-Nichols, D. S. Becvar, & A. Y. Napier (Eds.), *Handbook of family development and intervention* (pp. 279–298). New York: Wiley.

Bigner, J. J. (2006). Disclosing gay or lesbian orientation within marriage: A systems perspective. In W. C. Nichols, C. A. Everett, & R. E. Lee (Eds.), *When marriages fail: Systemic family therapy interventions and issues: A tribute to William C. Nichols* (pp. 85–100). Binghamton, NY: Haworth Press.

Bigner, J. J., & Bozett, F. W. (1990). Parenting by gay fathers. In F. W. Bozett & M. B. Sussman (Eds.), *Homosexuality and family relations* (pp. 155–176). New York: Harrington Park Press.

Bigner, J. J., & Jacobsen, R. B. (1992). Parenting behaviors of homosexual and heterosexual fathers. *Journal of Heterosexuality, 18,* 173–186.

Bigner, J. J., & Tasker, F. (Eds.). (2007). *Gay and lesbian parenting: New directions.* New York: Haworth Press.

Biller, R., & Rice, S. (1990). Experiencing multiple loss of persons with AIDS: Grief and bereavement issues. *Health and Social Work, 15,* 283–290.

Black, D., Gates, G., Sanders, S., & Taylor, L. (2000). Demographics of the gay and lesbian population in the United States: Evidence from available systematic data sources. *Demography, 37,* 139–154.

Blackwood, E. (1984). Sexuality and gender in certain Native American tribes: The case of the cross-gender females. *Signs, 10,* 27–42.

Blumstein, P., & Schwartz, P. (1983). *American couples.* New York: Morrow.

Boatwright. K. J., Gilbert, M. S., Forrest, L., & Ketzenberger, K. (1996). Impact of sexual identity development on career trajectory: Listening to the voices of lesbian women. *Journal of Vocational Behavior, 48,* 210–228.

Bohan, J. S., & Russell, G. M. (1999). Conceptual frameworks. In J. S. Bohan & G. M. Russell (Eds.), *Conversations about psychology and sexual orientation* (pp. 11–30). New York: New York University Press.

Bonello, K., & Cross, M. C. (2010). Gay monogamy: I love you but I can't have sex with only you. *Journal of Homosexuality, 57*, 117–139.

Bos, H. M. W., Van Balen, F., & Van Den Boom, D. C. (2004a). Experience of parenthood, couple relationship, social support, and child-rearing goals in planned lesbian mother families. *Journal of Child Psychology and Psychiatry, 45*, 755–764.

Bos, H. M. W., Van Balen, F., & Van Den Boom, D. C. (2004b). Minority stress, experience of parenthood and child adjustment in lesbian families. *Journal of Reproductive and Infant Psychology, 22*, 291–304.

Bosivert, D. (2007). Homosexuality and spirituality. In J. S. Siker (Ed.), *Homosexuality and religion: An encyclopedia* (pp. 32–44). Westport, CT: Greenwood Press.

Bowen, M. (1996). The use of family theory in clinical practice. *Comprehensive Psychiatry, 7*, 345–374.

Bozett, F. W. (1993). Gay fathers: A review of the literature. In L. D. Garnets & D. C. Kimmel (Eds.), *Psychological perspectives on lesbian and gay male experiences* (pp. 437–457). New York: Columbia University Press.

Bradford, J., & Ryan, C. (1991). Who we are: Health concerns of middle-aged lesbians. In B. J. Warsow & A. J. Smith (Eds.), *Lesbians at midlife: The creative transition* (pp. 147–163). San Francisco: Spinsters.

Brantner, P. A. (1992). When mommy or daddy is gay: Developing constitutional standards for custody decisions. *Hastings Women's Law Journal, 3*, 97–121.

Brown, L. B., Sarosy, S. G., Cook, T. C., & Quarto, J. G. (1997). *Gay men and aging*. New York: Garland.

Brown, L. S. (1994). *Subversive dialogues: Theory in feminist therapy*. New York: Basic Books.

Brown, L. S. (1995). Therapy with same-sex couples: An introduction. In N. S. Jacobson & A. S. Guttman (Eds.), *Clinical handbook of couple therapy* (pp. 274–291). New York: Guilford Press.

Brown, L. S. (1996). Ethical concerns with sexual minority patients. In R. P. Cabaj & T. S. Stein (Eds.), *Textbook of homosexuality and mental health* (pp. 897–916). Washington, DC: American Psychiatric Press.

Brown, S. L. (2000). The effect of union type on psychological well-being: Depression among cohabiters versus married. *Journal of Health and Social Behavior, 41*, 241–255.

Browning, C., Reynolds, A. L., & Dworkin, S. H. (1991). Affirmative psychotherapy for lesbian women. *Counseling Psychologist, 19*, 177–196.

Bryant, S., & Demian. (1994). Relationship characteristics of American gay and lesbian couples: Findings from a national survey. *Journal of Gay and Lesbian Social Services, 1*, 101–117.

Burch, B. (1986). Psychotherapy and the dynamics of merger in lesbian couples. In T. S. Stein & C. J. Cohen (Eds.), *Contemporary perspectives on psychotherapy with lesbians and gay men* (pp. 57–71). New York: Plenum Press.

Burch, B. (1997). *Other women: Lesbian/bisexual experience and psychoanalytic views of women*. New York: Columbia University Press.

Burda, J. M. (2004). *Estate planning for same-sex couples*. Chicago: American Bar Association.

Burda, J. M. (2008). *Gay, lesbian, and transgender clients: A lawyer's guide*. Chicago: American Bar Association.

Burke, P. (1993). *Family values: Two moms and their son*. New York: Random House.

Burke, T. W., Jordan, M. L., & Owen, S. S. (2002). A cross-national comparison of gay and lesbian domestic violence. *Journal of Contemporary Criminal Justice, 18*, 231–257.

Butler, B. (1990). *Ceremonies of the heart*. Seattle, WA: Seal Press.

Cabaj, R. P., & Klinger, R. L. (1996). Psychotherapeutic interventions with lesbian and gay couples. In R. P. Cabaj & T. S. Stein (Eds.), *Textbook of homosexuality and mental health* (pp. 485–502). Washington, DC: American Psychiatric Press.

Cahill, S. (2008). The disproportionate impact of antigay family policies on Black and Latino same-sex couple households. *Journal of African American Studies, 13*, 219–250.

Cahill, S., Ellen, M., & Tobias, S. (2002). *Family policy: Issues affecting gay, lesbian, bisexual and transgender families*. New York: Policy Institute of the National Gay and Lesbian Task Force.

Cahill, S., & South, K. (2002). Policy issues affecting lesbian, gay, bisexual, and transgender people in retirement: Different barriers compared to heterosexual peers. *Generations: The Journal of the Western Gerontological Society, 26*, 49–54.

Cahill, S., South, K., & Spade, J. (2000). *Outing age: Public policy issues affecting gay, lesbian, bisexual and transgender elders*. Washington, DC: Policy Institute of the National Gay and Lesbian Task Force Foundation.

Cahill, S., & Tobias, S. (2007). *Policy issues affecting lesbian, gay, bisexual, and transgender families*. Ann Arbor: University of Michigan Press.

Canary, D. J., & Stafford, L. (1992). Relational maintenance strategies and equity in marriage. *Communication Monographs, 59*, 243–267.

Card, C. (2007). Gay divorce: Thoughts on the legal regulation of marriage. *Hypatia, 22*, 24–38.

Caron, S. L., & Ulin, M. (1997). Closeting and the quality of lesbian relationships. *Families in Society, 78*, 413–419.

Carrington, C. (2002). *No place like home: Relationships and family life among lesbians and gay men*. Chicago: University of Chicago Press.

Cass, V. C. (1996). Sexual orientation identity formation: A Western phenomenon. In R. P. Cabaj & T. Stein (Eds.), *Textbook of homosexuality and mental health* (pp. 227–251). Washington, DC: American Psychiatric Press.

Caster, W. (2008). *The new lesbian sex book* (3rd ed.). New York: Alyson Books.

Causby, V., Lockhart, L., White, B., & Greene, K. (1995). Fusion and conflict resolution in lesbian relationships. *Journal of Gay and Lesbian Social Services, 3*, 67–82.

Cayouette, S. (1999). Running groups for lesbians. In B. Leventhal & S. Lundy (Eds.), *Same-sex domestic violence: Strategies for change* (pp. 233–243). Thousand Oaks, CA: Sage.

Center against Spouse Abuse. (2000). *Domestic violence report: An overview*. St. Petersburg, FL: Author.

Chambers, D. L., & Polikoff, N. D. (1999). Family law and gay and lesbian family issues in the twentieth century. *Family Law Quarterly, 33*, 523–542.

Chan, R., Brooks, R., Raboy, B., & Patterson, C. (1998). Division of labor between lesbian and heterosexual parents: Associations with children's adjustment. *Journal of Family Psychology, 12*, 402–419.

Chan, R., Raboy, B., & Patterson, C. (1998). Psychosocial adjustment among children conceived via donor insemination by lesbian and heterosexual mothers. *Child Development, 69*, 443–457.

Ciano-Boyce, C., & Shelley-Sireci, L. (2002). Who is mommy tonight? Lesbian parenting issues. *Journal of Homosexuality, 43*, 1–13.

Cini, M. A., & Malafi, T. N. (1991, March). *Paths to intimacy: Lesbian and heterosexual women's scripts of early relationship development.* Paper presented at the conference of the Association for Women in Psychology, Hartford, CT.

Clifford, D., Hertz, F., & Doskow, E. (2007). *A legal guide for lesbian and gay couples* (14th ed.). Berkeley, CA: Nolo.

Clunis, D. M., & Green, G. D. (1993). *Lesbian couples: Creating healthy relationships for the 90s.* Seattle: Seal Press.

Clunis, D. M., & Green, G. D (2000). *Lesbian couples: A guide to creating healthy relationships.* Seattle: Seal Press.

Cohler, B. J., & Galatzer-Levy, R. M. (2000). *The course of gay and lesbian lives: Social and psychoanalytic perspectives.* Chicago: University of Chicago Press.

Cole, S. W., Kemeny, M. E., Taylor, S. E., & Visscher, B. R. (1996). Elevated physical health risk among gay men who conceal their homosexual identity. *Health Psychology, 15*, 243–251.

Coleman, V. E. (1990). *Violence between lesbian couples: A between-group comparison* (Doctoral dissertation). Available from Dissertation Abstracts International (UMI No. 9109022).

Colgan, P. (1988). Treatment of identity and intimacy issues in gay males. In E. Coleman (Ed.), *Integrated identity for gay men and lesbians: Psychotherapeutic approaches for emotional well-being* (pp. 101–123). New York: Harrington Park Press.

Collins, D. (2008, October 11). State's high court backs gay marriage. *Dallas Morning News*, p. 6A.

Connolly, C. (2002). The voice of the petitioner: The experiences of gay and lesbian parents in successful second-parent adoption proceedings. *Law and Society Review, 36*, 325–347.

Connolly, C. M., & Sicola, M. K. (2005). Listening to lesbian couples: Communication competence in long-term relationships. *Journal of GLBT Family Studies: Innovations in Theory, Research, and Practice, 1*, 143–168.

Coombs, M. (1998). Sexual dis-orientation: Transgendered people and same-sex marriage. *UCLA Women's Law Journal, 8*, 217–266.

Corless, I. B. (2001). Bereavement. In B. R. Ferreu & D. Coyle (Eds.), *Textbook of palliative nursing* (pp. 352–362). New York: Oxford University Press.

Coss, C. (1991). Single lesbians speak out. In B. Sang, J. Warshow, & A. Smith (Eds.), *Lesbians at midlife: The creative transition* (pp. 132–140). San Francisco: Spinsters.

Craft, S. M., & Serovich, J. M. (2005). Family-of-origin factors and partner violence in the intimate relationships of gay men who are HIV positive. *Journal of Counseling and Development, 20,* 777–791.

Crisp, D., Priest, B., & Torgerson, A. (1998). African American gay men: Developmental issues, choices, and self-concept. *Family Therapy, 25,* 161–168.

Crocker, J., Major, B., & Steele, C. (1998). Social stigma. In D. Gilbert & S. Fiske (Eds.), *Handbook of social psychology* (Vol. 2, 4th ed., pp. 504–553). New York: McGraw-Hill.

Croteau, J. M., & Theil, M. J. (1994). Facing gay issues in counseling. *Education Digest, 59,* 25–28.

Cutrona, C., & Suhr, J. (1994). Social support communication in the context of marriage: An analysis of couples' supportive interactions. In B. R. Burleson, T. L. Albrecht, & I. G. Sarason (Eds.), *The communication of social support: Messages, interactions, relationships, and community* (pp. 113–135). Newbury Park, CA: Sage.

Dailey, T. (2001, March 6). *The negative health effects of homosexuality* (Insight No. 232). Washington, DC: Family Research Council.

D'Augelli, A. R., & Garnets, L. D. (1995). Lesbian, gay, and bisexual communities. In A. R. D'Augelli & C. J. Patterson (Eds.), *Lesbian, gay, and bisexual identities over the lifespan* (pp. 293–320). New York: Oxford University Press.

Davidson, A. G. (1991). Looking for love in the age of AIDS: The language of gay personals, 1978–1988. *Journal of Sex Research, 28,* 125–138.

Davies, D., & Neal, C. (1996). *Pink therapy: A guide for counsellors and therapists working with lesbian, gay, and bisexual clients.* Buckingham, UK: Open University Press.

Dean, L., Wu, S., & Martin. J. L. (1992). Trends in violence and discrimination against gay men in New York City, 1984–1990. In G. M. Herek & K. T. Berrill (Eds.), *Hate crimes: Confronting violence against lesbians and gay men* (pp. 46–64). Newbury Park, CA: Sage.

deBoer, D. (2009). Focus on the family: The psychosocial context of gay men choosing fatherhood. In P. L. Hammack & B. J. Bertram (Eds.), *The story of sexual identity: Narrative perspectives on the gay and lesbian life course* (pp. 327–346). New York: Oxford University Press.

Defense of Marriage Act, 1 U.S.C. § 7 (1996).

Diamond, L. M., & Savin-Williams, R. C. (2000). Explaining diversity in the development of same-sex sexuality among young women. *Journal of Social Issues, 56*, 297–313.

DiPlacido, J. (1998). Minority stress among lesbians, gay men, and bisexuals: A consequence of heterosexism, homophobia, and stigmatization. In G. Herek (Ed.), *Stigma and sexual orientation: Understanding prejudice against lesbians, gay men, and bisexuals* (pp. 138–159). Thousand Oaks, CA: Sage.

Downey, J., & Friedman, R. (1995). Internalized homophobia in lesbian relationships. *Journal of the American Academy of Psychoanalysis, 23*, 435–447.

Duclos, N. (1991). Some complicating thoughts on same-sex marriage. *Journal of Law and Sexuality, 31*, 51.

Dundas, S., & Kaufman, M. (2000). The Toronto Lesbian Family Study. *Journal of Homosexuality, 40*, 65–79.

Dupras, A. (1994). Internalized homophobia and psychological adjustment among gay men, *Psychological Reports, 75*, 23–28.

Dutton, D. G. (1994). The origin and structure of the abusive personality. *Journal of Personality Disorders, 8*, 181–191.

Dworkin, S. H., & Gutiérrez, F. J. (Eds.). (1992). *Counseling gay men and lesbians: Journey to the end of the rainbow*. Alexandria, VA: American Association for Counseling and Development.

Eldridge, N. S., & Gilbert, L. A. (1990). Correlates of relationship satisfaction in lesbian couples. *Psychology of Women Quarterly, 14*, 43–62.

Eliason, M. (1996). Lesbian and gay family issues. *Journal of Family Nursing, 2*, 10–29.

Elise, D. (1996). Lesbian couples: The implications of sex differences in separation-individuation. *Psychotherapy, 23*, 305–310.

Erich, S., Leung, P., Kindle, P., & Carter, S. (2005). Gay and lesbian adoptive families: An exploratory study of family functioning, adoptive child's behavior, and familial support networks. *Journal of Family Social Work, 9*, 17–32.

Eskridge, W. N., Jr. (2001). Equality practice: Liberal reflections on the jurisprudence of civil unions. *Albany Law Review, 31*, 641–672.

Eubanks-Carter, C., Burckell, L. A., & Goldfried, M. R. (2005). Enhancing therapeutic effectiveness with lesbian, gay, and bisexual clients. *Clinical Psychology: Science and Practice, 12*, 1–18.

Faderman, L. (1991). *Odd girls and twilight lovers: A history of lesbian life in twentieth century America*. New York: Columbia University Press.

Faderman, L. (1992). The return of butch and femme: A phenomenon in lesbian sexuality of the 1980s and 1990s. *Journal of the History of Sexuality*, *2*, 578–596.

Falco, K. L. (1991). *Psychotherapy with lesbian clients*. New York: Brunner/Mazel.

Farley, N. (1992). Same-sex domestic violence. In S. H. Dworkin & F. J. Gutiérrez (Eds.), *Counseling gay men and lesbians: Journey to the end of the rainbow* (pp. 231–242). Alexandria, VA: American Association for Counseling and Development.

Fassinger, R. E. (2000). Applying counseling theories to lesbian, gay, and bisexual clients: Pitfalls and possibilities. In R. M. Perez, K. A. DeBord, & K. J. Bieschke (Eds.), *Handbook of counseling and psychotherapy with lesbian, gay, and bisexual clients* (pp. 107–131). Washington, DC: American Psychological Association.

Fassinger, R. E., & Morrow, S. L. (1995). Overcome: Repositioning lesbian sexualities. In L. Diamant & R. D. McAnulty (Eds.), *The psychology of sexual orientation, behavior, and identity: A handbook* (pp. 197–219). London: Greenwood.

Feeney, J. A., Noller, P., & Hanrahan, M. (1994). Assessing adult attachment. In M. B. Sperling & W. H. Berman (Eds.), *Clinical and developmental perspectives* (pp. 128–152). New York: Guilford Press.

Feingold, A. (1990). Gender differences in effects of physical attractiveness on romantic attraction: A comparison across five research paradigms. *Journal of Personality and Social Psychology*, *59*, 981–993.

Franco, F. E. (1996). Unconditional safety for conditional immigrant women. *Berkeley Women's Law Journal*, *11*, 99–141.

Fredriksen, K. L. (1999). Family caregiving responsibilities among lesbians and gay men. *Social Work*, *44*, 142–155.

Friedman, L. (1997). Rural lesbian mothers and their families. *Journal of Gay and Lesbian Social Services*, *7*, 73–82.

Fulcher, M., Sutfin, E. L., Chan, R. W., Scheib, J. E., & Patterson, C. J. (2005). Lesbian mothers and their children: Findings from the Contemporary Families Study. In A. Omoto & H. Kurtzman (Eds.), *Recent research on sexual orientation, mental health, and substance abuse* (pp. 281–299). Washington, DC: American Psychological Association.

Gaines, S. O., Henderson, M. C., Kim, M., Gilstrap, S., Yi, J., Rusbult, C. E., et al. (2005). Cultural value orientations, internalized homophobia, and accommodation in romantic relationships. *Journal of Homosexuality*, *50*, 97–117.

Gallagher, M. (2004). (How) will gay marriage weaken marriage as a social institution: A reply to Andrew Koppelman. *University of St. Thomas Law Journal, 2*, 33–70.

Gallup Poll. (2006). Single U.S. public opinion polls: Same-sex marriages and civil unions. Retrieved January 1, 2011, from Religious Tolerance Web site: http://www.religioustolerance.org/hom_marp.htm.

Garnets, L. D., Hancock, K. A., Cochran, S. D., Goodchilds, J., & Peplau, L. A. (1991). Issues in psychotherapy with lesbians and gay men: A survey of psychologists. *American Psychologist, 46*, 964–972.

Garnets, L. D., & Kimmel, D. C. (1991). Lesbian and gay male dimensions in the psychological study of human diversity. In J. D. Goodchilds (Ed.), *Psychological perspectives on human diversity in America* (pp. 137–192). Washington, DC: American Psychological Association.

Gartrell, N., Banks, A., Reed, N., Hamilton, J., Rodas, C., & Deck, A. (2000). The National Lesbian Family Study: 3. Interviews with mothers of 5-year-olds. *American Journal of Orthopsychiatry, 70*, 542–549.

Gartrell, N., & Bos, H. (2010). U.S. National Longitudinal Lesbian Family Study: Psychological adjustment of 17-year old adolescents. *Pediatrics, 126*, 1–9.

Gartrell, N., Deck, A., Rodas, C., Peyser, H., & Banks, A. (2005). The National Lesbian Family Study: 4. Interviews with the 10-year-old children. *American Journal of Orthopsychiatry, 75*, 518–524.

Gartrell, N., Deck, A., Rodas, C., Peyser, H., & Banks, A. (2006). The USA National Lesbian Family Study: 1. Interviews with prospective mothers. *Feminism and Psychology, 16*, 175–192.

Gates, G., & Ost, J. (2004). *The gay and lesbian atlas*. Washington, DC: Urban Institute Press.

General Accounting Office. (2004). *Defense of Marriage Act: Update to prior report* (Document GAO-04-353R). Washington, DC: Author.

Girshick, L. B. (2002). *Woman to woman sexual violence: Does she call it rape?* Boston: Northeastern University Press.

Goldberg, A. E. (2010). *Lesbian and gay parents and their children: Research on the family life cycle*. Washington, DC: American Psychological Association.

Goldberg, A. E., Downing, J. B., & Sauck, C. C. (2008). Perceptions of children's parental preferences in lesbian two-mother households. *Journal of Marriage and Family, 70*, 419–434.

Goldberg, A. E., & Perry-Jenkins, M. (2007). The division of labor and perceptions of parental roles: Lesbian couples across the transition to parenthood. *Journal of Social and Personal Relationships*, *24*, 297–318.

Goldberg, A. E., & Sayer, A. (2006). Lesbian couples' relationship quality across the transition to parenthood. *Journal of Marriage and Family*, *68*, 87–100.

Golombok, S. (2000). Parents' sexual orientation: Heterosexual or homosexual? In S. Golombok (Ed.), *Parenting: What really counts?* (pp. 45–60). Philadelphia: Routledge.

Golombok, S., Perry, B., Burston, A., Murray, C., Mooney-Somers, J., & Stevens, M. (2003). Children with lesbian parents: A community study. *Developmental Psychology*, *39*, 20–33.

Gonsiorek, J. C. (1993). Mental health issues of gay and lesbian adolescents. In L. G. Garnets & D. C. Kimmel (Eds.), *Psychological perspectives on lesbian and gay male experience* (pp. 469–485). New York: Columbia University Press.

Gonsiorek, J. C., & Weinrich, J. D. (1991). The definition and scope of sexual orientation. In J. C. Gonsiorek & J. D. Weinrich (Eds.), *Homosexuality: Research implications for public policy* (pp. 1–12). Newbury Park, CA: Sage.

Gordon, L. E. (2006). Bringing the U-haul: Embracing and resisting sexual stereotypes in a lesbian community. *Sexualities*, *9*, 171–192.

Gottman, J. M. (1994). *What predicts divorce? The relationship between marital processes and marital outcomes*. Hillsdale, NJ: Erlbaum.

Gottman, J. M., Coan, J., Carrere, S., & Swanson, C. (1998). Predicting marital happiness and stability from newlywed interactions. *Journal of Marriage and the Family*, *60*, 5–22.

Gottman, J. M., & Levenson, R. W. (1992). Marital processes predictive of later dissolution: Behavior, physiology, and health. *Journal of Personality and Social Psychology*, *34*, 14–34.

Gottman, J. M., Levenson, R. W., Swanson, C., Swanson, K., Tyson, R., & Yoshimoto, D. (2003). Observing gay, lesbian and heterosexual couples' relationships: Mathematical modeling of conflict interactions. *Journal of Homosexuality*, *45*, 65–91.

Granvold, D. K., & Martin, J. I. (1999). Family therapy with gay and lesbian clients. In C. Franklin & C. Jordan (Eds.), *Family practice: Brief and systemic methods* (pp. 299–320). Pacific Grove, CA: Brooks/Cole.

Green, R.-J. (2002). Coming out to family . . . in context. In E. Davis-Russell (Ed.), *California School of Professional Psychology handbook of multicultural education, research, intervention, and training* (pp. 277–283). San Francisco: Jossey-Bass.

Green, R.-J. (2007). Gay and lesbian couples in therapy: A social justice perspective. In E. Aldarondo (Ed.), *Advancing social justice through clinical practice* (pp. 119–149). Mahwah, NJ: Erlbaum.

Green, R.-J., Bettinger, M., & Zacks, E. (1996). Are lesbian couples fused and gay male couples disengaged? Questioning gender straight jackets. In J. Laird & R.-J. Green (Eds.), *Lesbians and gays in couples and families* (pp. 185–231). San Francisco: Jossey-Bass.

Green, R.-J., & Mitchell, V. (2002). Gay and lesbian couples in therapy: Homophobia, relational ambiguity, and social support. In A. S. Gurman & N. S. Jacobson (Eds.), *Clinical handbook of couple therapy* (3rd ed., pp. 546–568). New York: Guilford Press.

Green, S. K., & Bobele, M. (1994). Family therapists' response to AIDS: An examination of attitudes, knowledge, and contact. *Journal of Marital and Family Therapy, 20,* 349–367.

Greenan, D. E., & Tunnell, G. (2003). *Couple therapy with gay men.* New York: Guilford Press.

Greene, B. (1994a). Ethnic minority lesbians and gay men: Mental health and treatment issues. *Journal of Consulting and Clinical Psychology, 62,* 243–251.

Greene, B. (1994b). Lesbian women of color: Triple jeopardy. In L. Comas-Diaz & B. Breene (Eds.), *Women of color* (pp. 389–427). New York: Guilford Press.

Greene, B. (1995). Lesbian couples. In K. Jay (Ed.), *Dyke life: From growing up to growing old—a celebration of the lesbian experience* (pp. 97–106). New York: Basic Books.

Greene, B. (2000). African American lesbian and bisexual women. *Journal of Social Issues, 56,* 239–249.

Greene, K., Causby, V., & Miller, D. H. (1999). The nature and function of fusion in the dynamics of lesbian relationships. *Affilia, 14,* 78–97.

Greenfield, S., & Thelen, M. (1997). Validation of the fear of intimacy scale with a lesbian and gay male population. *Journal of Social and Personal Relationships, 14,* 707–716.

Greenwood, G. L., Relf, M. V., Haung, B., Pollack, L. M., Canchola, J. A., & Catania, J. A. (2002). Battering victimization among a probability-based sample of men who have sex with men. *American Journal of Public Health, 92*, 1964–1969.

Griffen, D. W., & Bartholomew, K. (1994). Models of the self and other: Fundamental dimensions underlying measures of adult attachment. *Journal of Personality and Social Psychology, 67*, 430–445.

Grossman, A. H., D'Augelli, A. R., & Hershberger, S. (2000). Social support networks of lesbian, gay, and bisexual adults 60 years of age and older. *Journal of Gerontology: Psychological Sciences, 55B*, 171–179.

Grossman, A. H., D'Augelli, A. R., & O'Connell, T. S. (2001). Being lesbian, gay, bisexual, and 60 or older in North America. *Journal of Gay and Lesbian Social Services, 13*, 23–40.

Grossman, J. L. (2010). *In* United States v. Flores-Villar, *the Supreme Court will hear argument on the citizenship rights of non-marital children.* Retrieved from http://writ.news.findlaw.com/grossman/20101108.html.

Gruskin, E. P. (1999). *Treating lesbians and bisexual women: Challenges and strategies for health professionals.* Thousand Oaks, CA: Sage.

Gurman, A. S. (2008). *Clinical handbook of couple therapy* (4th ed.). New York: Guilford Press.

Haas, S. M. (2003). Relationship maintenance in same-sex couples. In D. J. Canary & M. Dainton (Eds.), *Maintaining relationships through communication: Relational, contextual, and cultural variations* (pp. 209–230). Mahwah, NJ: Erlbaum.

Haas, S. M., & Stafford, L. (1998). An initial examination of maintenance behaviors in gay and lesbian relationships. *Journal of Social and Personal Relationships, 15*, 846–855.

Haas, S. M., & Stafford, L. (2005). Maintenance behaviors in same-sex and marital relationships: A matched sample comparison. *Journal of Family Communication, 5*, 434–460.

Haldeman, D. C. (2000). Therapeutic responses to sexual orientation: Psychology's evolution. In B. Greene & G. L. Croom (Eds.), *Education, research, and practice in lesbian, gay, bisexual, and transgendered psychology: A resource manual* (pp. 244–262). Thousand Oaks, CA: Sage.

Haldeman, S. (2007). A queer fidelity: Reinventing Christian marriage. *Theology and Sexuality, 13*, 137–152.

Hall, M., & Gregory, A. (1991). Subtle balances: Love and work in lesbian relationships. In B. Sang, J. Warshow, & A. Smith (Eds.), *Lesbians at midlife: The creative transition* (pp. 122–133). San Francisco: Spinsters.

Hamberger, L. K. (1996). Intervention in gay male intimate violence requires coordinated efforts on multiple levels. In C. M. Renzetti & C. H. Miley (Eds.), *Violence in gay and lesbian domestic partnerships* (pp. 83–92). Binghamton, NY: Haworth Press.

Hargaden, H., & Llewellin, S. (1996). Lesbian and gay parenting issues. In D. Davies & C. Neal (Eds.), *Pink therapy: A guide for counselors and therapists working with LGB clients* (pp. 116–130). Philadelphia: Open University Press.

Harkless, L. E., & Fowers, B. J. (2005). Similarities and differences in relational boundaries among heterosexuals, gay men, and lesbians. *Psychology of Women Quarterly, 29,* 167–176.

Harper, G. W., Bruce, D., Serrano, P., & Jamil, O. B. (2009). The role of the Internet in sexual identity development of gay and bisexual male adolescents. In P. L. Hammack & B. J. Cohler (Eds.), *The story of sexual identity: Narrative perspectives on the gay and lesbian life course* (pp. 279–326). New York: Oxford University Press.

Harper, G. W., & Schneider, M. (2003). Oppression and discrimination among lesbian, gay, bisexual and transgendered people and communities: A challenge for community psychology. *American Journal of Community Psychology, 31,* 243–252.

Harris, J. I., Cook, S. W., & Kashubeck-West, S. (2008). Religious attitudes, internalized homophobia, and identity in gay and lesbian adults. *Journal of Gay and Lesbian Mental Health, 12,* 205–225.

Harry, J. (1984). *Gay couples.* New York: Praeger.

Hartman, A. (1999). The long road to equality: Lesbians and social policy. In J. Laird (Ed.), *Lesbians and lesbian families* (pp. 91–120). New York: Columbia University Press.

Harvey, J. H. (Ed.). (1998). *Perspectives on loss: A sourcebook.* Philadelphia: Brunner/Mazel.

Haslam, D. (2000). Analytical psychology. In D. Davies & C. Neal (Eds.), *Therapeutic perspectives on working with lesbian, gay, and bisexual clients.* Buckingham, UK: Open University Press.

Hatala, M. N., Baack, D. W., & Parmenter, R. (1998). Dating with HIV: A content analysis of gay male HIV-positive and HIV-negative personal advertisements. *Journal of Social and Personal Relationships, 15,* 268–276.

Hayes, J. A., & Gelso, C. J. (1993). Male counselors' discomfort with gay and HIV-infected clients. *Journal of Counseling Psychology, 40,* 86–93.

Heintz, A. J., & Melendez, R. M. (2006). Intimate partner violence and HIV/STD risk among lesbian, gay, and transgender individuals. *Interpersonal Violence, 21,* 193–208.

Hendrickson, M. (2007). Reaching out, hooking up: Lavender netlife in a New Zealand study. *Sexuality Research and Social Policy, 4,* 38–49.

Henry, W. P., Schacht, T. E., & Strupp, H. H. (1990). Patient and therapist introject, interpersonal process, and differential psychotherapy outcome. *Journal of Consulting and Clinical Psychology, 58,* 768–774.

Hequembourg, A., & Farrell, M. P. (1999). Lesbian motherhood: Negotiating marginal-main stream identities. *Gender and Society, 13,* 540–557.

Herdt, G. H., & Kertzner, R. (2007). I do, but I can't: The impact of marriage denial on the mental health and sexual citizenship of lesbians and gay men in the United States. *Sexuality Research and Social Policy, 3,* 33–49.

Herdt, G. H., & Koff, B. (2000). *Something to tell you: The road families travel when a child is gay.* New York: Columbia University Press.

Herek, G. M. (1993). Documenting prejudice against lesbians and gay men on campus: The Yale sexual orientation survey. *Journal of Homosexuality, 25,* 15–30.

Herek, G. M. (1995). Psychological heterosexism in the United States. In A. R. D'Augelli & C. J. Patterson (Eds.), *Lesbian, gay, and bisexual identities over the lifespan: Psychological perspectives* (pp. 321–346). New York: Oxford University Press.

Herek, G. M. (1996). Heterosexism and homophobia. In R. P. Cabaj & T. S. Stein (Eds.), *Textbook of homosexuality and mental health* (pp. 101–113). Washington, DC: American Psychiatric Press.

Herek, G. M. (2006). Legal recognition of same-sex relationships in the United States. *American Psychologist, 61,* 607–621.

Herek, G. M., Cogan, J. C., & Gillis, J. R. (2002). Victim experiences in hate crimes based on sexual orientation. *Journal of Social Issues, 58,* 319–339.

Herek, G. M., Gillis, J. R., & Cogan, J. C. (1999). Psychological sequelae of hate crime victimization among lesbian, gay, and bisexual adults. *Journal of Consulting and Clinical Psychology, 67,* 945–951.

Herman, E. (1994). *Psychiatry, psychology, and homosexuality.* New York: Chelsea House.

Hersoug, A. G., Hoglend, P., Monsen, J. T., & Havik, O. E. (2001). Quality of working alliance in psychotherapy: Therapist variables and patient/ therapist similarity as predictors. *Journal of Psychotherapy Practice and Research, 10,* 205–216.

Hertz, F. C., & Doskow, E. (2009). *Making it legal: A guide to same-sex marriage, domestic partnership and civil unions.* Berkeley, CA: Nolo.

Hickson, F. C., Davies, P. M., Hunt, A. J., Weatherburn, P., McManus, T. J., & Coxon, A. P. (1992). Maintenance of open gay relationships: Some strategies for protection against HIV. *AIDS Care, 4,* 409–419.

Hill, C. A. (1999). Fusion and conflict in lesbian relationships? *Feminism and Psychology, 9,* 179–185.

Hindy, C. G., & Schwarz, J. C. (1994). Anxious romantic attachment in adult relationships. In M. B. Sperling & W. H. Berman (Eds.), *Attachment in adults: Clinical and developmental perspectives* (pp. 179–203). New York: Guilford Press.

Hitchings, P. (1994). Psychotherapy and sexual orientation. In P. Clarkson & M. Pokorny (Eds.), *Handbook of psychotherapy* (pp. 119–134). London: Routledge.

Hogan, B., Carrasco, J. A., & Wellman, B. (2007). Visualizing personal networks: Working with participant-aided sociograms. *Field Methods, 19,* 116–144.

Hooyman, N. R., & Kramer, B. J. (2006). *Living through loss: Interventions across the lifespan.* New York: Columbia University Press.

Hostetler, A. J., & Cohler, B. J. (1997). Partnership, singlehood, and the lesbian and gay life course: A research agenda. *Journal of Gay, Lesbian, and Bisexual Identity, 2,* 199–230.

Hughes, T. L., Haas, A. P., & Avery, L. (1997). Lesbians and mental health: Preliminary results from the Chicago Women's Health survey. *Journal of the Gay and Lesbian Medical Association, 1,* 137–148.

Human Rights Campaign Foundation. (2002). *The family: Laws and legislation affecting gay, lesbian, bisexual and transgender families.* Retrieved from Human Rights Campaign Foundation Web site: http://www.hrc.org/ documents/SoTF.pdf.

Human Rights Campaign Foundation. (2005a). *Domestic partner benefits*. Retrieved from Human Rights Campaign Foundation Web site: http://www.hrc.org.

Human Rights Campaign Foundation. (2005b). *Nondiscrimination laws*. Retrieved from Human Rights Campaign Foundation Web site: http://www.hrc.org.

Human Rights Campaign Foundation. (2006). *Statewide marriage laws*. Retrieved from Human Rights Campaign Foundation Web site: http://www.hrc.org/Template.cfm?Section=Center&CONTENTID=2822.5&TEMPLATE=/ContentManagement/ContentDisplay.cfm.

Hunter, S. (1998). *Lesbian, gay, and transgendered youth*. Arlington: Judith Granger Birmingham Center for Child Welfare, University of Texas at Arlington.

Hunter, S. (2007). *Coming out and disclosure across the life span*. Binghamton, NY: Haworth Press.

Hunter, S., & Hickerson, J. (2003). *Affirmative practice: Understanding and working with lesbian, gay, bisexual, and transgender persons*. Washington, DC: National Association of Social Workers Press.

Iasenza, S. (1991). *The relations among selected aspects of sexual orientation and sexual functioning in females* (Doctoral dissertation). Available from Dissertation Abstracts International (UMI No. 9134752).

Iasenza, S. (1995). Platonic pleasures and dangerous desires: Psychoanalytic theory, sex research, and lesbian sexuality. In J. M. Glassgold & S. Iasenza (Eds.), *Lesbians and psychoanalysis: Revolutions in theory and practice* (pp. 345–373). New York: Free Press.

Iasenza, S. (1999). The big lie: Debunking lesbian bed death. *In the Family*, *4*, 8–11, 20, 25.

Iasenza, S. (2002). Beyond "lesbian bed death": The passion and play in lesbian relationships. *Journal of Lesbian Studies*, *6*, 111–120.

Igartua, K. J. (1998). Therapy with lesbian couples: The issues and the interventions. *Canadian Journal of Psychiatry*, *43*, 391–396.

Island, D., & Letellier, P. (1991). *Men who beat the men who love them: Battered gay men and domestic violence*. Binghamton, NY: Haworth Press.

Israel, T., Gorcheva, R., Walther, W. A., Sulzner, J. M., & Cohen, J. (2008). Therapists' helpful and unhelpful situations with LGBT clients: An exploratory study. *Professional Psychology: Research and Practice*, *39*, 361–368.

Israel, T., & Selvidge, M. M. D. (2003). Contributions of multicultural counselling to counselor competence with lesbian, gay, and bisexual clients. *Journal of Multicultural Counseling and Development, 31,* 84–98.

Istar, A. (1996). Couple assessment: Identifying and intervening in domestic violence in lesbian relationships. In C. M. Renzetti & C. H. Miley (Eds.), *Violence in gay and lesbian domestic partnerships* (pp. 93–160). New York: Harrington Park Press.

Jacobs, S. (1999). *Traumatic grief: Diagnosis, treatment, and prevention.* Philadelphia: Brunner/Mazel.

James, S. E. (2002). Clinical themes in gay and lesbian parented adoptive families. *Clinical Child Psychology and Psychiatry, 7,* 475–486.

James, S. E., & Murphy, B. C. (1998). Gay and lesbian relationships in a changing social context. In C. J. Patterson & A. R. D'Augelli (Eds.), *Lesbian, gay, and bisexual identities in families: Psychological perspectives* (pp. 99–121). New York: Oxford University Press.

Jayson, S. (2010, February 11). Internet changing the game of love: Friends are still the best cupids but dating sites are in hot pursuit. *USA Today,* p. 07b. Retrieved from http://www.usatoday.com/printedition/life/20100211/couplesmeet11_cv.art.htm.

Johnson, M. E., Brems, C., & Alford-Keating, P. (1997). Personality correlates of homophobia. *Journal of Homosexuality, 34,* 57–69.

Johnson, M. P., & Ferraro, K. J. (2000). Research on domestic violence in the 1990s: Making distinctions. *Journal of Marriage and the Family, 62,* 948–963.

Johnson, R. (1999). Groups for gay and bisexual male survivors of domestic violence. In B. Leventhal & S. E. Lundy (Eds.), *Same-sex domestic violence: Strategies for change* (pp. 215–228). Thousand Oaks, CA: Sage.

Johnson, S. M., & Greenberg, L. S. (1995). The emotionally focused approach to problems in adult attachment. In N. S. Jacobson & A. S. Gurman (Eds.), *Clinical handbook of couple therapy* (pp. 121–141). New York: Guilford Press.

Johnson, S. M., & O'Connor, E. (2002). *The gay baby boom: The psychology of gay parenthood.* New York: New York University Press.

Johnson, T. W., & Colucci, P. (1999). Lesbians, gay men, and the family life cycle. In B. Carter & M. McGoldrick (Eds.), *The expanded family life cycle: Individual, family, and social perspectives* (3rd ed., pp. 346–361). Boston: Allyn and Bacon.

Johnson, T. W., & Keren, M. S. (1996). *Creating and maintaining boundaries in male couples. Lesbians and gays in couples and families: A handbook for therapists* (pp. 231–250). San Francisco: Jossey-Bass.

Jones, D. A. (1996). Discrimination against same-sex couples in hotel reservations policies. *Journal of Homosexuality*, *31*, 153–159.

Jones, M. A., & Gabriel, M. A. (1999). Utilization of psychotherapy by lesbians, gay men, and bisexuals: Findings from a nationwide survey. *American Journal of Orthopsychiatry*, *69*, 209–211.

Jordan, J. V., Kaplan, A. C., Miller, J., Stiver, I. P., & Surrey, J. L. (1991). *Women's growth in connection: Writings from the Stone Center*. New York: Guilford Press.

Jordan, K. M., & Deluty, R. H. (1995). Clinical interventions by psychologists with lesbians and gay men. *Journal of Clinical Psychology*, *51*, 448–456.

Jordan, K. M., & Deluty, R. H. (2000). Social support, coming out, and relationship satisfaction in lesbian couples. *Journal of Lesbian Studies*, *4*, 145–164.

Jordan, M. (2007). Religion trouble. *GLQ: A Journal of Lesbian and Gay Studies*, *13*, 563–575.

Joslin, C. G., & Minter, S. P. (2008). *Lesbian, gay, bisexual and transgender family law*. New York: Thomson West.

Julien, D., Arellano, C., & Turgeon, L. (1997). Gender issues in heterosexual, gay and lesbian couples. In W. K. Halford & H. J. Markman (Eds.), *Clinical handbook of marriage and couples intervention* (pp. 107–127). New York: Wiley.

Julien, D., Pizzamiglio, M. T., Chartrand, E., & Bégin, J. (1995). *An observational study of communication in gay, lesbian and heterosexual couples*. Unpublished manuscript, University of Quebec, Montreal.

Kaiser Family Foundation. (2001). *Inside-out: A report on the experiences of lesbians, gays, and bisexuals in America and the public's view on issues and politics related to sexual orientation*. Menlo Park, CA: Author. Retrieved from Kaiser Family Foundation Web site: http://www.kff.org/content/2001/3193/LGBSurveyReport.pdf.

Kashubeck-West, S., Szymanski, D., & Meyer, J. (2008). Internalized heterosexism: Clinical implications and training considerations. *Counseling Psychologist*, *36*, 615–630.

Kelly, M. (1998). View from the field out in education: Where the personal and political collide. *Siecus Report*, *26*, 14–15.

Kennedy, E. D., & Davis, M. D. (1993). *Boots of leather, slippers of gold: The history of a lesbian community*. New York: Routledge.

Kirkpatrick, M. (1991). Lesbian couples in therapy. *Psychiatric Annals, 21,* 491–496.

Kitzinger, C., & Perkins, R. (1993). *Changing our minds: Lesbian feminism and psychology.* New York: New York University Press.

Klein, F., Sepekoff, B., & Wolf, T. J. (1985). Sexual orientation: A multi-variable dynamic process. *Journal of Homosexuality, 11,* 35–49.

Kleinberg, S., & Zorn, P. (1995). Rekindling the flame: A therapeutic approach to strengthening lesbian relationships. In J. M. Glassgold & S. Iasenza (Eds.), *Lesbians and psychoanalysis: Revolution in theory and practice* (pp. 125–143). New York: Free Press.

Klinkenberg, D., & Rose, S. (1994). Dating scripts of gay men and lesbians. *Journal of Homosexuality, 26,* 23–35.

Kohut, A. (2004). *Voters liked campaign 2004, but too much "mudslinging."* Washington, DC: Pew Research Center for the People and the Press. Retrieved November 12, 2008, from http://people-press.org/reports/pdf/233.pdf.

Krestan, J., & Bepko, C. (1980). The problem of fusion in the lesbian relationship. *Family Process, 19,* 277–289.

Kuehnle, K., & Sullivan, A. (2003). Gay and lesbian victimization: Reporting factors in domestic violence and bias incidents. *Criminal Justice and Behavior, 30,* 85–96.

Kurdek, L. A. (1988a). Relationship outcomes and their predictors: Longitudinal evidence from heterosexual married, gay cohabitating, and lesbian cohabitating couples. *Journal of Marriage and the Family, 60,* 553–568.

Kurdek, L. A. (1988b). Relationship quality of gay and lesbian cohabitating couples. *Journal of Homosexuality, 15,* 93–118.

Kurdek, L. A. (1989). Relationship quality in gay and lesbian cohabiting couples: A 1-year follow-up study. *Journal of Social and Personal Relationships, 6,* 39–59.

Kurdek, L. A. (1991a). Correlates of relationship satisfaction in cohabitating gay and lesbian couples: Integration of contextual investment, and problem-solving models. *Journal of Personality and Social Psychology, 61,* 910–922.

Kurdek, L. A. (1991b). The dissolution of gay and lesbian couples. *Journal of Social and Personal Relationships, 8,* 265–278.

Kurdek, L. A. (1991c). Sexuality in homosexual and heterosexual couples. In K. McKinney & S. Sprecher (Eds.), *Sexuality in close relationships* (pp. 177–191). Hillsdale, NJ: Erlbaum.

Kurdek, L. A. (1992). Relationship stability and relationship satisfaction in cohabitating gay and lesbian couples: A prospective longitudinal test of the contextual and interdependence models. *Journal of Social and Personal Relationships, 9,* 125–142.

Kurdek, L. A. (1993). The assessment of destructive arguing and personal conflict resolution styles in gay, lesbian, heterosexual nonparent and heterosexual parent couples. Unpublished manuscript, Wayne State University, Dayton, OH.

Kurdek, L. A. (1994a). Areas of conflict for gay, lesbian, and heterosexual cohabiting couples: What couples argue about influences relationship satisfaction. *Journal of Marriage and the Family, 56,* 923–934.

Kurdek, L. A. (1994b). Conflict resolution styles in gay, lesbian, heterosexual nonparent, and heterosexual parent couples. *Journal of Marriage and the Family, 56,* 705–722.

Kurdek, L. A. (1994c). The nature and correlates of relationship quality in gay, lesbian, and heterosexual cohabiting couples. In B. Greene & G. M. Herek (Eds.), *Lesbian and gay psychology* (pp. 113–155). Thousand Oaks, CA: Sage.

Kurdek, L. A. (1995a). Assessing multiple determinants of relationship commitment in cohabitating gay, cohabitating lesbian, dating heterosexual, and married heterosexual couples. *Family Relations, 44,* 261–266.

Kurdek, L. A. (1995b). Developing changes in relationship quality in gay and lesbian cohabitating couples. *Developmental Psychology, 31,* 86–94.

Kurdek, L. A. (1995c). Lesbian and gay couples. In A. R. D'Augelli & C. J. Patterson (Eds.), *Lesbian, gay, and bisexual identities over the lifespan: Psychological perspectives* (pp. 243–261). New York: Oxford University Press.

Kurdek, L. A. (1996). The deterioration of relationship quality for gay and lesbian cohabitating couples: A five-year prospective longitudinal study. *Personal Relationships, 3,* 417–442.

Kurdek, L. A. (1997a). Adjustment to relationship dissolution in gay, lesbian, and heterosexual partners. *Personal Relationships, 4,* 145–161.

Kurdek, L. A. (1997b). Relation between neuroticism and dimensions of relationship commitment: Evidence from gay, lesbian, and heterosexual couples. *Journal of Family Psychology, 11*, 109–124.

Kurdek, L. A. (1998a). The allocation of household labor in gay, lesbian, and heterosexual married couples. In D. L. Anselmi & A. L. Law (Eds.), *Questions of gender: Perspectives and paradoxes* (pp. 582–591). Boston: McGraw-Hill.

Kurdek, L. A. (1998b). Relationship outcomes and their predictors: Longitudinal evidence from heterosexual married, gay cohabiting, and lesbian cohabiting couples. *Journal of Marriage and the Family, 60*, 553–568.

Kurdek, L. A. (2000). Attractions and constraints as determinants of relationship commitment: Longitudinal evidence from gay, lesbian, and heterosexual couples. *Personal Relationships, 7*, 245–262.

Kurdek, L. A. (2001). Differences between heterosexual nonparent couples and gay, lesbian, and heterosexual parent couples. *Journal of Family Issues, 22*, 727–754.

Kurdek, L. A. (2003). Negative representations of the self/spouse and marital distress. *Personal Relationships, 10*, 511–534.

Kurdek, L. A. (2004). Are gay and lesbian cohabiting couples really different from heterosexual married couples? *Journal of Marriage and Family, 66*, 880–900.

Kurdek, L. A. (2005). What do we know about gay and lesbian couples? *Current Directions in Psychological Science, 14*, 251–254.

Kurdek, L. A. (2006). Differences between partners from heterosexual, gay, and lesbian cohabitating couples. *Journal of Marriage and Family, 68*, 508–528.

Kurdek, L. A. (2007). Avoidance motivation and relationship commitment in heterosexual, gay male, and lesbian partners. *Personal Relationships, 14*, 291–306.

Kurdek, L. A. (2008). Change in relationship quality for partners from lesbian, gay male, and heterosexual couples. *Journal of Family Psychology, 22*, 701–711.

Laird, J. (1999). Gender and sexuality in lesbian relationships: Feminist and constructionist perspectives. In J. Laird (Ed.), *Lesbians and lesbian families: Reflections on theory and practice* (pp. 47–89). New York: Columbia University Press.

Laird, J. (2000). Gender in lesbian relationships: Cultural, feminist, and construc-tionist reflections. *Journal of Marital and Family Therapy, 26*, 455–467.

Lambert, S. (2005). Gay and lesbian families: What we know and where we go from here. *Family Journal: Counseling and Therapy for Couples and Families, 13*, 43–51.

LAMBDA (2004). *Anti-violence project.* Retrieved from LAMBDA Web site: http://www.lambda.org/avp_gen.htm.

LaSala, M. C. (2004). Monogamy of the heart: Extradyadic sex and gay male couples. *Journal of Gay and Lesbian Social Services, 17*, 1–24.

Lassiter, P. S., Dew, B. J., Newton, K., Hays, D. G., & Yarbrough, B. (2006). Self-defined empowerment for gay and lesbian parents: A qualitative examina-tion. *Family Journal: Counseling and Therapy for Couples and Families, 14*, 245–252.

Laumann, E. D., Gagnon, J. H., Michael, R. T., & Michaels, S. (1994). *The social organization of sexuality: Sexual practices in the United States.* Chicago: University of Chicago Press.

Lawrence v. Texas, 539 U.S. 558 (2003). Retrieved from Cornell University Law School Web site: http://www.law.cornell.edu/supct/html/02-102.ZS.html.

Lazarus, R. S., & Folkman, S. (1984). *Stress, appraisal, and coping,* New York: Springer-Verlag.

Letellier, P. (1996). Twin epidemics: Domestic violence and HIV infection among gay and bisexual men. In C. M. Renzetti & C. H. Miley (Eds.), *Violence in gay and lesbian domestic partnerships* (pp. 69–82). Binghamton, NY: Haworth Press.

Lewis, G. B. (2005, November). *Thinking about gay marriage: Putting the moral condemnation back into morality policy.* Presentation at the Association for Public Policy Analysis and Management, Washington, DC.

Lewis, R. J., Derlega, V. J., Berndt., A., Morris, L. M., & Rose, S. (2001). An empir-ical analysis of stressors for gay men and lesbians. *Journal of Homosexual-ity, 42*, 63–88.

Liau, A., Millett, G., & Marks, G. (2006). Meta-analytic examination of online sex-seeking and sexual risk behavior among men who have sex with men. *Sexually Transmitted Diseases, 33*, 576–584.

Lie, G. Y., Schilit, R., Bush, J., Montagne, M., & Reyes, L. (1991). Lesbians in cur-rently aggressive relationships: How frequently do they report aggressive past relationships? *Violence and Victims, 6*, 121–135.

Linde, R. (1994). Impact of AIDS on adult gay male development: Implications for psychotherapy. In S. A. Cadwell, R. A. Burnhan, & M. Forstein (Eds.), *Therapists on the frontline: Psychotherapy with gay men in the age of AIDS* (pp. 25–31). Washington, DC: American Psychiatric Press.

Lockhart, L. L., White, B. W., Causby, V., & Isaac, A. (1994). Letting out the secret: Violence in lesbian relationships. *Journal of Interpersonal Violence*, 9, 469–492.

Long, J. K., & Pietsch, U. K. (2004). How do therapists of same-sex couples "do it"? In S. Green & D. Flemons (Eds.), *Quickies: Brief approaches to sex therapy* (pp. 171–188). New York: Norton.

Lott-Whitehead, L., & Tully, C. T. (1993). The family lives of lesbian mothers. *Smith College Studies in Social Work*, 63, 266–280.

Lund, D. A. (1999). Giving and receiving help during late life spousal bereavement. In J. D. Davidson & K. J. Doka (Eds.), *Living with grief: At work, at school, at worship* (pp. 203–212). Washington, DC: Hospice Foundation of America.

Lynch, J. M., & Murray, K. (2000). For the love of the children: The coming out process of lesbian and gay parents and stepparents. *Journal of Homosexuality*, 39, 1–24.

MacDonald, B. J. (1998). Issues in therapy with gay and lesbian couples. *Journal of Sex and Marital Therapy*, 24, 165–190.

Mackey, R. A., Diemer, M. A., & O'Brien, B. A. (2000). Psychological intimacy in the lasting relationships of heterosexual and same-gender couples. *Sex Roles*, 43, 201–227.

Mackey, R. A., Diemer, M. A., & O'Brien, B. A. (2004). Relational factors in understanding satisfaction in the lasting relationships of same-sex and heterosexual couples. *Journal of Homosexuality*, 47, 111–136.

Mackey, R. A., O'Brien, B. A., & Mackey, R. A. (1997). *Gay and lesbian couples: Voices from lasting relationships*. Westport, CT: Praeger.

Malley, M., & Tasker, F. (1999). Lesbians, gay men, and family therapy: A contradiction in terms. *Journal of Family Therapy*, 21, 3–29.

Mallon, G. P. (2000). Gay men and lesbians as adoptive parents. *Journal of Gay and Lesbian Social Services*, 11, 1–14.

Mallon, G. P. (2004). *Gay men choosing parenthood*. New York: Columbia University Press.

Markowitz, D. L. (2000). *The Vermont guide to civil unions* (2004). Montpelier, VT: Office of the Secretary of State.

Markowitz, L. M. (1991a). Dangerous practice: Inside the conversionist therapy controversy. *In the Family, 4,* 10–13, 25.

Markowitz, L. M. (1991b, January–February). Homosexuality: Are we still in the dark? *Family Therapy Networker,* 26–29, 31–35.

Martin, A. (1993). *The lesbian and gay parenting handbook.* New York: Harper-Collins.

Martin, A. (1998). Clinical issues in psychotherapy with lesbian-, gay-, and bisexual-partnered families. In C. J. Patterson & A. R. D'Augelli (Eds.), *Lesbian, gay, and bisexual identities in families: Psychological perspectives* (pp. 270–291). London: Oxford University Press.

Martin-Baró, I., Aron, A., & Corne, S. (1994). *Writings for a liberation psychology.* Cambridge, MA: Harvard University Press.

Marvin v. Marvin, 18 Cal.3d 660 (1976).

Matteson, D. R. (1996). Psychotherapy with bisexual individuals. In R. P. Cabaj & T. S. Stein (Eds.), *Textbook of homosexuality and mental health* (pp. 433–449). Washington, DC: American Psychiatric Press.

Matthews, A. K., Hughes, T. L., & Tartaro, J. (2006). Sexual behavior and sexual dysfunction in a community sample of lesbian and heterosexual women. In A. M. Omoto & H. S. Kurtzman (Eds.), *Sexual orientation and mental health: Examining identity and development in lesbian, gay, and bisexual people* (pp. 185–205). Washington, DC: American Psychological Association.

Matthews, C. R., & Lease, S. H. (2000). Focus on lesbian, gay, and bisexual families. In R. M. Perez, K. A. DeBord, & K. J. Bieschke (Eds.), *Handbook of counseling and psychotherapy with lesbian, gay, and bisexual clients* (pp. 249–273). Washington, DC: American Psychological Association.

Maurer, L. (1999). Transgressing sex and gender: Deconstruction zone ahead? *Siecus Report, 28,* 14–21.

Mays, V. M., Chatters, L. M., Cochran, S. D., & Mackness, J. (1998). African American families in diversity: Gay men and lesbians as participants in family networks. *Journal of Comparative Family Studies, 29,* 73–87.

Mays, V. M., & Cochran, S. D. (2001). Mental health correlates of perceived discrimination among lesbian, gay, and bisexual adults in the United States. *American Journal of Public Health, 91,* 1869–1876.

Mays, V. M., Cochran, S. D., & Rhue, S. (1993). The impact of perceived discrimination on the intimate relationships of black lesbians. *Journal of Homosexuality, 25*, 1–14.

McAllan, L. D., & Ditillo, D. (1994). Addressing the needs of lesbian and gay clients with disabilities. *Journal of Applied Rehabilitation Counseling, 25*, 26–35.

McClellan, D. L. (2001). The "other mother" and second parent adoption. *Journal of Gay and Lesbian Social Services, 13*, 1–21.

McClennen, J. C., Summers, A. B., & Daley, J. G. (2002). The lesbian partner abuse scale. *Research in Social Work Practice, 12*, 277–292.

McDougall, G. J. (1993). Therapeutic issues with gay and lesbian elders. *Clinical Gerontologist, 14*, 45–57.

McHenry, S., & Johnson, J. (1993). Homophobia in the therapist and gay or lesbian client: Conscious and unconscious collusion in self-hate. *Psychotherapy, 30*, 141–151.

McKenna, W., & Kessler, S. J. (2000). Retrospective response. *Feminism and Psychology, 10*, 66–72.

McKenry, P. C., Servovich, J. M., Mason, T. L., & Mosack, K. (2006). Perpetration of gay and lesbian partner violence: A disempowerment perspective. *Journal of Family Violence, 21*, 233–243.

McPhail, B. (2004). Questioning gender and sexuality binaries: What queer theorists, transgendered individuals, and sex researchers can teach social work. *Journal of Gay and Lesbian Social Services, 17*, 3–21.

McVinney, L. D. (1998). Social work practice with gay male couples. In G. P. Mallon (Ed.), *Foundations of social work practice with lesbian and gay persons* (pp. 209–227). Binghamton, NY: Haworth Press.

McWhirter, D. P., & Mattison, A. M. (1996). Male couples. In R. P. Cabaj & T. S. Stein (Eds.), *Textbook of homosexuality and mental health* (pp. 319–337). Washington, DC: American Psychiatric Press.

Meana, M., Rakipi, R. S., Weeks, G., & Lykins, A. (2006). Sexual functioning in a non-clinical sample of partnered lesbians. *Journal of Couple and Relationship Therapy, 5*, 1–22.

Metz, M. E., Rosser, B. R. S., & Strapko, N. (1994). Differences in conflict-resolution styles among heterosexual, gay, and lesbian couples. *Journal of Sex Research, 31*, 293–308.

Meyer, I. H. (1995). Minority stress and mental health in gay men. *Journal of Health and Social Behavior, 36*, 38–56.

Meyer, I. H. (2003). Prejudice, social stress, and mental health in lesbian, gay, and bisexual populations: Conceptual issues and research issues. *Psychological Bulletin*, *129*, 674–697.

Meyer, I. H., & Dean, L. (1998). Internalized homophobia, intimacy, and sexual behavior among gay and bisexual men. In G. M. Herek (Ed.), *Stigma and sexual orientation: Understanding prejudice against lesbians, gay men, and bisexuals* (pp. 160–186). Thousand Oaks, CA: Sage.

Miller, P. J. E., Caughlin, J. P., & Huston, T. L. (2003). Trait expressiveness and marital satisfaction: The role of idealization processes. *Journal of Marriage and Family*, *65*, 978–995.

Mills, T. C., Paul, J., Stall, R., Pollack, L., Canchola, J., Chang, Y., et al. (2004). Distress and depression in men who have sex with men: The urban men's health study. *American Journal of Psychiatry*, *161*, 278–285.

Milton, M., & Coyle, A. (1998). Psychotherapy with lesbian and gay clients. *Psychologist*, *11*, 73–76.

Mitchell, V. (2000). The bloom is on the rose: The impact of midlife on the lesbian couple. *Journal of Gay and Lesbian Social Services*, *11*, 33–48.

Modcrin, M. J., & Wyers, N. L. (1990). Lesbian and gay couples: Where they turn when help is needed. *Journal of Gay and Lesbian Psychotherapy*, *1*, 89–104.

Mohl, P. C., Martinez, D., Ticknor, C., & Huang, M. (1991). Early dropouts from psychotherapy. *Journal of Nervous and Mental Disease*, *179*, 478–481.

Moller, M. K. (2004, April 5). *Almost like being married*. Washington, DC: Cato Institute. Retrieved from http://www.cato.org/research/articles/moller-040405.html.

Morgan, K. S. (1997), Why lesbians choose therapy: Presenting problems, attitudes, and political concerns. *Journal of Gay and Lesbian Social Services*, *6*, 57–75.

Morgan, K. S., & Eliason, M. J. (1992). The role of psychotherapy in Caucasian lesbians' lives. *Women and Therapy*, *13*, 27–52.

Morrow, S. L. (2000). First do no harm: Therapist issues in psychotherapy with lesbian, gay, and bisexual clients. In R. M. Perez, K. A. DeBord, & K. J. Bieschke (Eds.), *Handbook of counseling and psychotherapy with lesbian, gay, and bisexual clients* (pp. 157–181). Washington, DC: American Psychological Association.

Murphy, B. C. (1994). Difference and diversity: Gay and lesbian couples. *Social Services for Gay and Lesbian Couples*, *1*, 5–31.

Murphy, D. E. (2004, March 18). San Francisco married 4,037 same-sex pairs from 46 states. *New York Times*, p. A-26.

Murray, V. M., Brown, P. A., Brody, G. H., Cutrona, C. E., & Simons, R. L. (2001). Racial discrimination as a moderator of the links among stress, maternal psychological functioning, and family relationships. *Journal of Marriage and the Family, 63*, 915–926.

Muzio, C. (1999). Lesbian co-parenting: On being/being with the invisible (m)other. In J. Laird (Ed.), *Lesbians and lesbian families: Reflections on theory and practice* (pp. 197–211). New York: Columbia University Press.

Nardi, P. M. (1999). *Gay men's friendships: Invincible communities*. Chicago: University of Chicago Press.

National Association of Social Workers. (1996). *Code of ethics*. Washington, DC: Author.

National Coalition of Anti-Violence Programs. (1998). *Lesbian, gay, bisexual and transgender domestic violence in 1999*. New York: Author.

National Coalition of Anti-Violence Programs. (2002). *Lesbian, gay, bisexual, and transgender domestic violence in 2002*. New York: Author.

National Coalition of Anti-Violence Programs. (2005). *The prevalence of LGBT domestic violence*. New York: Author.

National Gay and Lesbian Task Force. (2000). *Families*. Retrieved from National Gay and Lesbian Task Force Web site: http://www.ngltf.org.

National Gay and Lesbian Task Force (2005a). *Adoption/foster care laws in the United States*. Retrieved from National Gay and Lesbian Task Force Web site: http://www.ngltf.org/downloads/adoptionmap.pdf.

National Gay and Lesbian Task Force. (2005b). Second-parent/stepparent adoption in the United States [map]. Retrieved from National Gay and Lesbian Task Force Web site: http://www.ngltf.org/downloasds/second parentadoptionmap.pdf.

Neimeyer, R. A. (1998). *Lessons of loss: A guide to coping*. New York: McGraw-Hill.

Neisen, J. H. (1990). Heterosexism: Redefining homophobia for the 1990s. *Journal of Gay and Lesbian Psychotherapy, 1*, 21–35.

Nestle, J. (1992). *The persistent desire: A femme-butch reader*. Boston: Alyson Press.

Nichols, M. (1995). Sexual desire disorder in lesbian-feminist couples: The inter-sections of therapy and politics. In R. C. Rosen & S. R. Leiblum (Eds.), *Case studies in sex therapy* (pp. 161–175). New York: Guilford Press.

Norris, F. H., & Murrell, S. A. (1990). Social support, life events, and stress as modifiers of adjustment to bereavement by older adults. *Psychology and Aging, 5*, 429–436.

O'Brien, K. (1992). Primary relationships affect the psychological health of men at risk for AIDS. *Psychological Reports, 71*, 147–153.

O'Connell, A. (1993). Voices from the heart: The developmental impact of a mother's lesbianism on her adolescent children. *Smith College Studies in Social Work, 63*, 281–299.

Okun, B. G. (1996). *Understanding diverse families: What practitioners need to know*. New York: Guilford Press.

Ossana, S. M. (2000). Relationship and couples counseling. In R. M. Perez, K. A. Debord, & K. J. Bieschke (Eds.), *Handbook of counseling and psychother-apy with lesbian, gay, and bisexual clients* (pp. 275–302). Washington, DC: American Psychological Association.

Oswald, R., Gebbie, E., & Culton, L. (2001). *Report to the community: Rainbow Illinois survey of gay, lesbian, bisexual, and transgender people in central Illinois*. Urbana: University of Illinois.

Oswald, R. F. (2002). Inclusion and belonging in the family rituals of lesbian and gay people. *Journal of Family Psychology, 16*, 428–436.

Otis, M. D., Rostosky, S. S., Riggle, E. D. B., & Hamrin, R. (2006). Stress and relationship quality in same-sex couples. *Journal of Social and Personal Relationships, 23*, 81–99.

Otis, M. D., & Skinner, W. F. (1996). The prevalence of victimization and its effect on mental well-being among lesbians and gay people. *Journal of Homosexuality, 30*, 93–121.

Palmer, R., & Bor, R. (2001). The challenge to intimacy and sexual relationships for gay men in HIV serodiscordant relationships. *Journal of Marital and Family Therapy, 27*, 419–432.

Parks, C. A., & Humphreys, N. A. (2006). Lesbian relationships and families. In D. Morrow & L. Messinger (Eds.), *Sexual orientation and gender expression in social work practice* (pp. 216–242). New York: Columbia University Press.

Patterson, C. J. (1992). Children of lesbians and gay men. *Journal of Sex Research,* *30,* 62–69.

Patterson, C. J. (1994). Lesbian and gay families. *Current Directions in Psychological Science, 3,* 62–64.

Patterson, C. J. (1995a). Adoption of minor children by lesbian and gay adults: A social science perspective. *Duke Journal of Gender Law and Policy, 2,* 191–205.

Patterson, C. J. (1995b). Lesbian mothers, gay fathers, and their children. In A. R. D'Augelli & C. J. Patterson (Eds.), *Lesbian, gay, and bisexual identities over the lifespan: Psychological perspectives* (pp. 262–290). New York: Oxford University Press.

Patterson, C. J. (1996). Lesbian mothers and their children: Findings from the Bay Area Families Study. In J. Laird & R.-J. Green (Eds.), *Lesbians and gays in couples and families* (pp. 420–437). San Francisco: Jossey-Bass.

Patterson, C. J. (1997). Children of lesbian and gay parents. *Advances in Clinical Child Psychology, 19,* 235–282.

Patterson, C. J. (2000). Family relationships of lesbians and gay men. *Journal of Marriage and the Family, 62,* 213–220.

Patterson, C. J. (2001). Family relationships of lesbians and gay men. *Journal of Marriage and the Family, 62,* 1052–1069.

Patterson, C. J. (2002). Lesbian and gay parenting. In M.H. Bornstein (Ed.), *Handbook of parenting* (2nd ed., pp. 317–338). Mahwah, NJ: Erlbaum.

Patterson, C. J. (2006). Children of lesbian and gay parents. *Current Directions in Psychological Science, 15,* 241–243.

Patterson, C. J. (2007). Lesbian and gay family issues in the context of changing legal and social policy environments. In K. J. Bieschke, R. M. Perez, & K. A. Deford (Eds.), *Handbook of counseling and psychotherapy with lesbian, gay, bisexual, and transgender clients* (2nd ed., pp. 359–377). Washington, DC: American Psychological Association.

Patterson, C. J. (2009). Parental sexual orientation, social science research, and child custody decisions. In R. M. Galatzer-Levy, L. Kraus, & J. Galatzer-Levy (Eds.), *The scientific basis of child custody decisions* (2nd ed., pp. 285–306). Hoboken, NJ: Wiley.

Patterson, C. J., & Chan, R. W. (1996). Gay fathers and their children. In R. P. Cabaj & T. S. Stein (Eds.), *Textbook of homosexuality and mental health* (pp. 371–393). Washington, DC: American Psychiatric Press.

Patterson, C. J., Fulcher, M., & Wainright, J. (2002). Children of lesbian and gay parents: Research, law, and policy. In B. L. Bottoms, K. Bull, M. Kovera, & B. D. McAuliff (Eds.), *Children, social science, and the law* (pp. 176–199). New York: Cambridge University Press.

Patterson, C. J., Hurt, S., & Mason, C. (1998). Families of the lesbian baby boom: Children's contact with grandparents and other adults. *American Journal of Orthopsychiatry, 68*, 390–399.

Patterson, C. J., Sutfin, E. L., & Fulcher, M. (2004). Division of labor among lesbian and heterosexual parenting couples: Correlates of specialized versus shared patterns. *Journal of Adult Development, 11*, 179–189.

Patterson, D. G., & Schwartz, P. (1994). The social construction of conflict in intimate same-sex couples. In D. D. Cahn (Ed.), *Conflict in personal relationships* (pp. 3–26). Hillsdale, NJ: Erlbaum.

Paul, J. P. (1992). "Biphobia" and the construction of a bisexual identity. In M. Shernoff & W. A. Scott (Eds.), *The sourcebook on lesbian/gay health care* (2nd ed., pp. 259–264). Washington, DC: National Lesbian/Gay Health Foundation.

Pawelski, J., Perrin, E. C., Foy, J. M., Allen, C. E., Crawford, J. E., Del Monte, M., et al. (2006). The effects of marriage, civil union, and domestic partnership laws on the health and well-being of children. *Pediatrics, 118*, 349–364.

Peplau, L. A. (1991). Lesbian and gay relationships. In J. C. Gonsiorek & J. D. Weinrich (Eds.), *Homosexuality: Research findings for public policy* (pp. 177–196). Newbury Park, CA: Sage.

Peplau, L. A. (1993). Lesbian and gay relationships. In L. D. Garnets & D. C. Kimmel (Eds.), *Psychological perspectives on lesbian and gay male experiences* (pp. 395–419). New York: Columbia University Press.

Peplau, L. A., & Beals, K. P. (2004). The family lives of lesbians and gay men. In A. L. Vangelisti (Ed.), *Handbook of family communication* (pp. 233–248). Mahwah, NJ: Erlbaum.

Peplau, L. A., & Cochran, S. D. (1990). A relational perspective on homosexuality. In D. P. McWhirter, S. A. Saunders, & J. M. Reinisch (Eds.), *Homosexuality/heterosexuality: Concepts of sexual orientation* (pp. 321–349). New York: Oxford University Press.

Peplau, L. A., Cochran, S. D., & Mays, V. M. (1997). A national survey of the intimate relationships of African American lesbians and gay men: A look at commitment, satisfaction, sexual behavior, and HIV disease. In B. Greene

(Ed.), *Ethnic and cultural diversity among lesbians and gay men* (pp. 11–38). Thousand Oaks, CA: Sage.

Peplau, L. A., & Fingerhut, A. W. (2007). The close relationships of lesbians and gay men. *Annual Review of Psychology, 58,* 405–424.

Peplau, L. A., & Garnets, L. D. (2000). Women's sexualities: New perspectives on sexual orientation and gender. *Journal of Social Issues, 56,* 181–192.

Peplau, L. A., & Spalding, L. R. (2000). The close relationships of lesbians, gay men, and bisexuals. In C. Hendrick & S. S. Hendrick (Eds.), *Close relationships: A sourcebook* (pp. 111–123). Thousand Oaks, CA: Sage.

Perrin, E. C. (2002). Technical report: Co-parent or second-parent adoption by same-sex parents. *Pediatrics, 109,* 341–344.

Pesek, E. M. (2002). The role of support groups in disenfranchised grief. In K. J. Doka (Ed.), *Disenfranchised grief: New directions, challenges, and strategies for practice* (pp. 127–133). Champaign, IL: Research Press.

Peterman, L. M., & Dixon, C. G. (2003). Domestic violence between same-sex partners: Implications for counseling. *Journal of Counseling and Development, 81,* 40–48.

Pew Forum on Religion and Public Life. (2003). *Republicans unified, Democrats split on gay marriage: Religious beliefs underpin opposition to discrimination.* Washington, DC: Author.

Pope, M., & Schulz, R. (1990). Sexual attitudes and behavior in midlife and aging homosexual males. *Journal of Homosexuality, 20,* 169–177.

Powell-Cope, G. M. (1995). The experiences of gay couples affected by HIV infection. *Qualitative Health Research, 5,* 36–62.

Prager, K. (1995). *The psychology of intimacy.* New York: Guilford Press.

Price, P. B., & Jones, E. (1998). Examining the alliance using the psychotherapy process Q-set. *Psychotherapy: Theory, Research, Practice, Training, 35,* 392–404.

Prigerson, H. G., & Jacobs, S. C. (2001). Perspectives on care at the close of life. Caring for bereaved patients: "All the doctors just suddenly go." *JAMA, 286,* 1369–1376.

Prilleltensky, I. (1994). Empowerment in mainstream psychology: Legitimacy, obstacles, and possibilities. *Canadian Psychology/Psychologie Canadienne, 35,* 358–375.

Purcell, D. W., Camos, P. F., & Perrilla, J. L. (1996). Therapy with lesbians and gay men: A cognitive behavioral perspective. *Cognitive and Behavioral Practice, 3,* 391–415.

Rando, T. A. (1993). *Treatment of complicated mourning*. Champaign, IL: Research Press.

Reilly, M. E., & Lynch, J. M. (1990). Power-sharing in lesbian relationships. *Journal of Homosexuality*, *19*, 1–30.

Reimann, R. (1997). Does biology matter? Lesbian couples' transition to parenthood and their division of labor. *Qualitative Sociology*, *20*, 153–185.

Renzetti, C. (1992). *Violent betrayal: Partner abuse in lesbian relationships*. Newbury Park, CA: Sage.

Renzetti, C. (1996). The poverty of services for battered lesbians. *Journal of Gay and Lesbian Social Services*, *4*, 61–68.

Renzetti, C. M. (1997). Violence and abuse among same-sex couples. In A. P. Cardarelli (Ed.), *Violence between intimate partners: Patterns, causes, and effects* (pp. 70–89). Boston: Allyn and Bacon.

Richards, T., Wrubel, J., & Folkman, S. (1999–2000). Death rites in the San Francisco gay community: Cultural developments of the AIDS epidemic. *Omega: Journal of Death and Dying*, *40*, 335–350.

Richman, K. D. (2009). *Courting change: Queer parents, judges, and the transformation of American family law*. New York: New York University Press.

Richmond, B., & Ross, M. W. (2004). Responses to AIDS-related bereavement. *Journal of Psychosocial Oncology*, *12*, 143–163.

Riggle, E. D. B., Whitman, J. S., Olson, A., Rostosky, S. S., & Strong, S. (2008). The positive aspects of being a lesbian or gay man. *Professional Psychology: Research and Practice*, *39*, 210–217.

Roberts, A. L., Austin, S. B., Corliss, H. L., Vandermorris, A. K., & Koenen, K. C. (2010). Pervasive trauma exposure among U.S. sexual orientation minority adults and risk of posttraumatic stress disorder. *American Journal of Public Health*, *12*, 2433–2441.

Roberts, A. R. (2000). Crisis theory and crisis intervention. In A. R. Roberts (Ed.), *Crisis intervention handbook: Assessment, treatment, and research* (2nd ed., pp. 2–30). New York: Oxford University Press.

Rohrbaugh, J. B. (1992). Lesbian families: Clinical issues and theoretical implications. *Professional Psychology: Research and Practice*, *23*, 467–473.

Roisman, G. I., Clausell, E., Holland, A., Fortuna, K., & Elieff, C. (2008). Adult romantic relationships as contexts of human development: A multimethod comparison of same-sex couples with opposite-sex dating, engaged, and married dyads. *Developmental Psychology*, *44*, 91–101.

Rose, S. (2003). Community interventions concerning homophobic violence and partner violence against lesbians. *Journal of Lesbian Studies, 7*, 125–139.

Rose, S., & Zand, D. (2000). Lesbian dating and courtship from young adulthood to midlife. *Journal of Gay and Lesbian Social Services, 11*, 77–104.

Rose, S., Zand, D., & Cini, M. (1993). Lesbian courtship scripts. In E. D. Rothblum & K. A. Brehony (Eds.), *Boston marriages: Romantic but asexual relationships among contemporary lesbians* (pp. 70–85). Amherst: University of Massachusetts Press.

Rosenblum, D. M. (1991). Custody rights of gay and lesbian parents. *Villanova Law Review, 36*, 1665–1696.

Rosenbluth, S. C., & Steil, J. M. (1995). Predictors of intimacy for women in heterosexual and homosexual couples. *Journal of Social and Personal Relationships, 12*, 163–176.

Rosenfeld, M. J. (2007). *The age of independence: Interracial unions, same-sex unions, and the changing American family.* Cambridge, MA: Harvard University Press.

Rosenzweig, J. M., & Lebow, W. C. (1992). Femme on the streets, butch in the sheets? Lesbian sex-roles, dyadic adjustment and sexual satisfaction. *Journal of Homosexuality, 23*, 1–20.

Ross, C. E., Mirowsky, J., & Goldsteen, K. (1990). The impact of the family on health: The decade in review. *Journal of Marriage and the Family, 52*, 1059–1078.

Ross, M. W., & Rosser, B. R. (1996). Measurement and correlates of internalized homophobia: A factor analytic study. *Journal of Clinical Psychology, 52*, 15–21.

Rostosky, E. D., Riggle, E. D. B., Dudley, M. G., & Wright, M. L. C. (2006). Commitment in same-sex relationships: A qualitative analysis of couples' conversations. *Journal of Homosexuality, 51*, 119–221.

Rostosky, S. S., Riggle, E. D. B., Gray, B. E., & Hatton, R. L. (2007). Minority stress experiences in committed same-sex couple relationships. *Professional Psychology: Research and Practice, 38*, 392–400.

Rostosky, S. S., Riggle, E. D. B., Savage, T. A., Roberts, S. D., & Singletary, G. (2008). Interracial same-sex couples' perceptions of stress and coping: An exploratory study. *Journal of GLBT Family Studies, 4*, 277–299.

Rothblum, E. D. (1990). Depression among lesbians: An invisible and unresearched phenomenon. *Journal of Gay and Lesbian Psychotherapy, 1*, 67–87.

Rothblum, E. D. (2000). Sexual orientation and sex in women's lives: Conceptual and methodological issues. *Journal of Social Issues, 56*, 193–204.

Rothblum, E. D. (2006). "Somewhere in Des Moines or San Antonio": Historical perspectives on lesbian, gay and bisexual mental health. In R. M. Perez, K. A. Debord, & R. J. Bieschke (Eds.), *Handbook of counseling and psychotherapy with lesbian, gay, and bisexual clients* (pp. 57–80). Washington, DC: American Psychological Association.

Russell, G. M. (2000). *Voted out: The psychological consequences of antigay politics*. New York: New York University Press.

Russell, G. M., & Bohan, J. S. (2006). The case of internalized homophobia: Theory and practice. *Theory and Psychology, 16*, 343–366.

Russell, G. M., & Bohan, J. (2007). Liberating psychotherapy: Liberation psychology and psychotherapy with LGBT clients. *Journal of Gay and Lesbian Psychotherapy, 11*, 59–75.

Russell, G. M., & Richards, J. A. (2003). Stressor and resilience factors for lesbians, gay men, and bisexuals confronting antigay politics. *American Journal of Community Psychology, 31*, 313–328.

Rust, P. C. (1996). Monogamy and polyamory: Relationship issues for bisexuals. In B. A. Firestein (Ed.), *Bisexuality: The psychology and politics of an invisible minority* (pp. 127–148). Thousand Oaks, CA: Sage.

Rust, P. C. (2000). Bisexuality: A contemporary paradox for women. *Journal of Social Issues, 56*, 205–221.

Rutter, V., & Schwartz, P. (1996). Same-sex couples: Courtship, commitment, context. In A. W. Auhagen (Ed.), *The diversity of human relationships* (pp. 197–226). New York: Cambridge University Press.

Rutter, V., & Schwartz, P. (2000). Gender, marriage, and diverse possibilities for cross-sex and same-sex pairs. In D. H. Demo, K. R. Allen, & M. A. Fine (Eds.), *Handbook of family diversity* (pp. 59–81). New York: Oxford University Press.

Sanders, G. L., & Kroll, L. T. (2000). Generating stories of resilience: Helping gay and lesbian youth and their families. *Journal of Marital and Family Therapy, 246*, 433–442.

Scasta, D. (1998). Issues in helping people come out. *Journal of Gay and Lesbian Psychotherapy, 2*, 87–98.

Schacher, S. J., Auerback, C. F., & Silverstein, L. B. (2005). Gay fathers expanding the possibilities for us all. *Journal of GLBT Family Studies, 1*, 31–52.

Schilit, R., Lie, G. Y., & Montagne, M. (1990). Substance abuse as a correlate of violence in intimate lesbian relationships. *Journal of Homosexuality, 19,* 51–65.

Schreurs, K. M. G. (1993). Sexuality in lesbian couples: The importance of gender. *Annual Review of Sex Research, 4,* 49–66.

Schreurs, K. M. G., & Buunk, B. P. (1996). Closeness, autonomy, equity, and relationship satisfaction in lesbian couples. *Psychology of Women Quarterly, 20,* 577–592.

Schumm, W. R., Akagi, C. A., & Bosch, K. R. (2008). Relationship satisfaction for heterosexual women compared to lesbians and men in a sample of faith communities from Topeka, Kansas. *Psychological Reports, 102,* 377–388.

Scrivner, J. R., & Eldridge, N. S. (1995). Lesbian and gay family psychology. In R. H. Mikesell, D. Lusterman, & S. H. McDaniel (Eds.), *Integrating family therapy: Handbook of family psychology and systems theory* (pp. 327–345). Washington, DC: American Psychological Association.

Seacat, J. D. (2005). How the same-sex marriage debate may be affecting the health and well-being of gays and lesbians. *Division 44 Newsletter: Society for the Psychological Study of Lesbian, Gay, and Bisexual Issues, 21,* 7–8.

Segal-Sklar, S. (1996). Lesbian parenting: Radical or retrograde? In K. Jay (Ed.), *Dyke life: A celebration of the lesbian experience* (pp. 174–191). New York: Basic Books.

Shapiro, J. (1996). Custody and conduct: How the law fails lesbian and gay parents and their children. *Indiana Law Journal, 71,* 621–623.

Shernoff, M. J. (1995). Family therapy for lesbian and gay clients. In F. J. Turner (Ed.), *Differential diagnosis and treatment in social work* (pp. 911–918). New York: Free Press.

Shernoff, M. (1996). Gay men choosing to be fathers. In M. Shernoff (Ed.), *Human services for gay people: Clinical and community practice* (pp. 41–54). Binghamton, NY: Harrington Park Press.

Shildo, A. (1994). Internalized homophobia: Conceptual and empirical issues in measurement. In B. Geren & G. M. Herek (Eds.), *Lesbian and gay psychology: Theory, research and clinical application* (pp. 176–205). Thousand Oaks, CA: Sage.

Shildo, A., & Schroeder, M. (2002). Changing sexual orientation: A consumer's report. *Professional Psychology: Research and Practice, 33,* 249–259.

Siegel, S., & Walker, G. (1996). Connections: Conversations between a gay therapist and a straight therapist. In J. Laird & R.-J. Green (Eds.), *Lesbians and gays in couples and families: A handbook for therapists* (pp. 28–68). San Francisco: Jossey-Bass.

Silverstein, C., & Picano, F. (2003). *The joy of gay sex*. New York: Harper-Collins.

Simmons, T., & O'Connell, M. (2003). *Married-couples in unmarried-partner households: 2000*. Washington, DC: U.S. Census Bureau. Retrieved December 10, 2007, from http://www.census.gov/prod/2003pubs/censr-5.pdf.

Slater, S. (1995). *The lesbian family life cycle*. New York: Free Press.

Smith, D. M., & Gates, G. J. (2001). *Gay and lesbian families in the United States: Same-sex unmarried partner households: A preliminary analysis of 2000 United States census data*. Washington, DC: Human Rights Campaign.

Smith, R. B., & Brown, R. A. (1997). The impact of social support on gay male couples. *Journal of Homosexuality, 33*, 39–61.

*Sodomy laws in the U.S.* Retrieved February 2, 2011, from http://www.wordiq .com/definition/Sodomy_laws_in_the_United_States.

Soland, B. (1998). A queer nation? The passage of the gay and lesbian partnership legislation in Denmark, 1989. *Social Politics, 5*, 48–69.

Solomon, S. E., Rothblum, E. D., & Balsam, K. F. (2004). Pioneers in partnership: Lesbians and gay male couples in civil unions compared with those not in civil unions, and married heterosexual couples. *Journal of Family Psychology, 18*, 275–286.

Spencer, B., & Brown, J. (2007). Fusion or internalized homophobia? A pilot study of Bowen's differentiation of self hypotheses with lesbian couples. *Family Process, 46*, 257–268.

Stacey, J. (1998). Gay and lesbian families: Queer like us. In M. A. Mason, A. Skolnick, & S. D. Sugarman (Eds.), *All our families: New politics for a new century* (pp. 117–143). New York: Oxford University Press.

Stacey, J., & Biblarz, T. J. (2001). (How) does the sexual orientation of parents matter? *American Sociological Review, 66*, 159–183.

Stack, S., & Eshleman, J. R. (1998). Marital status and happiness: A 17-nation study. *Journal of Marriage and the Family, 60*, 527–536.

Stafford, L., & Canary, D. J. (1991). Maintenance strategies and romantic relationship type, gender, and relational characteristics. *Journal of Social and Personal Relationships, 8*, 217–242.

Stafford, L., Dainton, M., & Haas, S. M. (2000). Measuring routine and strategic relational maintenance: Scale revision, sex versus gender roles, and the prediction of relational characteristics. *Communication Monographs, 67*, 306–323.

Stein, E. (1999). *The mismeasure of desire: The science, theory, and ethics of sexual orientation.* New York: Oxford University Press.

Stein, T. S., & Cabaj, R. P. (1996). Psychotherapy with gay men. In R. P. Cabaj & T. S. Stein (Eds.), *Textbook of homosexuality and mental health* (pp. 423–432). Washington, DC: American Psychiatric Press.

Stiglitz, E. (1990). Caught between two worlds: The impact of a child on a lesbian couple's relationship. *Women and Therapy, 10*, 99–116.

Stokes, J., & Damon, W. (1995). Counseling and psychotherapy for bisexual men. *Directions in Mental Health Counseling, 5*, 4–15.

Stroebe, M. S., Hansson, R. O., Stroebe, W., & Schut, H. (2001). Introduction: Concepts and issues in contemporary research on bereavement research. In M. S. Stroebe, R. O. Hansson, W. Stroebe, & H. Schut (Eds.), *Handbook of bereavement research: Theory, research, and intervention* (pp. 3–22). Cambridge: Cambridge University Press.

Stout, D. (2009). House passes hate crimes bill. *New York Times.* Retrieved from http://thecaucus.blogs.nytimes.com/2009/10/08/house-passes-expanded-hate-crimes-bill/.

Sullivan, A. (1995). *Virtually normal: An argument about homosexuality.* New York: Knopf.

Sullivan, A. (2004). *Same-sex marriage, pro and con: A reader.* New York: Vintage Books.

Surrey, J. (1985). *Self-in-relation: A theory of women's development* (Work in Progress No. 13). Wellesley, MA: Wellesley College, Stone Center for Women's Development.

Swainson, M., & Tasker, F. (2005). Genograms redrawn: Lesbian couples define their families. *Journal of GLBT Family Studies, 1*, 3–28.

Swim, J. K., Pearson, N. B., & Johnson, K. E. (2007). Daily encounters with heterosexism: A week in the life of lesbian, gay, and bisexual individuals. *Journal of Homosexuality, 53*, 31–48.

Sycamore, M. B. (2004). *That's revolting: Queer strategies for resisting assimilation.* Brooklyn, NY: Soft Skull Press.

Szymanski, D. M., Kashubeck-West, S., & Meyer, J. (2008).Internalized heterosexism: A historical and theoretical overview. *Counseling Psychologist, 36,* 510–524.

Tasker, F. (2005). Lesbian mothers, gay fathers, and their children: A review. *Journal of Developmental & Behavioral Pediatrics, 26,* 224–240.

Tasker, F. L., & Golombok, S. (1997). *Growing up in a lesbian family: Effects on child development.* New York: Guilford Press.

Tasker, F. L., & Golombok, S. (1998). The role of co-mothers in planned lesbian-led families. *Journal of Lesbian Studies, 2,* 61–79.

Toder, N. (1992). Lesbian couples in particular. In B. Berzon & R. Leighton (Eds.), *Positively gay* (pp. 50–63). Berkeley, CA: Celestial Arts.

Todosijevic, I., Rothblum, E. D., & Solomon, S. E. (2005). Relationship satisfaction, affectivity, and gay-specific stressors in same-sex couples joined in civil unions. *Psychology of Women Quarterly, 29,* 158–166.

Tracy, J. K., & Junginger, J. (2007). Correlates of lesbian sexual functioning. *Journal of Women's Health, 16,* 499–509.

Turell, S. C. (2000). A descriptive analysis of same-sex relationship violence for a diverse sample. *Journal of Family Violence, 15,* 281–293.

Turner, P. H., Scadden, L., & Harris, M. B. (1990). Parenting in gay and lesbian families. *Journal of Gay and Lesbian Psychotherapy, 1,* 55–66.

Turteltaub, G. L. (2002, November). The effects of long-term primary relationship dissolution on the children of lesbian parents. *Dissertation Abstracts International: Section B: Sciences and Engineering, 63*(5-B), 2610.

Vanfraussen, K., Ponjaert-Kristoffersen, I., & Brewaeys, A. (2003). Functioning in lesbian families created by donor insemination. *American Journal of Orthopsychiatry, 73,* 78–91.

Von Schulthess, B. (1992). Violence in the streets: Anti-lesbian assault and harassment in San Francisco. In G. M. Herek & K. T. Berrill (Eds.), *Hate crimes: Confronting violence against lesbians and gay men* (pp. 65–75). Newbury Park, CA: Sage.

Wagner, G., Brandolo, E., & Rabkhi, J. (1996). Internalized homophobia in a sample of HIV gay men and its relationship to psychological distress, coping and illness progression. *Journal of Homosexuality, 32,* 91–106.

Wainright, J. L., & Patterson, C. J. (2006). Delinquency, victimization, and substance use among adolescents with female same-sex parents. *Journal of Family Psychology, 20,* 526–530.

Wainright, J. L., Russell, S. T., & Patterson, C. J. (2004). Psychosocial adjustment, school outcomes, and romantic relationships of adolescents with same-sex parents. *Child Development, 75,* 1886–1898.

Walters, S. D. (2000). Wedding bells and baby carriages: Heterosexuals imagine gay families, gay families imagine themselves. In M. Andrews, S. D. Schater, & C. Squire (Eds.), *Lines of narrative: Psychosocial perspectives* (pp. 48–63). New York: Routledge.

Wapenyi, K. (2010). Do lesbians get AIDS? Women who have sex with women, HIV/AIDS, and its mental health impact. *Journal of Gay and Lesbian Mental Health, 14,* 52–55.

Warner, M. (1999). *The trouble with normal.* New York: Free Press.

Weinberg, M. S., Williams, C. J., & Pryor, D. W. (1994). *Dual attractions: Understanding bisexuality.* New York: Oxford University Press.

Weinstock, J. S. (2004). Lesbian FLEX-ibility: Friend and/or family connections among lesbian ex-lovers. *Journal of Lesbian Studies, 8,* 193–238.

Weinstock, J. S., & Rothblum, E. D. (1996). What we can be together: Contemplating lesbians' friendships. In J. S. Weinstock & E. D. Rothblum (Eds.), *Lesbians and friendship: For ourselves and each other* (pp. 3–30). New York: New York University Press.

West, C. M. (1998). Lifting the "political gag order": Breaking the silence around partner violence in ethnic minority families. In J. L. Jasinski & L. M. Williams (Eds.), *Partner violence: A comprehensive review of 20 years of research* (pp. 184–209). Thousand Oaks, CA: Sage.

West, C. M. (2002). Lesbian intimate partner violence: Prevalence and dynamics. *Journal of Lesbian Studies, 6,* 121–127.

West, R., & Turner, L. H. (1995). Communication in lesbian and gay families: Building a descriptive base. In T. J. Socha & G. H. Stamp (Eds.), *Parents, children, and communication* (pp. 148–167). Mahwah, NJ: Erlbaum.

Wester, S. R., Pionke, D. R., & Vogel, D. L. (2005). Male gender role conflict, gay men, and same-sex romantic relationships. *Psychology of Men and Masculinity, 6,* 195–208.

Weston, K. (1996). *Render men, gender me: Lesbians talk sex, class, color, nation, studmuffins.* New York: Columbia University Press.

Weston, K. (1997). *Families we choose: Lesbians, gays, kinship,* 2nd ed. New York: Columbia University Press.

Wharton, G., & Phillips. I. (2004). *I do/I don't: Queers on marriage*. San Francisco: Suspect Thoughts Press.

White, M., & Epston, D. (1990). *Narrative means to therapeutic ends*. New York: Norton.

Wintemute, R., & Andenaes, M. (2001). *Legal recognition of same-sex partnerships: A study of national, European and international law*. Oxford, UK: Hart.

Witte, J., Jr. (2003). Ishmael's bane: The sin and crime of illegitimacy reconsidered. *Punishment and Society, 5,* 327–345.

Wood, J. T., & Inman, C. C. (1993). In a different mode: Masculine styles of communicating closeness. *Journal of Applied Community Research, 2,* 279–295.

Worden, J. W. (2002). *Grief counseling and grief therapy: A handbook for mental health practitioners* (3rd. ed.). New York: Springer.

Yep, G. A. (2002). From homophobia and heterosexism to heteronormativity: Toward the development of a model of queer interventions in the university classroom. In E. P. Cramer (Ed.), *Addressing homophobia and heterosexism on college campuses* (pp. 163–176). Binghamton, NY: Harrington Park Press.

Yep, G. A., Lovaas, K. E., & Elia, J. P. (2003). A critical appraisal of assimilationist and radical ideologies underlying same-sex marriage in LGBT communities in the United States. *Journal of Homosexuality, 45,* 45–64.

Young, I. (1995). *The Stonewall experiment: A gay psychohistory*. New York: Cassell.

Young, M. E., & Long, L. L. (1998). *Counseling and therapy for couples*. Pacific Grove, CA: Brooks/Cole.

Zacks, E., Green, R., & Morrow, J. (1988). Comparing lesbian and heterosexual couples on the circumplex model: An initial investigation. *Family Process, 27,* 471–484.

Zicklin, G. (1995). Deconstructing legal rationality: The case of lesbian and gay family relationships. *Marriage and Family Review, 21,* 55–76.

# Index

# About the Author

Ski Hunter is professor of social work at the University of Texas, Arlington. She lives in Dallas, Texas. She holds a bachelor's degree in political science, a master's degree in clinical psychology, an MSW, and a Ph.D. in social work. She is author of *Midlife and Older Lesbian and Gay Persons* (2005), *Coming Out and Disclosure across the Life Span* (2007), and *Effects of Conservative Religion on Lesbian and Gay Clients and Practitioners* (2011). She is coauthor, with M. Sundel, of *Midlife Myths: Issues, Research Findings, and Implications for the Helping Professions* (1989); with C. Shannon, J. Martin, and J. Knox, of *Lesbian, Gay, and Bisexual Youths and Adults: Translation of Knowledge for Practice* (1998); with S. Sundel and M. Sundel, of *Midlife Women* (2002); and with Jane Hickerson, of *Lesbian, Gay, Bisexual, and Transgender Youth and Adults: Issues for Practice* (2003). She has given many presentations and teaches a course on LGBT persons.